*For "Children Who Vary*
*from the Normal Type"*

# For "Children Who Vary from the Normal Type"

## Special Education in Boston, 1838–1930

*Robert L. Osgood*

Gallaudet University Press
Washington, D.C.

Gallaudet University Press
Washington, DC 20002

Photograph permissions: pp. 26 and 97—courtesy of Horace Mann School for
the Deaf; pp. 46 and 49—courtesy of Perkins School for the Blind; p. 101—
courtesy of Gallaudet University Archives; cover photo, pp. 17, 35, 74, 83, 108,
120, 131, and 139—courtesy of the Boston Public Library, Print Department.

*Library of Congress Cataloging-in-Publication Data*

Osgood, Robert L.
    For "children who vary from the normal type" : special education in Bos-
ton, 1838–1930 / Robert L. Osgood.
        p. cm.
    Includes bibliographical references and index.
    ISBN 1-56368-089-0
    1. Special education—Massachusetts—Boston—History—19th cen-
tury.   2. Special education—Massachusetts—Boston—History—20th
century.   3. Education—Massachusetts—Boston—History—19th century.   4. Education—Massachusetts—Boston—History—20th century.
I. Title.

LC3983.B7 O84 2000
371.9'09744'61—dc21                                        99-059168

# CONTENTS

# ACKNOWLEDGMENTS

I wish to express my heartfelt and long overdue thanks to a number of organizations and individuals who have all contributed in some way to this book's creation. I began my research several years ago for a doctoral dissertation; the project was supported in large part by the generosity of the Claremont Graduate School (now Claremont Graduate University) through a Claremont Graduate School Fellowship and a Linhardt Dissertation Fellowship. At that time I received a tremendous amount of support and constructive criticism from the members of my dissertation committee: Robert Dawidoff, Malcolm Douglass, and Mary Poplin, all of the Claremont Graduate School; and Helena Wall of Pomona College. This committee provided me with a great deal of latitude and flexibility in refining the topic to suit my own interests and discoveries. During the course of the research I relied heavily on the tireless patience and legwork of the staff of the Government Documents Department at the Boston Public Library. Similarly, the staffs at the Gutman Library of Harvard University and the Fingold Library at the Massachusetts State House were most helpful in directing me to possible sources. Particular thanks go to the library staff in the office of the Boston School Committee, who made me feel most welcome during several weeks of research there. The Honnold Library of the Claremont Colleges also provided excellent resources and opportunities for research, writing, and reflection. More recently, Aaron Schmidt of the Print Department of the Boston Public Library has generously assisted in the selection of the photographs included in the book.

Over the past two and one-half years I have worked closely with Gallaudet University Press. John Vickrey Van Cleve and anonymous reviewers offered constructive and insightful critique on earlier drafts. Special thanks goes to Ivey Pittle Wallace, whose expertise and professionalism not only made this a much better book but also rendered its preparation a delight. I have also appreciated the counsel and support of my colleagues at the Indiana University School of Education, especially Ed McClellan, Barbara Wilcox, Khaula Murtadha-Watts, Keith Morran, and Michael Cohen. Each in her or his own way has contributed directly to making the process of writing and revising easier and more productive. I also wish to thank

Dr. Moqim Rahmanzai, my good friend and colleague from Institut Teknologi Tun Hussein Onn, for his encouragement and advice during an extended period of writing in Malaysia during the 1997–98 academic year.

A significantly modified version of chapter 5 appeared as "Undermining the Common School Ideal: Intermediate Schools and Ungraded Classes in Boston, 1838–1900" in *History of Education Quarterly* 37 (winter 1997: 375–98). In addition, material drawn from several chapters formed the basis of "Becoming a Special Educator: Specialized Professional Training for Teachers of Children with Disabilities in Boston, 1870–1930," published in *Teachers College Record* 101 (fall 1999: 104–27). Much earlier versions of portions of this book also have been presented at annual meetings of the History of Education Society and the American Educational Research Association.

On a more personal note, this book would not have been possible without the love and support of my children, Laurel and Evan; my mother, Mary Anne Osgood; and my mother-in-law, Pearl Hinshaw, all of whom have been part of this long process every step of the way. This book honors the memory of my father, John Osgood, and that of my father-in-law, Randall Hinshaw; I only wish they were still alive to read and critique it. Finally, I wish to express my deepest love and affection for my wife, Elisabeth Hinshaw-Osgood, whose patience, advice, support, and love have been unwavering as she has watched my work develop and move towards publication. This book is dedicated to her.

*For "Children Who Vary*
*from the Normal Type"*

PART

1

# EDUCATION IN BOSTON

# 1

## INTRODUCTION

*All teachers on receiving a new class of children should give special study to the children who appear to be unusually dull or unresponsive in order to discover, if possible, the cause of the appearance. Mental defects amounting to feeble-mindedness in the scientific sense of the term are not always nor even usually the cause of apparent stupidity. Such causes as deafness, nearsightedness, and partial blindness may go unobserved for a time, but, when discovered, afford all necessary explanation. If, after the regular teacher has made a careful study of a case, and has become convinced that the cause of the apparent feeble-mindedness is beyond her power to discover or to remove, the case should be reported to the Superintendent of Public Schools, who will call in the expert services of the teachers of the special classes, and, if he deems it best, authorize the removal of the child to one of the special classes.*

EDWIN SEAVER, Superintendent of the Boston Public Schools, 1900

*To the maximum extent appropriate, children with disabilities, including children in public or private institutions or other care facilities, are educated with children who are nondisabled; and . . . special classes, separate schooling or other removal of children with disabilities from the regular educational environment occurs only when the nature or severity of the disability is such that education in regular classes with the use of supplementary aids and services cannot be achieved satisfactorily.*

Individuals with Disabilities Education Act, 1990

Throughout the history of special education, two fundamental yet conflicting positions have persisted regarding the education of students with disabilities: the belief, to varying degrees, that such children should

3

have opportunities to experience full integration in school with their non-disabled peers; and the belief, also to varying degrees, that such integration can be ill-advised, ineffective, or both.[1] The interplay and tension among these two beliefs has long constituted one of the defining characteristics of special education in the American public schools. Certainly, discussions on the placement and instruction of students with disabilities currently dominate professional and scholarly discourse in the field, with the 1990s having witnessed a plethora of commentary and research on the subject.

A number of scholars and practitioners have strongly supported more inclusive or integrative approaches to educating such children. Biklen, Stainback and Stainback, Wang, Will, Ferguson, Skrtic, and others argue that while inclusion is a practical, effective approach to placement and instruction, more importantly, the ethical and legal considerations in the pursuit of true equity in education demand it. Others, such as Kauffman, Fuchs and Fuchs, Lieberman, and Shanker caution against fully inclusive special education practices and recommend maintaining separate facilities and instructional settings, arguing that integration can fail to recognize, address, or respect the individual needs of certain children, especially those with severe disabilities.[2]

Issues related to the inclusion movement are obviously complex and intricately interconnected. Questions of equity, funding, technology, staffing, and curriculum directly affect the philosophy as well as practice of inclusion while raising other, much broader questions concerning the redefinition and reconceptualization of the public school experience along more integrative lines. Ultimately, untangling and addressing the many theoretical and practical problems and opportunities attending such changes in special and general education represents one of the greatest challenges for American schools as they enter the next century. To do so, however, is by no means an easy task; therefore, any and all avenues toward achieving a clearer picture and a more sophisticated yet functional understanding of the special education-general education dynamic thus should be considered and, if possible, pursued.

One potentially fruitful approach leads back to the past. Formal special education in the public schools possesses a long and fascinating history, with many of the problems, issues, conditions, and possibilities currently extant in special education (for example, labeling, placement, differentiations of status and power between special and general educators, appropriate curriculum and instructional methodology, teacher training, staff development, as well as social and psychological constructions of exceptionality) having been discussed widely among teachers, administrators, scholars, and parents for well over one hundred years. At the heart of these discussions has been the debate over the segregation and integration of students with formally identified disabilities in public schools. To examine this history is, in many ways, to catch a glimpse of ourselves in the mirror as we see how others before us struggled with similar questions, similar arguments, and similar hopes.

The past twenty years have seen a significant amount of historical scholarship in the field of special education. Sarason and Doris, Scheerenberger, Winzer, Trent, and Van Cleve and Crouch have prepared histories of a generalized nature, covering long periods of time and discussing a number of issues. Franklin, Tropea, Gelb, Lazerson, Richardson, and Osgood, among others, have explored more specific situations, locations, or themes that address in various ways the education of children formally identified as disabled. This body of scholarship clearly demonstrates the complexity of the subject and the value of historical research in understanding the nature of special education today. It is an important history and one that still needs much work—especially on public school special education's formative years in the late nineteenth and early twentieth centuries.[3]

The five decades between 1880 and 1930 witnessed a remarkable series of social, intellectual, psychological, and medical developments that not only changed education dramatically in the United States but also altered understandings and theories regarding disability and exceptionality. Social and educational progressivism, the child study movement, social Darwinism, Taylorism, the mental testing movement, immigration, urbanization, industrialization, compulsory education, technological advances: each are worthy of (and have received) intensive histories of their own. Yet they combined forces to turn a nascent, vague notion that students were indeed different from each other—with some much more different than others—into a noteworthy arm of public schooling known as special education, complete with its own terminology, theory, assumptions, tools, structure, practices, and specialized knowledge. The matrix of these complex social and intellectual forces, interacting with the more concentrated agencies of specific disabilities and/or specific aspects of education, suggests a wide range of questions, problems, and issues that can and should be addressed when trying to understand how special education has developed and how patterns of integration and segregation in the field have shifted over time.

Exploring these historical relationships can certainly be useful, not only in understanding that history in its own time and place but also in helping to understand similar relationships and issues today. To do so, a study concentrating on a single school system over an extended period represents a sound opportunity to engage in this subject with greater clarity and cohesion. This approach permits in-depth examination of specific conditions and programs, problems and solutions—an examination that in turn can suggest possible explanations for the nature and dynamics of special education's growth in public school systems. Focusing on a single school system also allows for close investigation into individual special education programs and their relations with each other, breaking down monolithic perceptions of special education by permitting more detailed studies of the myriad ways in which such programs have developed and operated.

The public school system of Boston, Massachusetts, constitutes a most instructive situation for exploring these developments as a case study. The Boston public schools followed a typical pattern experienced widely in nineteenth-century American education: the gradual yet inexorable growth of a system of graded schools and of a bureaucracy which wrestled with the advent of compulsory education, the expectations for efficient school management, and the challenges of increasing diversity and numbers among its students. All of these demanded constant adjustments in curriculum and administration. Concurrent with (and largely responsible for) these developments were the remarkable, even dramatic, changes in the nature of the city's economy, physical as well as intellectual environment, and population; again, a standard pattern for most major American cities at the time, especially those in the industrial North and Midwest. Boston both drew from and contributed to the widespread conversations addressing the development of public schooling during the latter 1800s and early 1900s, with its questions—and answers—to a large degree resembling those of many other American school systems.

Even so, Boston's public schools, including its special education programs, were fashioned by several factors unique to the city. To begin with, regional Boston provided national leadership in developing public school administration policy and practice. The first public high school, the first public graded school (in nearby Quincy), the earliest statewide compulsory education law and state board of education, and a dramatic administrative reorganization in 1876 all drew national attention to Boston, as did the efforts of a number of individuals (for example, Horace Mann, George Emerson, John Philbrick, Francis Wayland Parker, and David Snedden) who achieved national reputations for their work in, near, or with Boston's public schools. Such efforts established Boston as a model of innovation in education for the rest of the nation. In addition, the New England region, and Boston in particular, served as home for a number of individuals and institutions dedicated to improving the diagnosis, treatment, and education of individuals of all ages with disabilities. Thomas Hopkins Gallaudet, Samuel Gridley Howe, Edouard Seguin, Hervey Wilbur, and Walter Fernald were the most notable among many individuals who established and/or directed institutions for individuals with disabilities in the region. These institutions served as centers for teaching and research as well as easily accessible resources for Boston's school system as it built its special education programs. Strong leadership and fortuitous positioning gave Boston unusual opportunities to integrate special education into the public schools in an innovative as well as comprehensive fashion. As a result, by 1930 the Boston schools had a system of programs for students with identified disabilities considerably more mature and extensive than most if not all urban American school systems.

Thus, an important part of understanding the history of special education in American public schools involves ascertaining how Boston both differed from as well as exemplified the experiences of other cities addressing the need for special education at that time. The body of historical scholarship noted above demonstrates that Boston was just one of many cities to develop special education programs in the late nineteenth and early twentieth centuries. But with most of these histories either providing generalized overviews or emphasizing but one aspect of a system's special education initiatives, it is difficult to tell how closely the growth of special education in Boston resembled that of other cities. Consequently, the need clearly exists for substantial, detailed research of similar developments in other school systems to better understand the extent to which one may generalize the Boston experience. This study seeks to provide a framework for just such detailed eventual comparisons, functioning as a useful step toward a more comprehensive assessment of the origins of special education in the public schools of the United States.

This book is divided into two main sections: the first, encompassing chapters 2 through 4, describes developments in the city and its school system that prepared the groundwork for its special education programs. Chapter 2 describes the growth of the city of Boston, emphasizing demographic, economic, and intellectual developments that would have significant impact on the purposes and practices of public education in the city. Chapter 3 outlines the development of the city's public school system from its formal creation in 1789 through the 1920s, paying particular attention to its administrative structures, increasingly diverse student population, and the emergence of curriculum differentiation as a response to demographic, administrative, and pedagogical demands placed on the system. Chapter 4 then briefly reviews the role of medical, intellectual, and educational trends in the understanding, treatment, and education of individuals with disabilities, especially those with mental disabilities, as well as the role of the child study movement in the growth of special education in the public schools.

Part 2 of this study examines closely the emergence of individual programs in the Boston public schools that catered either directly or indirectly to students with formally identified disabilities: intermediate schools and ungraded classes; three separate programs for students with disciplinary problems; the city's groundbreaking day school for deaf children; special classes for the mentally retarded; and a variety of other programs for students with disabilities established between 1908 and 1913. Not only do these chapters describe the programs themselves, they also examine the rationales offered for their establishment and support.

Essentially, these rationales fell into four categories: the need to isolate children whose behavior or background elicited fear and/or contempt among school and civic authorities; the need to ensure efficiency in the operation and administration of the school system; the need to facilitate efficiency in the operation and administration of individual classrooms; and the desire to provide a specialized pedagogy to individual children identified as requiring one. The overlap, interplay, and friction between and among these various rationales is examined for each program. An understanding of these rationales and a specific knowledge of how each program was founded and implemented suggests that special education in the public schools of Boston arose from a dynamic matrix of needs, fears, hopes, and opportunities that emerged as public schools in the city became more structured and complex and as the schools became vested with ever-growing and ever-changing responsibilities.

Beginning in the 1830s with the introduction of intermediate schools, Boston began the systematic differentiation and segregation of its student population, with much of that effort responding to students' presumed intellectual, physical, or behavioral disabilities. The study of the development of these programs, which became an accepted, even definitive, part of the Boston public school system by the 1920s, can provide substantive perspective and insight into the origins and growth of public school special education in the United States.

This book concludes with a general discussion of ways in which the Boston experience with special education both exemplified and foreshadowed the emergence of certain core issues in special education that continue to characterize the field today.

Finally, an awareness of the author's intent and subjectivity is important in helping readers understand and interpret areas of emphasis as well as patterns of interpretation presented in the study. My goals in pursuing this line of historical inquiry are basic. As an historian, I wish to learn much more about a lively and crucial period in the history of American education and to understand better the origins of special education. As an educator, I am committed to the goal of achieving greater equity among students in the public schools; however, I hold a practical skepticism, grounded in my own teaching experiences, my research, and my conversations with other scholars and practitioners, about the feasibility of completely integrating children with disabilities in public school classrooms. This history simply seeks to add to our understanding of how special education has developed to its current state, with a particular focus on how questions regarding the integration, segregation, and instruction of exceptional students have been answered in other times. It attempts to disclose various beliefs about these children extant during the formative years of special education, and it seeks to determine the relative impact of the administrative needs of the school system and the educational needs of the student in forging special education in the public schools. Ultimately, this book tries to uncover possibilities and opportunities, either hinted at or initiated in the past, for making special education a little better for the parents, teachers, administrators, and especially students involved. In short, this study is an attempt to learn as much as possible to help address any inherent doubts and obstacles regarding the viability of fully integrating children with disabilities in the public schools of the United States.

# 2

## BOSTON 1630–1930:
## AN OVERVIEW

In 1630 John Winthrop and his fellow English colonists established a settlement on a small, narrow peninsula extending into Massachusetts Bay. Over the next three hundred years this community, named Boston in honor of many of the settlers' hometown, would undergo a profound transformation from a quiet, seventeenth-century coastal village to a major twentieth-century metropolitan area. The city's physical geography would alter considerably, its economy and population would grow and diversify, and its cultural and intellectual contributions would achieve international renown. In the process, Boston's development would manifest many of the persistent problems as well as the boundless energy that characterized American history into the early twentieth century. The following brief historical overview will emphasize those aspects of the city's growth most directly related to the evolution of the Boston public school system in order to provide necessary background on that system and its eventual introduction of special education programs.

### The Colonial Era

The earliest permanent European inhabitant of the Shawmut peninsula was William Blackstone, "a solitary, bookish recluse" who supported himself tending apple trees and a garden and trading with his Native American neighbors. In 1630 he invited Governor John Winthrop to relocate his struggling Massachusetts Bay Colony to the peninsula. Winthrop accepted, and on September 7, 1630, the settlement was officially named Boston by an act of the Colony's General Court. Blackstone eventually sold all but six acres of the peninsula to the Colony in 1634. The property consisted of three prominent hills, "dales and lowlands," bordered by some adjoining marshland, with the Charles River to the north and west. Speaking of Boston's early importance, a visitor stated that "this town, although it be neither the greatest or the richest, yet is the most noted and frequented, being the centre of the plantations where the monthly courts are kept."[1]

During the colonial era, Boston solidified its position as the administrative, cultural, and economic center of European New England. It served as the capital of the Massachusetts Bay Colony and later the colonial province of Massachusetts. The town also assumed leadership in religious and educational affairs, with numerous churches and schools (including the Boston Latin School, founded in 1635, and Harvard College, founded in nearby Cambridge in 1636) sustaining the region's intellectual and social life. In addition, Boston's natural harbor guaranteed that the town would continue as the area's commercial and financial heart. Finally, the town and many of its citizens played a vital role in the protracted struggles with England leading to the Revolutionary War and national independence.

## Economic, Social, and Intellectual Growth

For several decades following independence, the economy of Boston and its surrounding region underwent a dramatic transformation. In colonial times Boston's livelihood depended on sea trade, especially the sale of rum and slaves between New England, Africa, and England's colonies in the West Indies; the town thus functioned "as an integral part of the British imperial system." Fishing, smuggling, and shipbuilding constituted the other basic components of its economy. Regionally, agriculture and cottage industries were the primary economic enterprises. Following the Revolution, however, the triangular trade collapsed. That, coupled with an unsteady supply of regional products available for trade and the expansion of other American ports, reduced Boston's relative stature as an American seaport. To compensate, the city's merchants used much of the money previously invested in trade as capital for developing regional industries, which produced such goods as textiles and shoes. Boston thus became a major banking and financing center, second only to New York nationally. It supplied investment capital for much of New England's industrial growth (although its own industrial capacity grew relatively slowly). Between 1830 and 1860 Massachusetts, fueled largely by Boston money, experienced a tremendous industrial expansion along with a decrease in agricultural output.[2]

This regional shift from an agricultural to an industrial economy continued throughout the nineteenth century, and its impact on Boston was profound and lasting. Much of the town's increasing wealth was used to enhance the urban environment and improve contacts with outlying communities. More importantly, the steady growth of its population, which was largely encouraged by the economic expansion, began to affect the town's social and political character. In 1822 Boston adopted a city government, including a new city charter, a mayor's office, a board of aldermen, and a common council. During the 1820s, under the city's second mayor, Josiah Quincy, the municipal government was centralized, and numerous reforms, including efforts to improve public health and safety, were enacted. Throughout the nineteenth century, Boston and its environs urbanized while the economy expanded and diversified, eventually drawing hundreds of thousands of workers from rural New England, Canada, and overseas both into and near the city. Consequently its traditional image, long held by residents and visitors alike, as a homogenous, peaceful, self-contained community became obsolete. In its place arose a new image: that of a complex and thriving metropolis that in many respects reflected the continued, irreversible development of a more urban and industrialized nation.[3]

Boston's evolution into a major urban area was clearly illustrated by its geographic expansion. Early in the nineteenth century, the city began to manifest its urge to expand beyond the narrow confines of the original 783-acre peninsula. Boston used two basic tactics to accomplish this: altering the city's physical contours and repeatedly annexing neighboring areas and communities.

The original peninsula bordered a number of shallow bodies of water: West Cove, Mill Pond or North Cove, Town Cove, South Cove, and the Back Bay. Throughout the nineteenth century, the city undertook a series of landfill projects designed to ease the peninsula's congestion. By taking fill from a number of the peninsula's original hills as well as from other sources, the shallow marshy coves were systematically converted into usable land. Most of the projects required decades to complete, and thousands of workers were employed in the process. West Cove was filled over a period of sixty years; North Cove, twenty-five; East Cove, almost fifty; and South Cove, almost forty. Other fill projects included 250 acres in East Boston and Commonwealth Flats in South Boston. The most extensive project was that of the Back Bay, involving about 600 acres—almost as much as the other projects combined. Completed in 1894 after forty-seven years of work, the Back Bay fill cost over $1.6 million. These projects alone more than doubled the city's land area.[4]

Finding that acquiring property through landfill alone was insufficient, Boston's civic leadership also annexed several surrounding towns in order to gain land for residential and economic development as well as to increase the city's prestige and political clout in Massachusetts and in the nation's capital. Before 1640 Boston had claimed Noddle's Island and Breed's Island, the two areas comprising what is now known as East Boston. Dorchester Neck, also known as South Boston, was annexed in 1804. Another section of Dorchester, Washington Village, joined in 1855. The town of Roxbury was added in 1868 and in 1870 the rest of Dorchester. Then, on January 5, 1874, Boston annexed the communities of Charlestown, Brighton, and West Roxbury. The final annexation occurred on New Year's Day 1912 with the addition of nearby Hyde Park. All told, expansion through landfill and annexation had increased the city's total land area to over thirty thousand acres, more than thirty-eight times its original size.[5]

As Boston's land area increased, so did its population. The first official United States Census in 1790 recorded 18,320 residents of Boston; by 1830 61,392 people claimed Boston as their home. Over the next one hundred years the city grew at an often-startling rate, partly due to the city's emergence as a regional center and to annexation but also to rapidly increasing immigration. Table 1 lists increases in the population as recorded in the federal census between 1790 and 1930. The figures are for the city of Boston proper; it should be noted that the city's suburban areas grew at a rate almost three times that of the city between 1860 and 1930.[6]

Throughout this period of immense change, Boston maintained its position as an influential center for cultural and intellectual activity. The nineteenth century witnessed the blossoming of a number of religious, philosophical, literary, educational, and reform movements that both benefited from and contributed to the city's vitality. Boston continued as a stronghold of Congregationalism while supporting numerous other religious sects and faiths and serving as the spiritual capital of Unitarianism.

### TABLE 1
### Growth in Boston's Population

| Year | Population | Increase (%) |
|------|-----------|--------------|
| 1790 | 18,320 | .... |
| 1800 | 24,937 | 36.1 |
| 1810 | 33,787 | 35.5 |
| 1820 | 43,298 | 28.1 |
| 1830 | 61,392 | 41.8 |
| 1840 | 93,383 | 52.1 |
| 1850 | 136,881 | 46.6 |
| 1860 | 177,840 | 29.9 |
| 1870 | 250,526 | 40.9 |
| 1880 | 362,839 | 44.8 |
| 1890 | 448,477 | 23.6 |
| 1900 | 560,892 | 25.1 |
| 1910 | 670,585 | 19.6 |
| 1920 | 748,060 | 11.6 |
| 1930 | 781,188 | 4.4 |

*Source:* United States Bureau of the Census, *U.S. Census of the Population: 1960. Volume I: Characteristics of the Population. Part 23: Massachusetts* (Washington, D.C.: U.S. Government Printing Office, 1963), 23–28.

The city and its suburbs also boasted a large number of notable writers and other intellectuals, including novelists, poets, philosophers, and several leading members of the transcendental movement. Scholars of national and international fame were drawn to the area by Harvard College and Boston's intellectual and cultural reputation, moving the city to the forefront of American intellectualism and Harvard to the pinnacle of American higher education. The city also became an important publishing center and built a superb public library and art museum. And as a reflection of its energy, Boston provided both a home and a forum for important reformers and reform movements, particularly those concerning abolition, temperance, women's rights, and public health. As a community most proud of these achievements, Boston felt it deserved its identity as the Hub of the Universe.[7]

## Diversification of the Population

As the city underwent its tremendous growth it also experienced a dramatic diversification of its population, and to ascertain these important general characteristics—and evolution of those characteristics—of Boston's inhabitants is crucial to any subsequent discussion of the development of the Boston public schools. During the time Boston grew from a tiny Puritan village into a cosmopolitan urban center, the changing nature of its demographics would radically affect the purposes, configurations, and practices of the city school system.

Colonial Boston was overwhelmingly English in its lineage and restrictive in its acceptance of outsiders. The descendants of the original Bostonians reveled in their heritage; the consequent sense of moral superiority, together with severely limited occupational opportunities for newcomers, kept Boston a close-knit, culturally homogenous and exclusive community into the early 1800s. Nevertheless, a small number of outsiders did trickle into town before the Revolution, and their numbers would gradually increase throughout the early years of the new republic. Among the earliest of these were black slaves, first brought in from the West Indies in 1638. As of 1770 the number of blacks in the town stood at just under 1,000. By 1800, after Massachusetts had abolished slavery, the number of black Bostonians totaled 1,174, or 4.7 percent of the population. Other migrants included rural New Englanders in search of better opportunities and a minute number of European and other immigrants who had arrived over a long period of time. In 1820, two years before Boston officially became a city, the population had reached 43,300. Of these 1,690 were blacks and 5,161 were born outside the United States. While still a bastion of English culture and heritage, Boston's demography had begun to show some heterogeneity.[8]

During the 1830s newcomers continued to arrive at a steady pace, but it was during the 1840s and 1850s that the first great wave of immigration rolled through the city, changing it dramatically and shocking its long-time residents as well as its political leadership. A combination of factors, including the expansion of employment opportunities in the region and the turbulent social and political conditions of mid-century Europe, brought thousands of Europeans across the Atlantic. As a prominent eastern port, Boston had always received a large share of immigrants. Before the 1830s, however, most had sufficient resources to move through and beyond the city when they found Boston inhospitable and unpromising. Yet most of the immigrants of the 1840s and 1850s had barely been able to escape their homelands and found themselves in American ports with no possibility of moving on. They were stranded, most without money, marketable skills, or knowledge of American culture. Once a gateway, Boston had become by default a final destination.[9]

The vast majority of these new Bostonians came from Ireland. Political oppression and severe famine during the 1840s sent a tremendous stream of people from Ireland to the United States. By 1856, when the immigration wave receded somewhat, the port of Boston had received about 140,000 people from Ireland out of a total of some 265,000 immigrants. Many stayed; by 1855 more than 68,000 lived in Boston or in nearby towns. In Boston proper, natives of Ireland constituted almost 30 percent of the population—more than 46,000 people. During this period thousands of other immigrants also arrived: by the mid-1850s almost 6,000 Canadians, 5,000 from other parts of the British Isles, more than 3,000 from Germany, and 1,700 from other nations were residents of the rapidly growing city. Immigration at this time accounted for 38 percent of the city's denizens. Meanwhile, the number of blacks had increased to 2,160, or about 1.3 percent.[10]

Between 1860 and 1880, the rate of immigration slowed somewhat but nevertheless continued to alter Boston's demographic profile. Almost 88,000 persons of foreign birth lived in Boston in 1870; this number had increased to almost 115,000 by 1880, representing 35 percent and 32 percent of the population respectively. During this period, increasing numbers from northern Europe, especially Germany, immigrated to the city. Then, from 1880 until the outbreak of World War I in 1914, Boston was inundated with immigrants from all over the world, primarily from central, southern, and eastern Europe. This second wave, often referred to as the "new" immigration, brought a multitude of languages and customs as Italians, Russians, Slavs, and a host of other nationalities crowded into the city.

By the turn of the century, Boston was comprised largely of the foreign born or of native children born to immigrant parents. Although the percentage of Bostonians born outside the United States stayed at

**Aerial view of Boston looking out over Boston Harbor, as it appeared in 1860.**

approximately 35 percent between 1850 and 1920, the number of children whose parents were immigrants swelled from 46 percent in 1850 to 74 percent as of 1910. In 1900 almost 200,000 of the city's 560,000 people were non-natives. In 1910 there were 240,000 adult immigrants as well as 257,000 children with at least one immigrant parent, making almost half a million residents who claimed a distinctly non-American cultural and linguistic heritage in a city of 670,000. Even in 1930, well after the immigration rate had dropped significantly due to World War I and more restrictive immigration laws, over half of all Bostonians in a population of three-quarters of a million people were either first- or second-generation immigrants. In comparison, the number of black residents of Boston stayed well under 2 percent during the nineteenth century and under 3 percent until 1940.[11]

## The Lives of Immigrant Bostonians

These profound changes in demography manifested themselves in Boston's residential housing patterns and urban character. By the early 1800s the town had grown into a sizable community that actively sought to rearrange its topography and extend its political boundaries. As the number of its residents, dwellings, commercial structures, and streets increased, Boston found itself evolving into a city of distinct neighborhoods: the North End, the South End, Beacon Hill, Fort Hill, the financial district, the docks, the West End, and the Back Bay. The more the city's population diversified, the more closely these neighborhoods became identified with a particular ethnic, social, and/or economic status. When immigration intensified during the mid-nineteenth century, wealthier residents began to retreat, first to Beacon Hill, later to the Back Bay and the more distant, newly acquired sections of town. This migration left much of the historical heart of the city to the growing numbers of impoverished citizens and the ever-growing challenges of rapid urbanization.[12]

The Irish were the first immigrant group to arrive in large numbers, and their considerable poverty forced most of them to remain in what became the crowded neighborhoods near the landing docks, in the North End, and at the base of Fort Hill in the southeast corner of the peninsula. With a severe shortage of job opportunities, most Irish immigrants faced formidable obstacles in escaping these unhealthy surroundings. Consequently, many were forced to continue to live under demoralizing conditions. To make matters worse, they also had to face the often intense resentment of many native Bostonians who distrusted the religion, intentions, lifestyles, and rapidly increasing numbers of the Irish people. Barbara Solomon summarizes the general view of the Irishman held by "Yankees" at the time:

> The lowly peasant from the Emerald Isle was ignorant, shiftless, credulous, impulsive, mechanically inept, and boastful of the Old Country. The inclination toward drinking and related crimes . . . induced gloomy deprecations in New England. . . . The general view was bitter: "The Irishman fails to fit into the complex of our civilization, apparently for the reason that his talents are too little interwoven with the capacities which go to make up the modern successful man."[13]

Generations would be required to strengthen the status and wealth of those of Irish heritage in Boston, but slowly they were able to relocate in other neighborhoods and develop some all-important political influence. The first Irish mayor was elected in the 1880s, and by the early twentieth century the Irish had gained control of Boston politics. Even so, thousands and thousands of immigrants from Ireland continued to live in impoverished, dispiriting conditions.[14]

The hundreds of thousands of other immigrants who arrived throughout the late nineteenth and early twentieth centuries suffered from many of the same difficulties. With the great majority poor, unskilled, unfamiliar with American life and distrusted by nativists, they settled as best they could in the teeming immigrant neighborhoods of Boston. Though sharing an extremely crowded environment, most immigrant groups segregated themselves as much as possible, often to maintain some semblance of common culture and community support. By 1900 large numbers of Jews had settled in the West End; Italians in the North End, Germans in Roxbury, Russians in the North and West Ends, and the Irish in many places but especially South Boston. The city's black population remained mostly segregated in the West End and at the base of Beacon Hill, where they had lived for generations. The North End developed a reputation for housing the greatest variety of immigrants under the most unhealthy and dangerous conditions. Overcrowded tenements, open sewers, and widespread crime and disease plagued most of the immigrant neighborhoods, although to varying degrees.[15]

Much as the Irish before them, immigrants from southern and eastern Europe were often (and unfairly) criticized by nativist Bostonians, in part because the residents of immigrant neighborhoods were frequently held responsible for creating their dismal living conditions. Immigrant neighborhoods served as constant targets for reformers and city leaders who expressed ambivalent but generally negative views of the non-native population. From the late nineteenth century on, these ethnic groups (particularly the Italians) were subjected to harsh criticism for their religion, their supposed proclivity to crime and intemperance, and their alleged lack of respect for American values and institutions. Such attitudes led to the formation of an Immigration Restriction League during the 1890s. The Catholic Church, which eventually became the largest single religious organization in the city (it was the faith of most European immigrants), was continually attacked by nativists during the nineteenth century. In addition, negative generalizations about the innate characteristics of various ethnic groups proved quite popular well into the twentieth century. To emigrate to Boston may have been preferable to remaining in one's homeland, but for the majority of immigrants life in the city was difficult at best.[16]

## Education and the Betterment of Boston

These problems in urban development were repeated time and again throughout the United States as cities grew and immigration increased. Boston in many ways exemplified much of the nature of urbanization—the variety, the fears, the opportunities. The solutions offered to these problems of urbanization were many and varied. However, Boston and all great American cities believed strongly in the power of one new, crucial, and far-reaching tool as a panacea for much of what ailed urban life: the public school. As cities grew, so did their hope that the public schools could work wonders in addressing the seemingly insolvable problems that the city presented. Through the nineteenth century and well into the twentieth, the city of Boston emphasized the role of its school system in cleaning up urban blight and assuring the proper education of loyal, productive citizens.[17]

# 3

## BUILDING THE BOSTON PUBLIC SCHOOLS

The long history of public education in Boston began in 1635 with the founding of the city's first public school. From this single institution (the original Boston Latin School, open to young men interested in the ministry), Boston developed a massive, highly organized system of public education designed to accommodate and instruct its school-age population. That system struggled constantly to gain the support of the general public as well as adjust its purposes and structure to the rapid growth of the city's population and the greater diversity of its students. By the early 1900s the Boston public schools enrolled more than one hundred thousand students to whom it offered a remarkable variety of curricula and instructional settings, including numerous programs in special education.

Although colonial Boston supported a few "reading" and "writing" schools as well as the Latin School for its residents, the official history of the Boston public schools began with the passage of the Boston Education Act in 1789. This act created a formal system of separate "reading" and "writing" schools, established eligibility for school attendance, identified appropriate texts and, most importantly, created the Boston School Committee (BSC) to administer the system. Over the next 150 years, the BSC would oversee fundamental changes in the structure, policies, and practices of the Boston public schools that would both reflect and direct developments in the social, intellectual, and economic climate of the community and the region.[1]

Perhaps the most salient and obvious feature of the Boston public schools during this extended period was the dramatic growth in the number of students. This increase was a function not only of the growth of the city itself but also of the many deliberate efforts to bring more and more children within the influence of public education. Beyond the population increase, the addition of primary schools, the establishment of truancy laws, and especially the introduction and continuous extension of compulsory education laws all worked to bring students into the world of public schooling—a world which had been vested with great expectations and demands concerning the intellectual and especially the moral training of the city's youth. Between 1789 and 1930, the increase in the number of students enrolled in the Boston public schools mirrored the dramatic growth of the city itself. In 1789 about 600 students attended the schools; by the end of the first wave of immigration in 1855 there were more than 25,000. At the turn of the century, over 80,000 students attended the public schools in the city, with more than 129,000 enrolled as of 1930.[2]

An early boost to these increases occurred in 1818, when the school committee, after considerable debate, established a system of primary schools for children ages four to seven in order to instruct them in basic literacy and computational skills. By the late 1810s, Boston's demography had shown a notable rise in the number of residents and in the diversity of their ethnic origins. As newcomers arrived from rural New England, the Canadian territories, and Europe, many Bostonians became concerned over the growing number of new children who were ineligible for the public schools because of their inability to read. (Regulations required a child to be able to "read easy prose" to be admitted to the reading and writing schools.) This concern crystallized with the appearance of a letter from a Boston lawyer, James Savage, in the *Boston Daily Advertizer.* Published on April 21, 1818, Savage's letter reiterated the widely held belief that education was the most effective weapon against vice, crime, and poor citizenship in an increasingly urban Boston. Proclaiming that it was the town's duty to provide basic education—especially to the poorer classes—and that all children had a right to be schooled, Savage urged the town to develop primary schools toward that end. On May 25 of that year, a petition, signed by more than two hundred Bostonians and presented at a town meeting, requested the establishment of public primary schools for children aged four to seven as a place to obtain essential academic and moral instruction. A subcommittee of the BSC had already examined and decided against the proposition earlier, stating that it was beyond the responsibility of the town as well as too costly. Nevertheless, in June 1818 a committee formed by the town reported in favor of public primary schools. Yielding to pressure, the BSC established a primary school board on June

16 and gave it power to organize a primary school system. By this action the Boston public schools greatly expanded their accessibility and influence.[3]

## The Charge of Public Education

James Savage's letter supporting a system of primary schools manifested many privileged Bostonians' concern regarding the increasing numbers of poor and immigrant children. Beginning in the 1820s and extending over the next one hundred years, the city's civic and educational leadership remained adamant that the best way to stop the steady, persistent growth of poverty—and the closely related problems of crime, vice, and disease—was to build schools that would keep such children off the streets, isolate them from evil influences, and instruct them in the virtues of morality, honesty, and American citizenship.

During the early 1800s, prominent citizens of Boston considered and eventually undertook the development of a system of privately sponsored Sunday and charity schools designed to address the then-limited but nagging problem of immigrant poverty in the town. Led by the Boston Society for the Moral and Religious Instruction of the Poor and paralleling similar activity in other cities, especially New York, these efforts drew significant support from well-to-do Bostonians. Their support essentially reflected the belief that "in this way we strike at the foundation of the evils incidental to society, and with greater prospect of success than to reform the hardened offenders, —and yet through the children, not unfrequently the parent is reclaimed." Noah Webster, author of the most popular spelling text of the time, proclaimed in an 1819 letter that "the most efficacious mode of preventing crimes" was "to draw from the obscure retreats of poverty the miserable victims of ignorance and vice, to enlighten their minds and correct their evil habits, to raise them to the rank of intelligent, industrious, and useful members of society." This view of education as an effective medium of social and moral amelioration easily carried over into the realm of public schooling, whose leaders continued to assert the benevolent influence their schools would have on impoverished young Bostonians and their families for generations to come. George B. Emerson classically expressed this widespread attitude when he stated in 1847 that "unless [such children] are made inmates of our schools many of them will become inmates of our prisons."[4]

This generalized view manifested an important component of that drive—state, regional, and to some extent national—known as the common school movement. Complex in its characteristics and far-reaching in its influence, the common school movement in the United States emphasized the need for public schools to educate and acculturate the nation's youth: to provide them with basic literacy and computational skills, assure their capable participation in a democratic society, and convince them of the value of a life guided by a generalized Protestant morality and an unwavering loyalty to the nation and its political and economic ideals (as determined by educational leaders). The common school movement achieved perhaps its greatest initial acceptance in Massachusetts, where the persuasive arguments of many educators—especially James G. Carter—led directly to the establishment of a Massachusetts school fund in 1834 and a state board of education, headed by a superintendent, in 1837. While the legislature gave the new board and superintendent little power except to compile statistics, the legislation symbolized the region's hope that public schools would greatly assist in solving problems presented by changes in its demography and economy.[5]

The advent of the common school movement in Massachusetts and elsewhere would have a profound effect on the development of philosophical and ideological underpinnings of American education as well as on the organization and structure that public schooling would acquire during the nineteenth century. The leaders of the common school movement shared a particular worldview that powerfully shaped the assumptions and purposes guiding educational reform in nineteenth-century America; historian Carl Kaestle labeled this worldview "Native Protestant ideology." According to Kaestle, Native Protestant ideology consisted of

> ten strands or major propositions: the sacredness and fragility of the republican polity (including ideas about individualism, liberty, and virtue); the importance of individual character in fostering social morality; the central role of personal industry in defining rectitude and merit; the delineation of a highly respected but limited domestic role for women; the importance for character building of familial and social environment (within certain racial and ethnic limitations); the sanctity and social virtues of property; the equality and abundance of economic opportunity in the United States; the superiority of Ameri-

can Protestant culture; the grandeur of America's destiny; and the necessity of a determined public effort to unify America's polyglot population, chiefly through education.

To its advocates, common schooling represented a great opportunity to instill this particular set of values in students whose ethnic, cultural, religious, and linguistic backgrounds were becoming increasingly diverse— and thus upsetting to those in control of public policy.[6]

Common school reform was at its strongest in the years between 1830 and 1860, during which efforts to build and support common schools that could serve as a venue for teaching Native Protestant ideology to school-age children flourished. The nation's northern regions—stretching from Maine to the Mississippi River—experienced significant growth in the number of common schools as well as in the number of children attending them. Other individuals joined Horace Mann, the first Massachusetts secretary of the state board of education and common schooling's most forceful advocate, in proclaiming the virtues of government-operated, free public schools open to all social classes and supported largely through taxation. Mann and Carter in Massachusetts, Henry Barnard in Connecticut, Thaddeus Stevens in Pennsylvania, Calvin Stowe in Ohio, Caleb Mills in Indiana, and John Pierce in Michigan were among the most famous proponents of common school education, writing and speaking extensively on its merits and promise. Although the Southern regions of the United States lagged well behind in developing common schools, and while much of the activity of common school reform failed to move beyond rhetoric, the practical impact of common schooling did in fact reach large numbers of American school children during the 1800s. By 1860 the principle that tax-supported common elementary schools constituted a cornerstone in the creation of a civil, loyal, and moral citizenry had become well established, especially among the nation's educational leadership.

Boston was of course the home of the Massachusetts State Board of Education and its renowned first secretary. It was also the home of other influential intellects of the day who advocated social reform through education, notably Samuel Gridley Howe and George Emerson. The city's efforts in creating a system of city-operated primary schools and in offering privately sponsored infant and charity schools to its impoverished children drew nationwide attention and were perhaps second only to New York City's as an example to other urban school systems in the United States.

Horace Mann's advocacy of the oral method of instruction for deaf children was honored by renaming the Boston School for Deaf-Mutes as The Horace Mann School for the Deaf in 1877.

To say that Boston or even Massachusetts served as the primary source and sustenance of the common school movement would be to oversimplify the issue: the development of common schooling drew strength from a wide range of beliefs, conditions, aims, and activities that transcended the work done there, and so much of the actual practice—even essence—of common school reform emerged from the thousands of communities and school districts facing their own unique conditions and expectations. Nevertheless, much of the common school movement—including the articulation of the purposes of common school education, the development of school systems seeking to implement such education in a rapidly changing urban America, and the eventual abandonment of the common school ideal in favor of differentiated education as a response to demographic diversity—mirrored or even followed Boston's experience in building a system of compulsory public education.

Beginning with its creation of public primary schools, Boston's educational leadership constantly emphasized the critical importance of public schooling in preserving a stable, moral community. In 1852 Massachusetts enacted a law ordering all teachers at all levels in the state to teach their students "the principles of piety, justice, and a sacred regard to truth, love to their country, humanity and universal benevolence, sobriety, industry and frugality, chastity, moderation and temperance . . . and also to point out to them the evil tendency of the opposite vices." This law remained on the books and was cited as a valuable guideline in the superintendent's annual report of 1922. Superintendent of Schools John D. Philbrick expressed the idea more succinctly in 1857 when he called on the public to bring their schools "nearer to that standard of perfection which causes every pupil, by the influence of right motives, to do the right things at the right time and in the right manner." Moral education, also referred to as "character training" or as honing the "spiritual habits," remained a basic component of public school instruction. "As you pursue your education along whatever lines you may choose," advised a speaker to graduating grammar students in 1904, "always bear in mind that the development of good, strong qualities of character should be the most important element of that education." Superintendent Jeremiah Burke's 1924 report proclaimed, "The whole machinery of the school is prepared to move forward triumphantly for the development of spiritual habits; of unselfish conduct; of unfaltering loyalty to conviction; of moral robustness and vigor; of righteousness of living; and of the ability to distinguish between right and wrong."[7]

The maintenance of a stable community demanded that the public schools impress upon their students the values of good citizenship and patriotism. School officials stressed that this role was particularly important in Boston, where the population had become primarily immigrant by the early 1900s. They aimed to ensure that immigrant children would learn to understand, accept, and defend the "American" way of life. One supervisor, writing in 1898, spoke for most of the city's school leaders on this matter:

> [Immigrant children] need special care and attention in order that they may get right ideas of their relation to this country and what the city, State, and nation are doing to ameliorate the condition of all persons who seek a home on our shores. They show a strong desire to learn our language, and exhibit an earnest purpose to become thoroughly Americanized. The importance of the work to be done cannot be overestimated. The life of the Republic depends upon the *virtue* and *intelligence* of the people.[8]

"Americanization" was thus a cardinal theme of public schooling in the city, especially after 1890. In 1926 a special committee wrote of "good citizenship" and "social efficiency" as crucial dividends that would contribute to a stable, energetic, patriotic America:

> True citizenship means an intelligent understanding of one's obligations to the community, the state, the nation, and the world; a social attitude which holds one to an ideal of constructive endeavor rather than destructive criticism. . . . The necessary equipment for meeting one's duties and responsibilities as a citizen and in the home must include an understanding of the spirit of our democratic institutions and of the laws of the land, with the desire and the will to preserve and obey them. There must also be actively present the spirit of cooperation which grows out of the understanding of and sympathy with the other members of the various groups to which one may belong. Herein lies the key to the development of real social efficiency.[9]

Thus the task was clear, the agent named: the Boston public school system was expected to ensure the safety and loyalty of the community's citizens by bringing as many children as possible under the control of public education's beneficence. This was as true in the 1920s as in the 1820s, and it proved to be a powerful reassurance to those struggling with the growing size and diversity of the system that their struggles were important and their methods justified.

Hence, efforts to bring children of all eligible ages into the public school system had begun in earnest by the mid-nineteenth century. Although Massachusetts had always strongly urged basic education for its children, until well into the 1800s there existed no law specifically compelling attendance in a school. The first law directly addressing school attendance in Massachusetts took effect in 1836. It prohibited the employment in any factory of a child under age fifteen who had not attended school on a regular basis for at least three months in the year prior to employment. This law, Chapter 245 of the Acts of 1836, constituted the state's first child labor legislation. By 1850 the notion of appointing truancy officers to convince reluctant parents to send their children to a public school had taken firm hold. In that year the state passed a truant law enabling local school agencies "to make all needful provisions and arrangements concerning habitual truants and children not attending school." Even though school attendance was still voluntary, Boston responded with an ordinance strengthening the city's power to find truant boys and girls and place them in the classroom. Two years later the city appointed its first truant officers.[10]

In 1852 Massachusetts, with full support from the Boston School Committee, enacted the first comprehensive compulsory education law in the United States. The law (Chapter 240, Acts of 1852) stipulated that all youths in the state between ages eight and fourteen attend a public school for a minimum twelve weeks per year, at least six of which had to be consecutive. The law contained several qualifications, however. It exempted children who attended a private school, who received sufficient education at home, whose parents were too poor or otherwise unable to sustain their child's attendance, who had somehow "already acquired those branches of learning which are taught in common schools," or who due to physical or mental conditions were unable to benefit from instruction. The law carried a fine of twenty dollars for noncompliance; enforcement was erratic at best. Nevertheless, a crucial precedent had been set.[11]

Over the next several decades Massachusetts extended and strengthened its child labor and school attendance laws, becoming a national leader in developing the tradition of compulsory public education. In 1866 the state forbade the employment in any factory of any child aged ten to fourteen who had not attended school for at least six months prior to employment. Ten years later the act was extended to children working for any mercantile or mechanical concern. An 1873 state act increased the minimum period of compulsory attendance from twelve to twenty weeks but reduced the maximum age limit to twelve. Two years later that limit was again raised to fourteen. In 1889 thirty weeks became the minimum period of attendance, and poverty was no longer a permissible excuse to keep children from school. Meanwhile, the Boston School Committee had greatly increased the number of truant officers in order to ensure as full compliance with the laws as possible and to adjust to the tremendous increase in school-age youth in the city.

By 1911 Massachusetts required all children aged seven to fourteen to attend a local public (or sanctioned private) school for the "entire time public day schools are in session," that is, from early September to late June. Children aged fourteen to sixteen who were illiterate were also required to attend. Shortly thereafter compulsory attendance came to include all children between seven and sixteen. As of 1914 no child under fourteen could work for wages during regular school hours. At this time the law also stipulated that "no physical or mental condition which is capable of correction, or which renders the child a fit subject for special instruction at public charge in institutions other than the public day schools, shall avail as a defense . . . unless . . . the defendant has employed all rea-sonable measures for the correction of the condition or the suitable in-struction of the child." Thus by the 1910s Massachusetts and its capital city sought to bring virtually every person of school age under the umbrella of formal schooling.[12]

The dramatic changes in the size and demography of the public school system in Boston quickly rendered the organizational structure cre-ated by the 1789 Education Act obsolete. The creation of primary schools was among the first of many structural and administrative changes that the state, the city, and the school committee initiated in order to make the system more comprehensive and manageable. By 1930 the Boston public schools had undergone a series of major bureaucratic reorganizations. It also had implemented a sweeping restructuring of its method of student classification. These efforts followed logically from the growing emphasis on building an efficient, economical, and effective system of public educa-tion, one that could satisfy the declared purposes of public schooling as well as the expectations of the community.

## Growth of Bureaucracy: The Business of Education

The drive to improve the efficiency of the school system led to a series of initiatives affecting the schools' top-level administration. The Boston School Committee was restructured in 1835 to include two representatives from each city ward; by doing so officials hoped to provide sufficient super-vision over the steadily growing number of schools. In 1851, following years of debate, the BSC authorized the establishment of the office of su-perintendent of schools. In 1855 the school committee dissolved the Pri-mary School Board. This board had become a strong, independent body with over 190 members by the early 1850s, one for each primary school; however, it lost a protracted struggle for power with the school committee, which had sought to gain autonomous control over all the public schools. In 1866 the grammar school principals obtained direct supervision of the primary schools in their respective districts to facilitate primary school su-pervision.

In 1876 and again in 1905 the school committee itself underwent significant reorganization. By 1875 the BSC had swelled to an unwieldy membership of 116 due to the addition of wards through annexation. On

January 1, 1876, a state law reduced the BSC's membership to the mayor plus twenty-four members elected at large in order to streamline the decision-making process. Thirty years later the state, which retained ultimate power of all local school committees in Massachusetts, again restructured the BSC by cutting its membership to five. To assist in administration, a board of supervisors was created in 1876. In 1906 a board of superintendents, comprised of six assistant superintendents, replaced the board of supervisors.[13]

A fundamental principle guiding these developments was that the school system should exhibit the systematic logic of a well-tuned, well-oiled machine. In 1883 J. L. Pritchard published an article in *Education* entitled "City Management of Public Schools." Pritchard contended that "the best machine is that which does its work most evenly, most speedily, with the least friction, with the least possibility of derangement, and with the least waste of material employed." This view epitomized those of Boston's school leaders from Superintendents Nathan Bishop and John Philbrick in the 1850s to Jeremiah Burke in the 1920s, and it was a cornerstone in the construction of urban school systems across the nation. In his first semiannual report as superintendent, dated December 30, 1851, Bishop expressed the general theme that the schools should be organized and run as a business, emphasizing practicality in the organization of classrooms, textbook selection and distribution, and teacher selection. "Such a system," he observed, "should contain ample provisions for giving to every child in the city an education of the best quality, in the shortest time, and at the smallest expense." Over fifty years later, the BSC's annual report for 1905 included an extensive section on the "Application of Modern Business Methods to Educational Activities." In explaining their rationale for establishing many of the numerous special education programs to be discussed in this study, Boston's educational leadership would constantly cite their desire to assure a businesslike efficiency and economy in the system's operation.[14]

## The Graded Classification of Students

The desire to operate an efficient system of public education was both strong and durable, yet achieving such factorylike efficiency proved more and more problematic as the student population became more diverse and the expectations for public schools grew more extensive and demanding. Tensions between efficient administration and the realities of the classroom had existed almost from the beginning of the system itself; as the nineteenth century progressed these tensions emerged as a central concern for teachers and administrators alike. A key question thus persisted for decades: how can diverse classrooms function efficiently and effectively, using as little money and other resources as possible?

The single most important response to this question was the introduction of the graded classification of students in 1847. Traditionally the schools had been organized as reading and writing schools, separate institutions in separate facilities with different teachers. In the 1820s these schools were partially consolidated under the "double-headed" system, which brought the schools closer together physically yet maintained their separate status. When the primary schools opened, their students were grouped according to achievement in a single class for all subjects. These early attempts at formal classification functioned adequately in an era when enrollment was relatively small and cultural and linguistic background relatively homogenous. As the public school population grew and diversified, however, school officials found that a more efficient approach was necessary.

In 1847 the BSC initiated its new approach to student classification, one that would have a profound effect on the evolution of the school system and on the eventual development of special education. In that year the school committee introduced the "single-headed" or graded system of grammar school organization at the new Quincy School in central Boston. Under this plan the dual reading and writing divisions in grammar instruction were merged into a single classroom under one master. Instead of the complex and often inconsistent classification characteristic of the "double-headed" system, this new approach opted for pupils at a grammar school to be assigned, according to age and achievement, to one teacher who would instruct the same class for the entire year. The Quincy School was the first fully graded grammar school in the city, even though the "double-headed" plan had been publicly criticized as early as 1830. With the graded system the Boston School Committee hoped to bring some order and logic into a public school system that by then cried out for both. Within fifteen years, most of the city's grammar schools had adopted the approach; primary school grading began in 1857 and was completed in just a few years. By the 1880s the classification of students according to age under a single teacher for a single year, with regular advancement along with their classmates through the elementary grades, had become an ingrained, widely applauded feature of the Boston public schools, nationally noted and imitated.[15]

As the graded system of school organization and student classification developed, however, Boston school officials had to learn to cope with and adjust to the practical effects of a rigid, prescribed system designed to move as many children as possible up the educational ladder in an efficient manner. Into the early twentieth century the graded approach, while a source of great pride, also generated a great deal of consternation as teachers, administrators, and the school committee learned that a huge, diverse school population could not fit neatly into their carefully crafted schemes of lockstep instruction and promotion. The committee's efforts to achieve and maintain operational and instructional efficiency eventually required the abandonment of the ideal of common education for all in favor of differentiated curricula and the establishment of a wide variety of segregated, specialized instructional settings—all of which would contribute significantly to the emergence of a special education for students with disabilities in the Boston public schools.

Recognition of some of the practical implications of the graded system appeared soon after its inception. In 1859 Superintendent John Philbrick, who as principal of the Quincy School had guided the introduction of graded classification and would eventually become a nationally prominent leader in public education, observed that "in the most perfectly graded school, there is always a top and a bottom to every class." Accordingly, he maintained that under the graded system "school tasks should be graduated neither to the inability of the weakest and dullest, nor to the ability of the strongest and brightest, but to the mediocrity of the mass. In schools as well as in government, 'the greatest good to the greatest number,' is the guiding principle ever to be kept in view." However, not all school critics shared this position. During the late 1870s and early 1880s, the "rigidity" and "inelasticity" of the graded system and its imposed curriculum came under intense attack for its alleged disrespect for the individuality of each student. Philbrick's suggestion that schools should cater to mediocrity was likened by critics such as Burke Hinsdale and Charles Francis Adams Jr. to an attempt to "make equal the legs of the lame" or to move children down an assembly line in order to "receive the same mental nutriment in equal quantities and at fixed times." Another critic argued that "the ideal of the system is to take a key and wind up at the centre and have the whole mechanism, to the very circumference, tick, and strike, and move with unchanged regularity."[16]

Despite such criticisms, the graded system continued to operate, receiving strong support from education professionals. But eventually these same professionals, especially teachers, came to recognize the difficulties of forcing a diverse student population into preconceived strata. Between 1890 and 1900, graded classification was the object of much discussion as educators identified its problems and tried to fashion viable solutions. The fundamental difficulty, according to these educators, was the impossibility of providing quality, individualized instruction to classrooms full of large numbers of children whose abilities differed so greatly. "However carefully the pupils of a school may be classified," stated the board of supervisors in 1890,

> it is impossible to put fifty or more under the instruction of one teacher in any grade, and expect equally good work from all members of the class. Some are older and more mature, capable of closer application and more independent effort; others, although younger, have keener and more active minds than a majority of their classmates. The dull but faithful pupil will, for a while, make a heroic effort to measure his steps with those of his more favored mates. Until he fully recognizes his inferiority, he will struggle to overcome it; but inevitably the struggle becomes a hopeless one and his effort is relaxed.[17]

Seven years later Superintendent Edwin Seaver acknowledged that under the graded system of instruction "the grades have a tendency to level down as well as to level up; superior minds may be injured quite as much as inferior minds are helped by the constant enforcement of an 'average' rate and standard of work." Seaver was an experienced teacher and former headmaster at Boston's English High School who had been appointed superintendent in 1880 during a most difficult and divisive time in the school system's history. As a strong believer in not only efficient school governance but also in nascent progressivist approaches to school instruction, Seaver compared school children to plants who required different kinds and amounts of fertilizer at different times for optimum growth, concluding that "a rigidly uniform course of study for all children is as absurd as a uniform course of fertilization for all vegetables." Concern was

A primary-grade classroom in the Hancock School, a public school for girls located in the North End, c. 1892. More than one-third of the students in this school were enrolled in ungraded classes by the turn of the century.

expressed for both the slower pupils who, it was feared, would struggle to keep pace, and for the unusually bright pupils who required more stimulating studies which they could "easily do, and need to do in order to keep their minds open and alert. . . . The more machine-like a graded school becomes in its operations, the more these two evils of over-pressure and under-work appear." Philbrick thus understood what graded classification involved. He did not, however, view a curriculum designed for the mediocre with the skepticism and negativity his more experienced successors did.[18]

To some school officials, the graded system's lack of concern for individual students could also be seen in the forced march of children through a system demanding constant, predictable advancement to a higher grade. The 1890 supervisor's report described how pupils were commonly shuffled, promoted, or rearranged without regard to their educational needs so as to obey regulations, follow guidelines, and satisfy practical demands for classroom space. Such movement within the system troubled all levels of the public schools and, according to this report, clearly demonstrated the sacrifice of the child to the machinery of the system. It was a view of the schools that persisted after the late 1870s and gradually became more accepted by teachers as well as administrators.[19]

## Adjustments in Graded Classification

Professional educators in Boston still firmly believed that graded instruction constituted an absolute necessity for any effective operation of their public school system. Nonetheless, faced with the logistical and instructional drawbacks inherent in graded classification, they also recognized that some adjustment was required. In a seminal declaration, Edwin Seaver stated, "The official duty of the supervising powers is to operate the machinery of graded instruction: but in so doing there should be a large discretion lodged with those powers to encourage and assist all teachers in their efforts to promote the education of individual pupils through other means than those afforded by the regular official courses of study."

Responding to and reflecting this philosophy, the school system over the last several years of the nineteenth century moved toward the definitive differentiation, based on academic ability and achievement, of regular elementary school students. By 1895 several schools had experimented with staggered (rather than end-of-the-year) student promotions as well as with intraclass groupings frequently readjusted to best suit the instructional needs of the teacher and pupils. Such steps recalled the earlier nineteenth-century practices of the one-room district school.[20]

More pronounced, however, was the call for separate facilities and programs for "special" groups of pupils. Seaver suggested "enrichment" studies for brighter children as the best means to individualize the curriculum so that "all youth of superior mental endowments and moral worth can be prepared for the highest walks of honor and usefulness." Such studies were implemented mostly in the form of elective subjects in the higher grammar levels and secondary schools. For the elementary schools, officials gave more attention to coping with "dull" students who were viewed as suffering from overwork or as holding back the majority of their classmates. In 1890 the supervisors, calling for in-class differentiation of children, claimed that "pupils able to push forward at a more rapid pace should be allowed to do so unhindered by classmates less able or less ambitious." By 1897 school officials had begun to argue strongly for unique allowances for its academically struggling elementary students. Wrote Superintendent Seaver:

> There are in every school faithful pupils of excellent spirit—pupils quite as well worth educating for their own sake and that of the com-

munity as are their more brilliant classmates—whose intellectual parts are not equal to the effort of keeping pace with the main body of the class. Such pupils oftentimes are able to do three studies well, but not four, or to do four well, but not five. These pupils should be permitted and encouraged to undertake each year only so many studies as they can do well, and to take as much longer time to earn the diploma as they may need.

The schools also saw the need to provide suitable learning environments for students who due to reasons of physical ailment could not keep up with the curriculum: "What such pupils need is a reduced amount of work giving employment for regular but moderate periods of time. . . . The number of pupils, chiefly girls, who need to be treated in the way just described, is probably much larger than teachers generally expect."[21]

In a thorough report on this issue Supervisor Sarah Arnold, a strong proponent of individualized study catering to the specific needs of the child, applauded the fact that "in some primary buildings, from two to four rooms . . . are arranged for pupils who deviate from the standard classification. 'Advanced first,' 'beginning second,' classes are met in these buildings, as the children's attainments determine. The pupils are sent on as fast as possible." Arnold recommended that a written record of each child in "the army of 'specials'" in the public schools be kept to inform an assistant teacher in any schoolhouse of their special problems. "Knowing the child's histories, and their individual records, she can place them where their special needs will be met, removing them from time to time, as their necessities dictate." This approach, Arnold said, would serve to individualize a child's education while also rendering graded classification more efficient.[22]

## Movement toward Curriculum Differentiation

The various issues surrounding student diversity and school efficiency had elicited comments and concern among school officials almost from the beginning of the graded system of student classification. Many of these comments referred specifically to a student's "natural" abilities—or lack thereof. School officials also frequently considered how differences in student background and presumed "interest"—and the consequent expectations regarding their future employment—could or should affect decisions regarding the selection and implementation of curriculum. Over time there emerged a series of calls to acknowledge such differences among students and to differentiate the curriculum accordingly.

In 1858 the Boston School Committee took vivid note of the differences that existed among students. Its annual report for that year proclaimed that teaching students with dramatically diverse abilities and from suspect backgrounds constituted a most difficult challenge. That same year Superintendent John Philbrick described how two teachers took different approaches to coping with diversity in their classrooms. "One teacher of large experience," he wrote, worked hard "to keep the dull ones from falling back,—while those of premature mental development, with large heads on small bodies, are judiciously restrained, till their physical growth can come up with their intellectual; another does not discriminate, and each is allowed to go his own pace."[23]

By 1871 the school committee was advocating a differentiated education based on home life and background. In its annual report the BSC argued, "But we have to consider that the widely differing conditions of parents determines in a great measure the needs and opportunities of their children; and no program can be established that will be the best for all classes of pupils. . . . With these things in mind we shall better understand the extreme difficulty of adhering to one unvarying programme of study for all pupils, and perhaps be satisfied that it is as undesirable as it is difficult." The report then explained that primary grades and "the first part of Grammar School" should have a common curriculum for all pupils, but by the time a student had "reached the age of twelve or thirteen years" a differentiated curriculum might be appropriate. The committee's 1876 report reiterated this belief. "Up to that point where the elementary instruction needed by all, whatever their after-course in life may be, is acquired, there can be no question as to the wisdom of uniformity of instruction," stated the committee. "But in the subsequent conduct of education it becomes a question, whether it would not be desirable to put boys whose circumstances oblige them to cease their school attendance at age fourteen, under a different regimen from that which should be pursued by those who intend to pass through the High School." The report then suggested differentiating the grammar school curriculum, providing different instruction to those headed for high school and those headed for the workforce. Over the next twenty years those suggestions were realized as Boston, like the rest of Massachusetts and like much of the rest of the country, initiated extensive programs in manual training, industrial education, pre-vocational education, and vocational education. "Adaptation and mobility are the touchstones by which the modern school system may be tested," proclaimed Assistant Superintendent Augustine L. Rafter in 1914. "Perhaps no city in the land has recognized this principle of differentiation in its schools to the extent that Boston has."[24]

As differentiating curriculum on the basis of student background and anticipated postschool employment became accepted, so did the belief that differences in the mental and physical abilities of students also demanded that the schools differentiate curricula appropriately. Many statements emanating from school authorities discussed the impact of diverse student ability on the graded classification system, as noted earlier. By the early 1900s the notion that diverse ability was a basic condition of the public school population and that the schools should respect such diversity for purposes of both economy and pedagogy had become entrenched in Boston. In an extensive essay on the subject, Superintendent Stratton Brooks argued that differences in ability, background, and future needs among Boston's school children were profound and that the school had a responsibility to recognize this. "In recent years," he wrote, "the recognition of differences among children has resulted in many modifications in education. Educators have endeavored to determine what differences exist and in what way the educational machinery needs to be modified in order best to promote the welfare of each individual pupil." Speaking specifically to the question of ability, the next superintendent, Franklin Dyer, offered the following extended observation:

> To meet the needs of children who vary from the normal type is one of the leading purposes of our school system. This has not been found so expensive as it was expected to be, because as children who require especial and individual attention were removed from the ordinary classes and the group of children under regular teachers became more homogenous, the teachers could handle larger groups more effectively than they could when the children were not so well classified. When teachers are required to give a large portion of their time to children who have special needs, mass teaching becomes difficult and exhausting, and a group of thirty-five children under such conditions is more burdensome than a group of forty-five that is homogenous. It is therefore economical in every way to establish classes for children who are exceptional.[25]

Clearly the efficiency of the school system was at stake, but it was more than that. Brooks' expressed concern for "the welfare of each individual pupil" was echoed by Superintendent Jeremiah Burke in 1922:

> There are radical differences in the qualities that go to make up the so-called normal child. Humanely and sanely these differences and peculiarities are becoming recognized in the life of the school. In place of rigid and uniform courses of study, curricula are being modified and reconstructed to satisfy the varying aptitudes and capacities of boys and girls, of groups of children, all equally deserving, all endowed with equality of rights and entitled to equality of opportunity.[26]

This position would eventually become firmly implanted in the official "Philosophy of Education" of the Boston schools, as Burke described in 1931.

> We must have a variety of courses—diverse avenues of instruction—to meet the needs and capacities of children. Therefore Boston, perhaps in the lead of American cities, is offering these opportunities in different types and classes of schools. The rigid and uniform courses of the older days . . . are replaced today with curricula adapted to the peculiar aptitudes and capacities of children.[27]

The diversity of student backgrounds, assumed vocational needs, and intellectual and physical ability thus would have a dramatic impact on the administration of the school system as well as the instruction carried on in individual classes and schools—an impact that would be directly responsible for the development of programs for students with disabilities. In 1871 the Boston School Committee had issued a prescient observation:

> There is something fascinating to the mind, we are fully aware, in the idea of rounding each department of a system, and of deploying masses of pupils by right lines in a column; the wiser idea, however, is to regard all rules but as general directions, to be observed in a liberal spirit, and to be administered for the benefit of individuals rather than for the pleasure or glory of the ruler.[28]

This pronouncement contains the key to understanding how and why programs for students with disabilities eventually would take hold in Boston. The "fascination" with a "round" system and "right lines" generated sustained efforts to address the obstacles that student diversity placed in front of the educational machinery. Even so, genuine concern for individual students and a persistent desire among many to design instruction that truly would be "for the benefit of individuals" also contributed to such efforts. Consequently, the story of the birth and growth of special education in Boston is to a great extent the story of the interplay, overlap, and collision between these two fundamental principles of education to which the Boston schools claimed allegiance so insistently.

# 4

## THE EMERGENCE OF SPECIAL EDUCATION

The profound and fundamental changes in public education that took place in Boston during the nineteenth and early twentieth centuries reflected similar developments in public schools throughout the United States. The common school movement, the crusade for a businesslike efficiency in public school systems, and the rise of progressive education and child study were all national movements that dramatically affected the development of public education and educational research. As the Boston public schools paid greater attention and developed more sophisticated understandings of the differences among schoolchildren, their deliberations and efforts drew upon a significant, dynamic body of research on and experience with individuals with disabilities. Centered primarily in private and public institutions during the 1800s, the education of children with disabilities—particularly those with deafness, blindness, and mental retardation—attracted considerable attention from doctors, educators, politicians, and eventually the public.

By the early 1900s, "special education" had moved into the public schools, not just in Boston but in a significant number of other cities as well. The development of special education as a notable component of public schooling owed much to the growth and dissemination of research on the etiology and pedagogy of disability. As the concept of special education emerged and sharpened, the Boston public schools began putting it to extensive use; by the 1920s the city's public school system had seven separate programs enrolling thousands of students with formally identified disabilities. This chapter briefly summarizes the contexts of research and practice out of which the concept of a special education for students with disabilities arose and moved into the world of public schools.

42

## Notions of Educability: The Deaf and the Blind

In 1817 the Connecticut Asylum for the Education and Instruction of Deaf and Dumb Persons opened its doors in Hartford. The asylum was the first of a multitude of institutions opened during the 1800s in the United States that aimed to provide residence, treatment, and education to individuals with formally identified disabilities. Arising out of a complex mixture of reform movements in medicine, education, and humanitarianism, these institutions offered space and resources for individuals—mostly children and adolescents—whose families could not or would not keep them at home or who were deemed incapable of participating in or contributing to mainstream society. Such institutions hosted teachers, doctors, and intellectuals who believed strongly in the educability of the disabled; they supplied opportunities for research, observation, and experimentation that helped develop understanding of disability and constructions of educability for these particular populations. The work done within these institutions would later find its expression and modification in the education offered to children with disabilities in the public schools by the early twentieth century.

That the Connecticut Asylum initiated institution-based special education in the United States is no surprise. Education of the deaf had been discussed and carried out for generations in Europe, so the evidence that deaf students could benefit from carefully planned instruction—that they were, in fact, educable—had existed for generations as well. Since the seventeenth century the belief that deaf people could reason and learn even though they lacked speech had been posited and accepted by many. The work of Melchor de Yebra and Juan Pablo Bonet in Spain, Anthony Deusing in Holland, and Abbé Charles Michel de l'Épée in France, to name only a few, had proposed methods of instruction and advanced the ideas of signing and of liberal education for the deaf. When Thomas Hopkins Gallaudet decided to establish a school for the deaf in the United States, he traveled to Europe to observe the teaching methods being used in schools for deaf children there. In France he enlisted the services of Laurent Clerc, a deaf individual who taught at the Royal Institute for the Deaf in Paris. Together with Gallaudet and Mason Fitch Cogswell, Clerc helped found the Connecticut Asylum using five thousand dollars in funds from the state of Connecticut. It became the American Asylum at Hartford in May 1819 (and is now known as the American School for the Deaf).

Similar institutions in other states soon followed. By 1880 there were fifty-five institutions, many of which received financial support from state governments, providing education to deaf individuals. Numerous founders of and teachers at these other institutions trained at Hartford.[1]

Until the 1860s these schools relied almost exclusively on the use of manual signs for teaching and communication. Then, in the late 1860s, schools emphasizing the oral method of instruction opened in New York City (the New York Institution for the Improved Instruction of Deaf-Mutes, later the Lexington School for the Deaf) and Northampton, Massachusetts (the Clarke Institution for Deaf-Mutes). The oral method had originated in Germany and constituted a pointed alternative to signing both as a means of communication and as a statement on the nature of the relationship between the deaf and hearing communities. Clerc's and Gallaudet's staunch advocacy of manualism was countered by Horace Mann and Samuel Gridley Howe, who visited Europe in 1843 and prepared a glowing report on oral instruction in German and Prussian schools. The report, included in Horace Mann's *Seventh Annual Report* as secretary of the Massachusetts State Board of Education, led to a "firestorm" of controversy regarding the proper education of deaf people. Oralism found its most influential advocate in Alexander Graham Bell, who for the next several decades argued forcefully in its favor as a means to integrate the deaf community more effectively with the world of the hearing and reduce what he considered the highly negative effects of a segregated deaf culture that relied on signing as an exclusionary means of communication.[2]

The pitched battle between oralism and a combined method of communication based on signing was fully joined by the 1870s; it yielded serious, at times even bitter, confrontations between and among educators of the deaf in the professional literature, at professional conferences, and in the popular press. The combined method drew strength from near-universal acceptance of the use of signing as established at the American School for the Deaf and employed by most residential institutions for the deaf in the United States. Proponents of the combined method argued that signing was a legitimate, albeit alternative, method of communication among people. While recognizing the value of speechreading and speaking, combinists insisted that signing could serve not only as a valuable means of communication and instruction but also as a unifying and distinguishing feature of a valid and honorable deaf culture. Proponents of oralism believed that the combined method, with its heavy emphasis on a sign language mysterious to all but a few, worked only to segregate, ostracize, and stigmatize deaf individuals within mainstream society. Taking the view that deafness was an undesirable disability to be overcome rather than a cultural feature to be celebrated, Bell and other oralists maintained that deaf people needed to demonstrate their capacity to communicate with hearing persons as an important step toward participating as fully as possible within the hearing world. While Edward Miner Gallaudet (son of Thomas Hopkins Gallaudet) and Bell led their respective movements, virtually everyone involved in deaf education or associated with deaf individuals accepted one view or the other in this highly polarized debate. Professional journals, associations, and conferences provided the forums for intense, often heated discussions. Especially strong for several decades after 1880, the controversy over whether a combined approach or oralism represents the best way in which deaf students should learn continues to this day as a defining issue in deaf education.[3]

During the nineteenth century, the controversy over methods of instruction and communication effectively underscored the by-then accepted view that deaf individuals were not only entitled to an education but also fully capable of acquiring a sophisticated and extensive one. All issues regarding deaf education were widely discussed through periodicals such as the *American Annals of the Deaf* and the Little Paper Family, a collection of publications from many of the institutions for the deaf, as well as through regional and national organizations such as the New England Gallaudet Association, various state organizations, and the National Association of the Deaf. To punctuate these developments, the National Deaf-Mute College (later Gallaudet University) was established in 1864 to educate a leadership elite that could advance the interests and position of the deaf community in American society. By 1900 any doubts regarding the advisability or plausibility of providing high-quality education to deaf individuals of all ages had been dramatically reduced.[4]

A similar pattern of development evolved in the education of blind persons. As with deaf education, the origins of progress in the education of blind individuals were found in Europe. Denis Diderot, who had written philosophically oriented tracts on deafness, did so on blindness as well; his work informed that of Valentin Haüy, whose efforts in the eighteenth century drew attention from royalty and the public. Haüy is credited with establishing in 1784 the first formal school in the world for blind

The Perkins Institution for the Blind was located on Broadway between G and H Streets in South Boston from 1839 until 1912. During the 1910s the school contributed personnel and other resources to the conservation of eyesight classes in the Boston schools. Reprinted by permission of Perkins School for the Blind.

individuals. In 1832 Louis Braille developed his system of raised symbols to make reading possible for blind individuals, the first of many such systems created in the nineteenth century. In that same year the Massachusetts Asylum for the Blind, which soon came to be known as the Perkins Institution in honor of an early benefactor, was established with Samuel Gridley Howe as its director.

Howe, like Gallaudet, traveled to Europe to research educational methods and to recruit teachers for his institution. The school had received a charter as well as six thousand dollars from the state in 1829 to assist its efforts to educate indigent children; it opened with six students. The New York School for the Blind also opened in 1832, with another in Pennsylvania commencing the following year. By 1900 thirty-seven schools for the blind existed; some of these also taught deaf individuals. Typically these schools combined academic study with work in manual and vocational training and in music. Reading and writing of course required specialized instructional methods, usually utilizing tactile devices such as three-dimensional maps, manipulatives, and raised type. Howe believed strongly in the importance of physical exercise and music, especially singing. Various types of raised type existed in addition to Braille, some of which used the regular alphabet or a modified version. Braille, with its system of six-dot symbols, eventually became dominant by 1900. Efforts were made to normalize the education of the blind as Howe and others believed that "we should endeavor to make them, in their habits and temperament, as like the seeing as possible. . . ." Institutions for the blind throughout the United States followed Howe's lead and employed similar approaches in their educational programs. As with deaf education, the education of the blind received boosts from national associations such as the American Association of Instructors of the Blind as well as from the work and products of the American Printing House for the Blind. However, a national institution of higher education for blind students was never established; instead, postschool efforts focused on developing work or trade skills.[5]

Of special note was the instruction of those who were both deaf and blind. Howe was instrumental in the education of Laura Bridgman, who became a well-known figure in the early nineteenth century. Of even greater fame was Helen Keller, another deaf-blind individual who was referred to the Perkins Institution by Alexander Graham Bell and who made great strides under the tutelage of Anne Sullivan. Their personal educational struggles and accomplishments generated great interest as Howe and Sullivan worked exhaustively to develop methodological approaches that would address the sensory impairments of their students. Thus, beliefs in the educability of blind individuals and the wherewithal to conduct that education grew strong as well, although these advances took place somewhat later than those regarding the education of the deaf.[6]

## Social Constructions and Notions of Educability: The Mentally Retarded

The obvious and relatively specific nature of the physical disability related to deafness and blindness most likely made it easier to develop, implement, and adjust specific educational programs tailored to the needs of deaf as well as blind individuals. There did exist serious concerns on the part of some regarding the implications of abnormality and hence the moral character of deaf and/or blind individuals in light of some assumed causes of deafness and blindness. However, any effect these concerns had on the plausibility or advisability of educating such individuals was limited to ideas about what they should learn, not whether they could—or should. The accomplishments of deaf education and blind education during the nineteenth century reinforced the belief that individuals who were deaf or blind—or both—were entitled to and capable of receiving extensive education.

The situation regarding the education of individuals with mental disabilities was far more complicated. The evolution of understanding regarding the definition and etiology of mental retardation and the educability of those considered mentally disabled has taken place over centuries (and of course has even yet to reach a definitive conclusion). While specific programs of education were being developed for the deaf and the blind in Europe, the understanding of how mental retardation related to constructs of insanity, mental illness, and immorality was only beginning to receive consideration. Institutions or "asylums" for those considered insane, or possessed, or who exhibited an obvious lack of intellectual ability had existed in Europe as early as the sixteenth century. These institutions housed individuals with a dramatically wide range of mental disabilities, conditions, behaviors, and/or attitudes that threatened the sensibilities of the general population. By the early nineteenth century, mental retardation had begun to be separated conceptually from insanity, if only slightly. Philippe Pinel, Jean E. D. Esquirol, and Jean Marc Gaspard Itard pioneered work in France with their attempts to treat more humanely and even educate individuals exhibiting mental subnormality. Itard's work with Victor, "the wild boy of Aveyron," drew international attention—even if it did convince many that mentally disabled people were ineducable.[7]

The two individuals most responsible for bringing theory and practice of the education of the mentally retarded to the United States were Samuel Gridley Howe and Edouard Seguin. Having successfully established a school for the blind and being always interested in the causes of the powerless, Howe determined that a school for "idiots" needed to be established.* On his visit to Europe with Horace Mann, Howe also investi-

---

* Part of these developments included the initial application of clinical labels used to describe or explain the severity of mental disability. By the mid 1800s the term "idiot" was used by Esquirol, Howe, and Eduoard Seguin to refer to an individual with, in Seguin's

Samuel Gridley Howe's efforts led to the founding of the Perkins Institution for the Blind in 1832 and the Massachusetts Asylum for Idiotic and Feeble-minded Youth in 1851. Both institutions played significant roles in building special education programs in the Boston schools. Reprinted by permission of Perkins School for the Blind.

gated European efforts to address idiocy; he became convinced that people previously thought uneducable could in fact be educated, and he was particularly impressed with the work of Seguin. After two years as leader of a commission investigating the educational opportunities for "idiots" in Massachusetts, Howe managed to persuade the state's legislature to establish a state school for "idiotic and feeble-minded children." Following its initial experimental run, the Massachusetts School for Idiotic and Feeble-Minded Youth opened its doors on a permanent basis in 1851. Within five years the states of Rhode Island, Pennsylvania, and New York had followed suit. The development of institutions designed to house and educate individuals with mental retardation was well under way.[8]

Most of these institutions relied heavily on the work of Eduoard

words, "grave cerebral incapacity" who "knows nothing, can do nothing, cannot even desire to do anything"—an individual who today might be considered severely or profoundly mentally retarded. Howe also used the terms "fools" and "simpletons" to refer to moderate and mild levels of cognitive disability respectively. These labels would evolve as understandings and constructions of mental retardation evolved, as they continue to do today.

Seguin in designing educational programs for their students. Seguin had worked with Esquirol and Itard in Paris at the Bicêtre and Salpetrière institutions. In 1846 he published *Traitement Moral, Hygiène et Éducation des Idiots,* in which he defined idiocy, identified its etiology, and presented a plan for the education of "idiots." In 1848 Seguin relocated to the United States and soon became associated with the Pennsylvania School for Idiotic and Feeble-Minded Children. In 1866 he published his seminal *Idiocy: And Its Treatment by the Physiological Method.* This tract, which reiterated many of his ideas from his 1846 publication, advocated applying a "sense-training" approach to the education of individuals with mental retardation. Drawing on the ideas of Jean Jacques Rousseau and Johann Pestalozzi, Seguin developed a highly structured program that relied heavily on the use of touch through motor exercises. Physical exercise, music, speech acquisition, and other activities using "a sequence of movement training, discrimination training, classification, object association, and logical operations" were stressed, as were visual and auditory stimuli. The goal was to train the child's muscular system, nervous system, and senses, followed by work on "intellectual functions, and finally moral faculties." It was a highly structured, carefully sequenced program demonstrating the belief that sensory rather than cognitive or intellectual approaches would work best with this population of students. Seguin ultimately hoped to raise the student from his or her "filthy and degrading habits" into a child "capable of observing all the properties of life."[9]

Seguin's sensory and moralistic approach to the education of mentally retarded individuals gained wide attention and respect during the latter half of the nineteenth century. By the early 1900s, most education for the mentally retarded was based on Seguin's physiological method. Maria Montessori's exemplary work with impoverished children in Rome drew significantly on Seguin's work, highlighting the extent to which sensory-based education could be and was being applied to all children during the progressivist years of the early twentieth century. Alfred Binet also incorporated Seguin's method in developing "tasks" for his early intelligence tests. In addition, Seguin's work not only "formed the basis for training programs in most institutions for the mentally retarded" but also proved fundamental to the development of special class curricula in the public schools. Education for children with mental disabilities thus would owe a great debt to Seguin for the specific method as well as for the evidence and conviction that individuals with even severe mental retardation were capable of benefiting from formal instruction.[10]

The emerging conviction that effective education for mentally retarded individuals was possible occurred concurrently with changing beliefs regarding not only the value of such instruction but also its necessity. As Seguin's methods and influence took hold, medical, psychological and social constructions of mental retardation moved through a series of paradigmatic shifts, from charitable optimism during the reform-minded first half of the nineteenth century to more negative perceptions of the potential and character of the mentally disabled. Such shifts reflected developments in both broad constructions of mental abnormality as well as more specific articulations of intellectual disability. Long lumped together with the entire range of mental conditions seen as abnormal, the notion of mental deficiency slowly began to emerge as its own construct, distinctive from, yet still associated with, mental illness and moral degeneracy. Steven Gelb describes a process of collecting "mental deficiency" under the successive umbrellas first of "moral derangement," then "moral idiocy," then "moral insanity," and finally "moral imbecility" as the nineteenth century progressed. By 1880 "moral imbecility" was "applied broadly to persons whose behavior was judged socially deviant in both the presence and the absence of other signs of mental or physical disability." According to Gelb, "moral" was quite broadly defined during this time, and these labels bore in his words a "nebulous" quality that reflected the uncertain understanding of the relationship among heredity, intelligence, and personal morality. The evolution of the use of these terms thus became a function of changes in psychological, clinical, and medical models of intellect, disease, mental illness, and morality as doctors, educators, religious leaders, and others struggled to understand how the mind worked and how social and personal behavior and accomplishment reflected the health of the body, intellect, and soul.[11]

Predictably, attempts to resolve these issues led in turn to changes in societal attitudes and beliefs regarding individuals exhibiting mental retardation. The work of Howe and Seguin, grounded in social reform movements and in a strong spiritual concern for the more helpless members of society, had contributed to a more optimistic and compassionate view of "idiots." After the Civil War, however, suspicion over the character and presumed lack of productivity among this class of individuals led to more pessimistic and negative perceptions of the mentally retarded, perceptions grounded in a belief that such individuals constituted a serious burden to society and required segregation in isolated institutions. Between 1900 and 1920, the term "mental defective" became well established, and public policy—including educational policy—constructed this class of citizens no longer as just a burden but as a menace, "the control of which was an urgent necessity for existing and future generations." No longer merely associated with social pathology, individuals with mental retardation thus came to be considered the direct cause of it. By the early 1900s Walter E. Fernald, director of the Massachusetts State School for the Feeble-Minded, was advancing the notion that immoral behavior largely resulted from mental deficiency:

> A very large proportion of the feeble-minded persons, even the well-trained higher-grade cases, eventually become public charges in one way or another. No one familiar with the mental and physical limitations of this class believes that any plan of education can ever materially modify this fact. The brighter class of the feeble-minded, with their weak will-power and defective judgment, are easily influenced for evil, and are very likely to become prostitutes, vagrants, or petty criminals. They are powerless to resist the physical temptations of adult life, and should be protected from their own weakness and the cupidity of others. Especially should they be prevented from marriage and the reproduction of their kind.

Fernald and Henry Herbert Goddard led a chorus of expressed concern over individuals who were mildly mentally retarded, stating that such individuals were quite numerous, too invisible to identify easily, and highly susceptible to immoral impulses and influences. Although still connected to criminal behavior, mental deficiency had emerged as a powerful construct, separate from illness or depravity, that demanded serious attention and study from educators, scientists, and civic leaders.[12]

## The Mental Testing and Eugenics Movements

Fueling developments in understanding and constructing mental retardation was the ascendancy of science and scientific investigation as means to better understand the mind and its effect on human behavior. One result was that psychology arose as a distinct scientific discipline during the late nineteenth century; another was that "scientifically" derived explanations and prescriptions for social problems became quite popular. Such developments led to two movements directly related to the study, treatment, and control of mental retardation: the mental testing movement and the eugenics movement. These would have a profound effect on the evolution of social and educational policy and practice geared toward individuals with disabilities in the early twentieth century.

Although the mental testing movement can be traced to the work of Francis Galton in England in the 1860s and 1870s, Alfred Binet's work in France just after the turn of the century provided the most direct stimulus to the development and use of intelligence tests in the United States. The French government commissioned Binet to create an instrument that would identify students in the French public schools who were thought to be in need of specialized instruction due to exceptionally poor performance in school. With his colleague Théophile Simon, Binet developed a series of tasks designed to test processes of reasoning using a variety of practical activities. Before Binet died in 1911 he had published the original version of his scale (in 1905) as well as two revisions; the 1908 version was the first to assign each task with an age level, leading to the development of the concept of mental age. In 1912 William Stern, a German psychologist, advanced the notion of an intelligence quotient (IQ)—the ratio of the measured mental age to the actual chronological age of the child. The IQ became a fundamental feature of all subsequent intelligence tests as well as an enormously influential concept in psychology and education.[13]

Binet insisted that his scale should be used only as a general guide for identifying children with intellectual disabilities, and that the IQ should not be "perverted and used as an indelible label" because it was but one number representing a highly complex entity. Nevertheless, his cautions were ignored. During the 1910s, American psychologists—most notably Lewis Henry Terman and H. H. Goddard—latched on to the concept of the IQ and intelligence testing, vesting them with remarkably broad applications. Binet's scale was imported, translated, advertised, and used along the very lines against which he had cautioned so strongly. Instead of being merely a helpful diagnostic tool suggesting certain possible characteristics of a certain group of children, the Binet scale evolved into a powerful and ubiquitous instrument, administered to millions of adults as well as school children; it was then used to make sweeping, definitive judgments regarding the capabilities and character of entire racial and ethnic groups. By 1930 mental testing had become a multimillion dollar business as well as an embedded feature of both policy and practice in the public schools of the United States.

As of 1910 concern over the rate of failure and retention of American public schoolchildren had become serious and widespread. Leonard P. Ayres's *Laggards in Our Schools,* published in 1909, effectively captured the spirit of the time: great distress over the "retardation" (holding back) of pupils for failing to make sufficient academic progress, and a firm belief that a scientific and efficiency-minded solution to the problem was necessary. The desire to sort children and offer a differentiated curriculum based on that sorting had gained remarkable strength, and the intelligence test provided a supposedly objective, scientific, and foolproof means of doing just that. In 1911 a translated version of the Binet-Simon scale was administered in the public schools of Vineland, New Jersey, the home of one of the nation's most prominent institutions for the mentally retarded and of H. H. Goddard, who arranged the first English translation of the scale. Goddard saw enough to become a strong supporter of intelligence testing; during 1912–13 he engaged in extensive mental testing of thousands of immigrants arriving at Ellis Island off the coast of New York City. The results of this testing led him to claim that certain European ethnic groups were genetically disposed toward inferior intellectual capabilities. Thereafter Goddard wrote and published prolifically on the educationally and socially predictive value of intelligence tests, arguing that they could and should drive social as well as educational policy. It was Lewis Terman, however, who transformed the Binet-Simon scale into the predominant mental measurement instrument in the United States, the Stanford-Binet revision of 1916. Working out of Stanford University, Terman revised the Binet-Simon scale by increasing its length to ninety tasks and extending its age range to adults. The Stanford-Binet test of 1916 quickly became the standard against which all other individualized intelligence tests were judged; over the next several years it was used with steadily increasing frequency in school districts across the nation. Terman and Goddard continued to argue vociferously that the intelligence test was an objective, valid, and reliable tool which school districts could use to identify "defective" students and increase the efficiency of public school administration.[14]

However, a major roadblock to the widespread use of intelligence testing in schools could be found in its individualized nature. By 1920 the possibilities of using intelligence tests in schools seemed endless, but its practical application in schools required tests that could be administered to large groups, thus saving both time and money. Terman argued that group testing was not only desirable but also highly practical and held great promise for the future:

> Binet's "methode de luxe" has been so simplified that any intelligent teacher can use it in a way to enlarge greatly her knowledge of a given child. The group examination methods now in process of development may be expected to add still further to the popularity of intelligence tests as an aid in the more accurate grading and in the wiser educational guidance of school children. "A mental test for every child" is no longer an unreasonable slogan.[15]

Terman based his optimism to a great extent on the work of Robert M. Yerkes of Harvard University. Yerkes was responsible for developing mass-produced group intelligence tests that were administered to hundreds of thousands of army recruits during World War I. This initial full-scale attempt to administer group intelligence testing caught the attention of public school professionals and resulted in a multitude of such tests being prepared by psychologists and used in the schools. The 1920s witnessed tremendous growth in the use of intelligence tests in public education as mass production and greater ease of training the testers promised a less expensive, more efficient means of administering them. By 1930 millions of children in thousands of school districts were being sorted and differentiated on the basis of their IQ score. In 1922–23, for example, over eight hundred thousand copies of the National Intelligence Test—developed by a group of psychologists under Terman's leadership—were sold.[16]

The widespread use of intelligence testing reflected a belief that the tests were crucial instruments in developing and implementing educational and social policy. But the tests were seen as much more than just useful scientific instruments; to many proponents, the stories the testing data told about various groups in society were at least as important. To Goddard, Terman, Yerkes, and others, the tests provided infallible proof that intelligence was a fixed trait, passed on genetically, that clearly stamped certain groups as significantly more intelligent than others. Goddard and Terman argued for years to a convinced public that intelligence tests demonstrated the intellectual inferiority of African Americans, southern Europeans, and eastern Europeans, and that their inherited inferior state demanded legislative and other social action designed to curb their negative influence on American society. Carrying the seal of science and objectivity, intelligence tests supplied the rationale for the severely restrictive national immigration laws passed in 1924 as well as for the tracking of students of "inferior" heritage into low-level paths of schooling, including the special or ungraded classes for "mentally defective" children in public schools across the country.

The results of intelligence testing gave further credence and impetus to the eugenics movement. Defined by Francis Galton in 1883 as "the science which deals with all the influences that improve the inborn qualities of the race," eugenics sought to scientifically engineer superior human beings as a key means to eliminate serious societal problems such as vice, crime, poverty, poor health, and disability. Intense interest in the science of genetics and in the implications of Darwin's theory of evolution on social progress instigated the eugenics movement, which advocated both the purposeful practice of "promot[ing] the birth of healthy well-endowed, superior individuals (*positive eugenics*) as well as "prevent[ing] the procreation of defectives or degenerates" (*negative eugenics*). Assuring that heredity determined not only physical features but also intelligence and character, eugenics advocates supported efforts to negotiate exclusive "breeding" among people deemed genetically superior as well as to reduce if not eliminate breeding among those presumed genetically inferior. Eugenics represented a widely accepted policy to combine scientific knowledge and advances with social reform efforts.[17]

The eugenics movement both embodied and strengthened prevailing negative beliefs about persons with disabilities, catalyzing efforts to segregate, isolate, and significantly reduce the population of those considered physically, intellectually, or morally defective. Not surprisingly, Goddard and Terman proved tireless advocates of eugenics while warning the public about the "menace" of the mental defective, the alleged strong association of mental defect and consequent criminality with nonwhite races and ethnic groups from southern and eastern Europe, and the need for increased institutionalization of "defective" individuals. Alexander Graham Bell argued a similar theme regarding deaf individuals: he expressed publicly and widely a staunchly negative view of deafness, recommending against marriage and procreation of deaf individuals as well as the creation of deaf communities. Bell was an avid proponent of the eugenics movement; he saw it as a means of significantly reducing the scourge of deafness in society. Isolation, institutionalization, and sterilization of genetically defective individuals, all part and parcel of the eugenics perspective, drew wide support and acclaim during the late nineteenth and early twentieth centuries. Eugenics also established an intriguing tone of negativity toward disability, one that was shaded by optimism regarding the ability of science to drastically reduce, and ultimately eliminate, disability from society. Although some leading figures, notably Fernald and Goddard, would later recant their enthusiastic support of eugenics and the genetic determinism of "defect," the power of the eugenics movement was unmistakable.[18]

## Public Schools and Disability: The Early 1900s

Changing constructions of mental retardation and the advent of the mental testing and eugenics movements clearly affected the response of public schooling to the presence of disability among its student population. During the1800s the educability of individuals with mental retardation had been demonstrated repeatedly in private schools as well as in state and private institutions; descriptions of successful instruction of the "feeble-minded" filled journals and other publications. When the impetus for educating such children shifted from humanitarianism to social control, the public schools became deeply involved in that instruction. By the 1920s compulsory education laws, which typically had exempted the "mentally deficient" child from public school attendance, began to demand it. Since so many children believed to belong to this group were first- or second-generation immigrants, their exposure to public education was considered crucial to ensure their acculturation and direct them to perform their desired economic and social functions in the community.

Even before compulsory education laws required their attendance, many children with mental disabilities had been attending public schools (evidence from Boston, for example, suggests they had been doing so for decades). Their presence created problems for teachers and administrators as they sought to provide an education deemed appropriate but also wished to operate classrooms efficiently and economically. The solution was to create separate instructional settings, usually referred to as "special" or "un-graded" classes, that would allow these children to attend public school but would also keep them from disrupting the regular classroom through their behavior or their excessive demands on a teacher's time. Walter

Fernald, by then a nationally recognized expert on the subject of mental defect, argued that "there are many reasons why such classes should be established as part of the public-school system in large centers of population in this country." He cited the low cost and convenience of creating these classes, which would then provide the "much lower plane, . . . hand-work and manual training," and slower pace that had proven successful in educating mentally retarded students. Implying that their inclusion in the public schools was essential to maintaining social order and to steering these children away from potential vice and crime, Fernald said that special classes could help "many of the slightly feeble-minded" to "be educated and developed to the point of supporting themselves, and of becoming desirable members of the community." His belief that public education could help achieve these goals was strong; more significantly, he also argued that "every American child has the right to be educated according to his need and capacity." Fernald's opinions represented the powerful suspicions, as well as the guarded hope, that many educators and medical officers felt toward individuals with disabilities.[19]

E. R. Johnstone, superintendent of the New Jersey Training School for Feeble-Minded Children at Vineland, adamantly supported the concept of special classes in the public schools in his comments to the National Education Association's Special Department in 1908. Johnstone's address used a broad application of "special class" to include those designed for students with severe hearing or vision impairments; however, he focused his discussion primarily on classes for "mental defectives." Johnstone argued that the functions of such classes were many: as a place to shunt students who disrupted regular classes and unfairly monopolized the teacher's time; as a "clearing-house" where all children causing trouble or holding back "normal" students could be sent until "closer differentiation and separation" could be completed; and especially as a "laboratory for the public-school classes." To Johnstone, this last function was especially significant: he noted that "teachers in the primary grades go to the special class teacher to learn how she accomplishes, with subnormal children, results which they find difficult to obtain with their normal children." "I firmly believe," he stated, "that our most advanced ideas on educational procedure will come from the study of 'special' children and their mental processes." Johnstone's comments reflected the multiple purposes of efficiency, economy, pedagogy, and control that came to characterize special class work in urban school systems throughout the nation.[20]

By 1930 most public school systems in the larger cities had some system of special education in place, boosted largely by the extension of compulsory education laws to include many children with disabilities and the consequent increase in their school attendance. The handful of classes for the mentally retarded found in American public schools in 1900 grew dramatically in number over the next thirty years, 1918 to 1927 being the busiest period. In 1927, 218 cities had special or ungraded classes for about fifty-two thousand children labeled "mental handicapped." Much of this increase can be directly attributed to the advent of group intelligence tests during the early 1920s that greatly facilitated the "scientific" identification of children presumed to be mentally deficient. These programs did not replace the traditional institutions, which continued to enroll the most severe cases of individuals with mental disabilities and to suffer from overcrowding. Rather, these special classes recognized and opened the door for "mild" or "moderate defectives" who, through the advent of extensive mental testing and the experience of classroom instruction, came to the attention of educators and caused great concern on the part of many. The special class for the noninstitutionalized mentally retarded child thus became an important means to realize the social control that the public schools were expected to provide.[21]

## The Role of Progressive Education and Child Study

The increasingly complex understandings of and mechanisms for accommodating public school students with disabilities did not just come from specialized research or from the decades of educational experience garnered in institutions and other specialized schools. The more generic developments in progressive education—from the concept of social efficiency to that of child study—also fundamentally affected the public school response to the identification and education of these children. The Boston public schools' insistence on efficiency and economy in management and instruction, and its increasing expressions of concern for the individual child and the need to differentiate and personalize the curriculum accordingly, arose directly from these substantive changes in educational theory and practice during the late nineteenth century and especially the early twentieth century.[22]

As discussed in the previous chapter, efficiency in the school office as well as in the classroom had long represented an important goal of Boston school officials. As the city's schools moved into the twentieth century, efficiency came to mean more than a mere emphasis on good business practices. The growth of curriculum differentiation reflected, among other things, a desire to use the school as an effective agent of social engineering, where students would be grouped (or tracked) on the basis of their presumed postschool employment and subjected to an appropriate school curriculum. In addition, the schools continued their role as a vehicle for maintaining social control over certain classes of students, a function receiving at least as great attention in the early twentieth century as it did in the mid-nineteenth. As Herbert Kliebard has observed,

> Efficiency became more than a byword in the educational world; it became an urgent mission. That mission took the form of enjoining curriculum-makers to devise programs of study that prepared individuals specifically and directly for the role they would play as adult members of the social order. To go beyond what someone had to know in order to perform that role successfully was simply wasteful. Social utility became the supreme criterion against which the value of school studies was measured.[23]

Much of this efficiency movement was driven by the notion of scientific management. Sociologist Edward Ross and "the so-called father of scientific management," Frederick Taylor, each wrote generally about efficiency in society and business yet wielded a powerful influence on the thoughts and practices of educational administrators. John Franklin Bobbitt worked scientific management into his study of curriculum, exemplified by his widely read 1912 publication, *The Elimination of Waste in Education*. Other writers, commissions, and committees investigated deeply and published frequently on ways to make schools and their curriculum more efficient and economical in their operation—especially with regard to their "products," the students whose occupations needed to be predetermined to suit the economy and whose character needed to be molded to ensure stability. Again, Ayres's *Laggards in Our Schools* was a clarion call for administrators fretting over the waste of so many children repeating grades in school due to inefficient classification and curriculum differentiation. One of the leading proponents of this approach, David Snedden, resided in Boston as commissioner of education in Massachusetts for many years before moving on to Teachers College at Columbia University in 1916.

Efficiency, economy, and scientific management became educational watchwords of the greatest importance to Boston school officials during the late 1800s and early 1900s.

This progressivist spirit in education and the emphasis on the use of science to find solutions to educational problems encompassed another generalized movement critical to the development of education for individuals with disabilities in the public schools: the child-study movement. During the late 1800s, interest in the education and needs of the individual child strengthened noticeably. This interest was stimulated largely by the work of G. Stanley Hall, who believed that science and the scientific method could and should be applied to the study of children with great effect, arguing that therein lay the key to making schools more active, vital, and meaningful places to learn. Hall's work emphasized a romanticized view of childhood but also demonstrated how "science" could be used to unlock the mysteries of children's minds and to guide educators in developing more effective schools, just as Colonel Francis Wayland Parker had done in the Quincy, Massachusetts, public schools near Boston. Hall's notions of childhood, including his elaborate (and at the time highly attractive) theory of "cultural epochs,"* signaled an intense interest in the needs and interests of the individual child as well as a strong belief that using a scientific approach to child study could contribute to greater "individualization" of school curriculum.[24]

The child study movement, like that for efficiency and scientific management in education, spread nationwide. According to Kliebard, "child study flourished in the 1890s," with state associations being formed and the National Education Association devoting much time and energy to the idea. Hall himself taught at Harvard in the early 1880s, and his lectures on pedagogy there took place "on Saturdays so that Boston school teachers could attend." As the nineteenth century came to a close, the child's needs, as well as those of the teachers, administrators, or the school system itself, assumed an important position in deliberations and debates

---

*As Kliebard explains, "Culture epochs theory posited the notion that the child recapitulates in his individual development the stages that the whole human race traversed throughout the course of history." Hall commented that "to understand either the child or the race we must constantly refer to the other," thus underscoring the dual importance of the study of child development. See Kliebard, 44–45.

in Boston regarding educational reform and the purposes of public schooling. Child-study and its close correlate, child-centered education, gained even wider renown through the work of John Dewey and the ascendancy of progressive education during the early 1900s.[25]

Efficiency, scientific management, child-study, and child-centered education coexisted uneasily in the public school systems of the United States, and Boston's experience was no exception. The performance and behavior of individual students constituted an important consideration for those trying to make teaching and administration more economical and effective, while the sacrifice of the individual student's needs and best interests to the school system troubled many of the city's teachers and school administrators. These conflicting agendas, however, found a mutual home in special education. Children with disabilities demanded individual attention at the expense, it was argued, of the great majority of students in a given classroom. Their presence rendered traditional instruction inefficient and expensive when factoring in the cost of a teacher's time and the need for certain children to repeat grades. Yet these children also needed to be in school so that the city could maintain close scrutiny and control over their lives and their futures. Curriculum differentiation, as manifested in the segregation of these children, was consequently a cornerstone in the effort to keep the children in school as well as keep those schools efficient and economical. But such segregation also satisfied the desires of child-study advocates and others who supported a child-centered education. In isolated settings, with smaller classes and specially trained teachers, the individual needs of children with disabilities could be met, freeing the regular classroom from the complications and distractions of educating them.

The tension and interplay among these various agendas characterized the development of programs that accommodated students with disabilities. The fear and consequent segregation of many students in the public schools, mirroring the institutionalization of the deaf, the blind, and the mentally disabled, began in earnest in Boston in the late 1800s; as the nineteenth century drew to a close, the calls for greater efficiency, greater economy, and greater attention to individual students grew as well. By the early 1900s, fear, control, efficiency, economy, scientific management, the scientific study of the individual child, and child-centered education all claimed a place in the development of programs for students with a wide range of identified physical, mental, and behavioral disabilities. The growth of these programs reflected both local conditions and priorities as well as national educational and other intellectual trends. Part 2 will explore these programs individually, examining the development of each in terms of how these agendas interacted to shape the program into its own particular configuration. In doing so, those aspects of Boston's experience that exemplified national events—as well as those that may have been unique to the city or to a given program—will begin to emerge, casting a little more light on how special education in the public schools originated and how those origins have shaped the nature and dynamics of the field today.

# PART 2

# SPECIALIZED EDUCATION
# PROGRAMS

# 5

## INTERMEDIATE SCHOOLS AND
## UNGRADED CLASSES

The nineteenth century constituted a period of profound change for public schools in Boston as they adjusted their purposes and organization to
suit the increasing social, cultural, and economic diversity of the city. The
school leadership determined early in the century that the ideal of a common education for all of Boston's children was ill-advised in practice. Beginning in 1820, when the school system was small and loosely defined,
the Boston School Committee heard calls for a separate program to accommodate students who, in the opinion of many, did not belong in the regular primary or grammar schools because of their age and background. As
the system grew more complex and sophisticated and the student population more diverse, the demand for such a program persisted and was eventually realized. Initially manifested as monitorial schooling for older illiterate children, this segregated program began in 1838 as intermediate
schools, or schools for special instruction.

In 1879 these schools were discontinued and replaced by ungraded
classes in the grammar schools. Serving essentially the same kinds of students as the intermediate schools, the ungraded classes fit more efficiently
into the highly regimented graded classification system of the late nineteenth century, serving a limited but useful function as a repository for
students who did not readily fit in a regular classroom. Until the early
1920s, the ungraded classrooms provided teachers and administrators with
a convenient instructional safety valve for a system that felt strongly the
pressure to educate children whose presence inhibited the ability to achieve
the goal of a smoothly and efficiently operated school system. To examine
the history of the intermediate schools and ungraded classes is both to
glimpse the educational lives of thousands of the city's school children and

to witness an urban school system's struggle to realize its goals while coping with the demands those goals presented.

## Poverty, Cultural Difference, and the Monitorial School

The establishment of primary schools in 1818 clearly demonstrated the Boston School Committee's desire to extend public elementary schooling to as many of Boston's children as possible. This action also reflected the BSC's conviction that such schooling was of tremendous importance to the well-being of the city. Within two years the committee reinforced the seriousness of that conviction when discussions arose over the lack of public school opportunities for a particular segment of the school-age population: illiterate children between the ages of seven and fourteen. According to regulations, children could not attend the grammar schools unless they were at least seven years old and "able to read easy prose" (a skill that was typically acquired in the home or other private setting at the time). While primary schools were formed to provide basic reading and writing instruction to younger students ages four to seven, there still existed in the community a significant number of children over seven who had either failed to get such education in Boston or who had come from other parts of North America or overseas and had not received any reading or writing instruction, at least in English.

Concern focused particularly on the "idle and vagrant" children whose numbers appeared to be growing at an alarming rate. A subcommittee of the Primary School Board, expressing "great surprise and grief," called attention to hundreds of children ages seven to fourteen who were unqualified to enter the grammar schools:

> Some of these are truants; some of them employed in street-begging, and all of them ignorant; and if nothing is done for them, they seem destined forever to remain ignorant, and vicious, and wretched.
>
> These children, be it remembered, were born in as free and as happy a land as the earth affords, and have, as we believe, undeniable claims on the public munificence for such an education as will enable them to know, defend, and enjoy the civil, religious, and social privileges of which they are born the distinguished heirs; and not only so, but if they are permitted to remain in their ignorance, insubordination, and vicious habits, they will not only go quickly to destruction

themselves, but by their pernicious example and influence, they will draw many others after them to the same deplorable ruin.

The subcommittee then recommended that formal schooling presented the most promising solutions to these growing dangers:

> A lively interest in the welfare of these unhappy youth, (which we believe is also felt by a humane and virtuous public,) has led us to consider whether something could not be done for their relief and the public good, both in a moral and social view; and the result of our reflections has been, that one or more schools might be opened at a trifling expense to the town, and instructed by persons competent to teach and govern them; and that nearly all these children, whose names, ages, and places of residence we are already in possession of, may be induced to attend, and thus escape the evil to which they are now exposed.[1]

During the 1820s and into the 1830s the Boston School Committee sporadically employed monitorial schooling to combat the disturbingly visible "evil" of older, illiterate, idle children as well as to economize public education. As conceived by its chief advocate, Joseph Lancaster, the monitorial system offered urban schools an apparent opportunity to educate large numbers of children inexpensively. Simply put, the system involved a headmaster instructing a group of older students in the basic curriculum. The older students, or "monitors," would in turn impart that information in a regimented fashion to much larger groups of younger children. Also known as the Lancastrian system, this method gained wide use in many urban school districts, most notably those of New York City and Philadelphia, where it was envisioned as a superb solution to the constant pressures of high costs, overcrowded classrooms, and disruptive students.[2]

Boston first tested the Lancastrian approach in the early 1820s. A Primary School Board semiannual report of April 1824 noted that a monitorial school had been opened perhaps as early as 1820 on Fort Hill, a notorious slum area, in an attempt to provide instruction to older illiterate youngsters. The report stated that "it succeeded remarkably well [and] was doing great good to the pupils and to society" before being forced to close when its master resigned. The BSC, "for some reason, not known to the Committee," did not secure another teacher and closed the school. In that same report, however, the Primary School Board decried the fact "that in this city a considerable number of youth should be suffered to grow up

destitute of the advantages secured to the children generally, and be aban-
doned to idleness, vagrancy, ignorance, and crime. . . . [This] reflects no
honor on the citizens or our institutions, and demands prompt attention."
Supported by Mayor Josiah Quincy, the BSC then opened another monitorial school in 1827. In April of that year a committee report offered lav-
ish praise of monitorial schools, suggesting they would be a panacea for
problems of student motivation and behavior. It also suggested that monitorial schooling be introduced into all the primary schools. After reporting
positively on such schools in other cities, the committee sanctioned the
establishment of others in Boston the following year. By 1829 twelve primary schools employed the Lancastrian system. A report of a standing
committee of the Primary School Board observed that of these "none are
reported as having decidedly deteriorated since its adoption; some are represented as improved under it; and others are represented as doubtful, or
equal to their former state."[3]

The popularity of the Lancastrian system in the United States was
short-lived. Although the Primary School Board organized a subcommittee to investigate whether to employ the system in all the primary schools,
a variety of problems, such as the securing of suitable schoolrooms and
doubts about its effectiveness, caused the "indefinite postponement of the
whole subject." The Lancastrian system soon fell into disfavor nationally,
partly due to the growing acceptance of other educational methods, partly
due to realizations that the method was ineffective in controlling costs and
delivering instruction. By the early 1830s, only an occasional attempt to
use monitorial instruction took place in Boston, and little if any mention
of it was made by school officials thereafter.[4]

## Founding of Intermediate Schools

The failure of monitorial schooling led school officials and concerned citizens to explore other alternatives. In the early 1830s a number of citizens
petitioned the BSC to open "intermediate schools" that could offer primary instruction to older illiterate children without exposing them to
younger primary students. The BSC showed great reluctance to open such
schools, mainly because of an entrenched fiscal conservatism that feared
the specter of even greater expenditures for primary education. In 1831
the committee failed to act definitively on a formal request to establish

intermediate schools. Two years later, however, it did adopt an order to permit "all children over eight years of age, who are *not* qualified by their attainments," to attend grammar schools but only with the permission of the subcommittee of the grammar school in question. Once enrolled such children were segregated as much as possible from the regular students and were taught by older boys. This segregation continued for the child until he or she had acquired sufficient skills to join the lowest class of the grammar school. Even so, the committee did on occasion experiment with the idea of segregated schools. Records indicate that an intermediate school for children older than seven was organized in May 1833 in the Mill Dam neighborhood near the North End and another in East Boston two years later. A third, also in East Boston, received consideration in 1836, but it is not clear whether it actually opened, and the other two existed only briefly.[5]

By 1837 the debate over the education of illiterate children older than seven had become intense. In 1835 the Common Council of Boston received a petition requesting the creation of four intermediate schools for boys and girls at least eight years old and unqualified for the grammar schools. The council referred it to the school committee, which then officially restated the order that such children could be "admitted by a special permit from the Sub-Committee of the School" and denied the petition. In March 1837 the Committee on Public Instruction of the Common Council examined the issue of "idle, vicious, and indolent children" closely. The result was a report claiming that (1) the "special permit" provision negated any need for a separate system of intermediate schools; (2) that the need for such schools would anyway disappear "after a few months" once the eligible children received the necessary instruction, thus rendering the expenditure of substantial start-up costs unwise; and (3) that the availability of intermediate schools might cause parents to neglect sending "their children to the Primary Schools at a proper age." The committee's chair, B. A. Gould, closed by saying that "your Committee cannot but hope that gentlemen will cease to urge the establishment of intermediate Schools; as they are unanimously of the opinion that it is inexpedient for the City to establish such schools."[6]

Nevertheless the number of impoverished older children in the streets continued to increase, causing concerned citizens to press their efforts for a public school solution to the problem. Another formal request (or "memorial") to the city council, dated October 1837 and filed on behalf of the Society for the Prevention of Pauperism, reiterated the belief that the city had to take steps to curb the idleness of children. Noting the "*juvenile* character" of participants in recent street rioting and asserting that "time has greatly increased too the difficulties and dangers to which all of them are exposed," the memorial requested the establishment of intermediate schools: "We would pray, then, that one of these schools may be established and tried, with such a teacher and under such provisions as the character of the children may seem to require." It also asked for the appointment of "some agent to look after all vagrant and exposed children." Although in December the council agreed to appoint an agent, it denied the request for an intermediate school, citing the March report as support for its decision. The committee hoped that the grammar schools could instruct "special permit" students for the presumed brief time required.[7]

Despite the persistent contention that intermediate schools were not necessary, public pressure regarding the "threat" of these children persisted to the point where the council and the school committee finally acquiesced. In March 1838 a city council order granted the Primary School Board permission to admit into one school in each of the districts "any child who is more than seven years of age, and is not qualified for admission to the Grammar Schools." Because the schools were designed for children coming from overseas and suffering from "misfortune or neglect," the board decided that one school in each of four mostly immigrant districts, specifically "Nos. 2, 5, 7, and 8, will be sufficient at the present time." Joseph Wightman, in his *Annals of the Boston Primary School Committee*, praised the passage of this order "after nearly twenty years [of] unremitted effort."[8]

## Intermediate Schools, 1838–1879

The Primary School Board assumed that about 700 children were "proper subjects" for the four new intermediate schools, or "schools for special instruction," a figure that proved a considerable underestimate. Indeed, once the schools opened their enrollment increased rapidly. By November 1838, 963 students, or about 13 percent of the total school population, attended them. Within five years there were ten such schools; by 1854 they numbered thirty-two, including one for blacks only, five for boys, and four for girls, with a combined enrollment of almost 2,000. After the 1850s the number of these intermediate schools leveled off, although complete data on them during this period are unavailable. A city document shows that as of May 1857 thirty-one schools for special instruction—including eight for boys, seven for girls, and sixteen coeducational—existed in eighteen districts. Most of them were located in those neighborhoods experiencing a surge of immigration: Fort Hill, the North End, and the West End. At this time these schools enrolled 1,674 students, with 582 over the age of ten.[9]

Documents indicate that the schools over time acquired a negative reputation. By the 1850s, they had come to serve poor immigrant children almost exclusively "by the natural process of selection—by age, intelligence, and residential location." Teachers often resisted serving in the schools, causing the Primary School Board to consider in 1845 whether intermediate school instructors "ought to receive a larger compensation than the others." One reason for this negative image may have been the high turnover among students: the data from 1854 also show that there had been "2,720 changes in six months!!" through admissions and discharges of students in these schools, which averaged a total of under two thousand in total daily attendance.[10]

Few records exist which describe the actual nature of life in intermediate schools, but John Philbrick visited some early in his tenure as superintendent. One he found "extraordinar[il]y" successful, with "pupils . . . trained to cleanliness and good manners . . . really civilized and refined." In another he discovered "slovenly urchins . . . little better than semibarbarians." Philbrick attributed the difference to the relative skills of the teachers in charge. The superintendent also suggested limiting their class size to forty and recommended against a full introduction of the graded classification system into the schools because of their "peculiar" character. While some intermediate schools did experiment with graded instruction, most found that because of the wide range of background and ability among students a more flexible approach was necessary. Commenting on the diversity in the intermediate schools, Philbrick described the materials used in the basic curriculum as "somewhat miscellaneous" and observed that "the teachers in these schools have an arduous and difficult task to perform, and they need special encouragement and assistance."[11]

School officials generally expressed ambivalent attitudes toward the intermediate schools throughout their existence. On the one hand they

John Philbrick, superintendent of the Boston public schools from 1856 to 1878, oversaw the development of intermediate schools and the Horace Mann School for the Deaf.

praised them for being "very useful" and indispensable, and the schools continued to receive funding. On the other hand, authorities often proclaimed their desire to promote students out of them as rapidly as possible and even to get rid of the intermediate schools altogether. The 1857 BSC report acknowledged the schools' role in serving students "naturally dull and slow of comprehension" and in shielding the "tender and unsophisticated children of the Primary Schools" from older intermediate school attendees. However, that same report commented that intermediate children should be transferred whenever possible to the regular grammar schools "so as to become in all respects the *subjects* of influence, and not the *leaders* of it," as well as to keep them "in the regular march of promotion." The "constant effort of the Committee," revealed the report, "is to dispense with [intermediate schools] as soon as it can be judiciously done."[12]

In light of these comments it is not surprising that the 1857 city report on intermediate schools agreed that they should be discontinued. It declared that they had somehow lost their original purpose of serving "overgrown and backward children, who, it was hoped, might . . . be prepared for entrance into the grammar schools, in the shortest possible time." The report lamented that teachers kept their better students from advancing to grammar schools in order to give the teachers "a good appearance at the examinations." It also claimed the following irregularities:

> This is not the only point in which the original design of this class of schools seems to have been perverted, for the custom soon obtained of sending from Primary Schools all the backward and ill-favored children, as soon as they arrived at the age of eight years, into this class of schools. Teachers of the Primary Schools have often been known to state that certain children, who were giving them more than ordinary trouble, would soon be old enough to be sent off to the Schools for Special Instruction. It is evident that the present system offers too great an inducement to Primary School teachers to neglect certain pupils, who may soon, according to the rules, be sent to an Intermediate School, and imposes upon the latter class of teachers an undue share of labor and trouble. The very existence of such a class of schools, composed of children whose early education and moral instruction have been neglected, or who have not been favored by an ordinary share of intellectual endowments, naturally tends to abuses which no regulations, however stringent, can prevent.

The report continued by saying that it could find "little evidence" suggesting intermediate school students enjoyed "rapid development of the intellectual powers." It said that the schools' disadvantages were "sufficiently obvious" and that the "unfortunate" intermediate school students could surely benefit "from the association with children of active intellects and good manners. . . . [T]hese unfortunate children, especially, need such an advantage, and we see no reason why they should be deprived of these valuable means of improvement."[13]

Although intermediate schools remained an official component of the school system (as specified in chapter 9, section 4 of the 1865 regulations), they were mentioned little if at all in official records through the 1870s. Then, in 1879, the school committee announced that the schools for special instruction had undergone a thorough review. In summarizing that review, the BSC indicated the negative characteristics and reputation with which these schools had become saddled. While praising them generally, the committee commented that the schools "were peculiarly unfortunate in occupying an isolated position" and did not have "a recognized place in the school system." The BSC also asserted that the schools contained "in general, only the less promising children" and that "the selection of teachers for them seems to have been made, in most cases, with less than usual care. Add to this the fact that they had been sometimes turned into a kind of Botany Bay, to which transgressors were banished from Primary and Grammar Schools, and it is not surprising that they were found to be in an unsatisfactory condition, and that a radical change appeared to be needed."

At the end of 1879 the intermediate schools were dissolved, and their students were reclassified into a new category, that of the "ungraded classes of Grammar Schools."[14]

## Ungraded Classes, 1879–1900

The discontinuation of the intermediate schools did not constitute a move to abandon segregation of older illiterate children from younger primary pupils. "There are grave objections," wrote the BSC, "which all parents will appreciate, to the intimate association with very young children of those much older and more mature, and the separation, therefore, provided for and secured by the Intermediate Schools was an excellent thing." Rather, the reorganization into ungraded classes, just one part of a major reorganization of the public school system during the late 1870s, reflected a desire to place the education of intermediate students under much closer supervision. As part of the grammar schools, the ungraded classes came under the immediate control of grammar school principals, an arrangement thought "certain to secure a more steady and effective supervision" that would then rectify the problems facing the schools. The school committee believed that "this change will commend itself to all whose judgment is of any value." Moreover, it was hoped that the closer association with the grammar schools would encourage ungraded class students to work harder and emulate the regular students, thus providing "a healthy moral incentive." The ungraded classes became an official component of the graded Boston public school system as of 1880.[15]

The next two decades proved to be a period of significant growth for the ungraded classes. The 1881 statistics showed 665 ungraded class pupils, or 2.7 percent of the just over 25,000 grammar school pupils. Of the fifty grammar schools in the city, fifteen offered an ungraded class; both single-sex and coeducational ones existed, usually depending on the pattern of their host grammar schools. By 1900 thirty-three out of fifty-seven

### TABLE 2
### Yearly Growth Rate of Ungraded Classes

| Year | Number of Classes | Number of Students | Percentage of Total |
|------|------|------|------|
| 1881 | 15 | 665 | 2.7 |
| 1882 | 19 | 839 | 3.3 |
| 1883 | 17 | 834 | 3.0 |
| 1884 | 21 | 930 | 3.4 |
| 1885 | 21 | 850 | 3.2 |
| 1886 | 23 | 918 | 3.3 |
| 1887 | 23 | 934 | 3.3 |
| 1888 | 23 | 981 | 3.4 |
| 1889 | 26 | 1171 | 3.9 |
| 1890 | 25 | 1247 | 4.2 |
| 1891 | 23 | 1226 | 4.2 |
| 1892 | 23 | 1415 | 4.8 |
| 1893 | 25 | 1646 | 5.5 |
| 1894 | 28 | 1568 | 5.1 |
| 1895 | 28 | 1669 | 5.2 |
| 1896 | 28 | 1842 | 5.6 |
| 1897 | 30 | 1867 | 5.5 |
| 1898 | 34 | 2058 | 5.8 |
| 1899 | 35 | 2232 | 6.2 |
| 1900 | 33 | 2318 | 6.2 |

grammar schools had ungraded classes holding over 2,300 students, or just under 6.2 percent of grammar school enrollment. Table 2 presents the growth rate of the ungraded classes between 1881 and 1900.

According to available statistics, ungraded classes served children mostly between the ages of ten and thirteen, with a few fourteen or older. In 1894 the statistics on the classes began listing the ratio of male to female ungraded students. Not surprisingly the majority were boys, ranging from 54.4 percent male in 1896 to a high of 65 percent in 1894 and standing at approximately 60 percent male in 1900. It is important to note, however, that even with such increases not all children eligible for the classes were assigned to them. Superintendent Edwin Seaver's annual report of 1890 expressed great dismay that

> the presence of considerable—sometimes large—numbers of these old children in the regular primary classes is one of the most deplorable consequences of grading strictly and exclusively by scholarship tests. . . . The evil influences exerted on younger children by those who have outgrown the primary school are too well known to need description.
> So in every district, let the overaged children be removed from the primary schools, bodily, and placed in special classes where they may be fitted by special treatment to join the regular classes in the grammar school as soon as possible.

Clearly, the policy of bringing as many children as possible under the control and influence of public schooling underscored the limits of ungraded class availability during this period of the school system's rapid growth.[16]

## Student Characteristics

The regulations covering the ungraded classes broadened the eligibility requirements for attendance beyond those for the intermediate schools. In 1885 admission regulations stipulated that the ungraded classes were for the instruction of "children who, from age or other reason, are unqualified for the regular classes of Primary and Grammar Schools." Thus a student could be placed in an ungraded class for a variety of reasons other than being eight or older and needing to acquire literacy skills. The selection process itself was only vaguely defined, probably consisting of a subjective teacher recommendation approved by the school principal. This expansive approach toward eligibility and selection made it easier for teachers and administrators to use the classes as an instructional option for students who either created difficulties in the regular classroom or could not keep pace with the programmed march up the educational ladder.[17]

Consequently, the ungraded classes included a highly diverse collection of students. A board of supervisors report observed that ungraded class students "have simply lacked opportunities. They have become advanced in age without the corresponding mental development; they are new arrivals from foreign shores, where they have had no educational advantages, or they have been thrown back by sickness, and need much help and encouragement. Some of them, as is often the case in other classes, may be morally as well as intellectually weak." Observers used other vivid terms in describing ungraded class pupils: "backward and peculiar," "dull . . . yet honest and industrious," "boys and girls who know little of books and much of the rough and tumble of life," students "who, from laziness, irregularity in attendance, or viciousness, have become obnoxious." Although school regulations specifically stated that "no child shall be placed in an ungraded class for misconduct," the BSC acknowledged that "there are reasons for believing that many pupils who are unruly . . . and troublesome to their teachers are placed in these classes." The hope was that ungraded classes would provide smaller settings "where the advancement of industrious children will not be held in check by those who are idle, disorderly, or irregular in their attendance." In effect, then, the ungraded classes became a catchall for students who for whatever reason could not perform satisfactorily in the regular grades as well as for older children who needed to learn basic skills but also, it was believed, had to be kept apart from younger pupils.[18]

## Curriculum in the Ungraded Classes

The highly diverse characteristics of ungraded class students presented a considerable challenge to curriculum planning and instruction. Although the stated intent of the ungraded classes was to provide basic primary instruction to older children as preparation for the grammar schools, ungraded class teachers came to understand that the extreme diversity found in their classrooms made standardized, traditional instruction virtually impossible. Instead of implementing a standard primary curriculum, the ungraded classes were forced to keep class size relatively low and to take a more eclectic approach to teaching and classroom management.

From the inception of ungraded classes in 1879, class size constituted an important consideration. The regular public school classroom generally had sixty or more children in the latter nineteenth century. By the late

1800s, regulations set a maximum of fifty-six per class, but that limit was frequently ignored. School officials agreed that because of the age and background of ungraded class children a smaller class size was necessary. Intermediate schools had tried to hold enrollment to forty pupils per teacher, and in the early 1880s the ungraded class maximum was set at thirty-five to provide more individualized instruction. The board of supervisors stated the case for this decision in 1885:

> Here, in charge of a teacher who has not more than thirty-five pupils, they can receive the individualized attention they need and, if they have the capacity, be brought up to the standard of the Grammar class where they naturally belong. Their mental and physical condition demands a consideration that they cannot receive in a Primary classroom, where they will aimlessly repeat work with little children, to whose companionship they are as ill-suited as they are to the Primary-School desks and chairs.

In 1887 the board reiterated its conviction that in the ungraded class students "may receive more personal attention, be more sympathetically treated, and the sooner the better prepared for the other classes of the school. . . . The teacher is thus enabled to do for them individually what cannot be done in the graded classes." The need to keep the student/ teacher ratio in ungraded classes as low as possible remained an accepted tenet among school officials for the duration of the classes' existence; in 1911 the school committee reduced the limit from thirty-five to thirty. It should be noted, however, that ungraded classes often numbered much more than regulations permitted, as statistics suggest and some authorities pointed out.[19]

The purpose of keeping enrollment in ungraded classes relatively low was to allow teachers to exercise greater flexibility in implementing curriculum. Over time the ungraded class curriculum evolved into two fundamental components: basic primary instruction and English language instruction. Documents revealed precious few specifics about how such instruction was carried out. Superintendent Edwin Seaver described ungraded class activity in vague terms in his report of 1899, noting only that students received "special attention" to be "fitted soon to join the regular classes" or get "what little instruction they are capable of." A 1913 school document explained that in late 1912 the ungraded classes at the Hancock Grammar School in the North End still had "no course of study. . . . The individual teachers did the best they could with their respective groups without supervision or close cooperation." Ungraded class instruction most likely varied considerably depending on the conditions and diversity found within each individual class.[20]

One vivid description of an ungraded class survives: a brief report regarding the introduction of a manual training program into a class of boys. This report was written by the teacher and included in the board of supervisors' annual report for 1889. The author detailed how he used scissors, knives, and other simple tools to get his students more interested in school and "as an incentive to good conduct and good lessons." The teacher related that "the class was a difficult one, composed chiefly of backward and peculiar pupils, between eight and fifteen years of age, in a district where a large proportion of the charity of the city is expended." Tools were used two or three times a week and given only to students who had shown good effort and behavior. The boys made a number of small objects out of cardboard, paper, and wood, with many of the students bringing their own materials. The teacher claimed that manual training eliminated truancy as well as the need for corporal punishment. The board of supervisors concurred, saying that "a new avenue of interest was opened to the most unresponsive and irresponsible pupils, which proved to be a way to an awakened interest in their regular work and right relations with the school." Given the great popularity of manual training during the late nineteenth and early twentieth centuries—especially with immigrant and/or struggling students—and given the reported success of this experiment, it is quite likely that manual training was an oft-used component of instruction in many ungraded classes.[21]

That same board of supervisors report also raised the issue of disciplinary methodology, pleading for the use of a gentle, positive, and sympathetic treatment of ungraded class students. But reliable information on methods of discipline and motivation in ungraded classes is virtually nonexistent. Approaches probably varied greatly depending on the teachers, students, principals, and schools involved. The board of supervisors indicated that in some ungraded classes

> teachers have been so illogical in their methods as to visit the returning truant with exasperating punishment, thus increasing the difficulty of reclaiming him. It has been found over and over again that a word of welcome, or an act of kindness, may do more to cure truancy than the last resource of penal authority. To give the ragged boy clean and whole clothing, to aid him in any way to present a respectable appearance, to give him a germ of self-respect, and to put

confidence in him as a helper, will do more toward making him a faithful and manly pupil than any expression of scorn or rebuke, or any attitude of shame and disgrace.

Despite this humanitarian plea and the claims of the teacher that manual training eliminated the need to use corporal punishment to reduce truancy, there is no evidence of any set policy being established or followed regarding discipline or motivation in the ungraded classes.[22]

## Ungraded Classes and Immigrant Education

For virtually all of their history, the predominant participant in the majority of ungraded classes was the child who either came from overseas or was born to immigrant parents. As immigration to Boston increased, so did the percentage of such children in the ungraded classroom. Statistics reveal that the traditional focus on poor children of foreign parentage carried over from the intermediate schools. Most ungraded classes were organized in the grammar schools of Boston's impoverished immigrant neighborhoods, especially the North End, West End, and Fort Hill. The Eliot and Hancock Grammar schools, enrolling boys and girls respectively, were located in the heart of the crowded North End and always had the largest number of ungraded pupils; in 1881 almost one-third of all such students were in these two schools. In 1893, 40 percent of all boys at the Eliot School and 37 percent of all girls at the Hancock School attended ungraded classes. By 1899 these classes enrolled more students than any one of the other six traditional grades in the Hancock, Eliot, and Bigelow schools, all of which were located in immigrant neighborhoods.[23]

The importance of the ungraded class to the schooling of immigrants had thus become obvious, and school officials paid close attention to the classes' nature and purpose in relation to immigrant education from the 1880s into the 1900s. In 1887 the board of supervisors suggested that the ungraded classes represented a possible means to acclimate immigrant children to the schools and introduce them to the English language. Two years later the board wrote that "some of these classes are made up of children of many nationalities; a fusing and unifying motive is at once essential; we must Americanize them." In 1890 the Boston School Committee clearly indicated its belief that a primary function of the ungraded classes

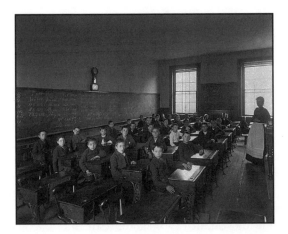

A primary classroom in the Eliot School for boys located in the North End, c. 1892. With its sister institution, the Hancock School, the Eliot School was a showcase and proving ground for ungraded class instruction.

was to provide a suitable opportunity for immigrant children to learn English and learn how to become Americans.[24]

In 1895 and in 1898 Supervisor Walter S. Parker, whose supervisory district included large numbers of immigrant children, filed two reports that closely examined the relationship between the ungraded classes and the schooling of immigrants. His 1895 report noted that the great need for ungraded classes in these districts was "apparent to anyone visiting the schools. . . . In most cases the classes are composed of pupils who have recently come to our country from abroad. They have no knowledge of our language, either spoken or written; many of them have not attended school in their native land." In his 1898 report Parker revealed that his supervisory area included twenty-seven ungraded classes with "over a thousand pupils who need special instruction on account of lack of knowledge of our language. They are received into the several schools from all the countries of Europe, although Russia and Italy supply the larger number. They are of all ages from five to seventeen years, in all stages of development." He left no doubt that he considered the ungraded class to be of paramount importance in public school efforts to assimilate and educate the tremendous influx of immigrant children into Boston.[25]

Language instruction clearly constituted a core component of such efforts, receiving considerable attention from school officials by the last decade of the nineteenth century. Walter Parker stressed, not surprisingly, that English instruction should be considered a fundamental component of the curriculum for ungraded classes in heavily immigrant districts. Although many students of foreign parentage knew no English, "the masters and teachers, without exception, testify to their great eagerness to learn our language, and to their earnestness of purpose to become Americans. They are for the most part docile and tractable. They need and deserve able, skilful instruction." Parker went on to suggest "that a special course of reading be planned for these classes, and books furnished for supplementary reading which are particularly adapted to their needs, and the course of study be somewhat modified in its application to them."[26]

The following year, in 1896, Parker testified to the dual purposes of the acquisition of literacy skills and the introduction to English that shaped ungraded class instruction. "The schools in that part of the city have a double task to perform," he wrote. "They have not only the regular subjects . . . but they have the additional difficulty of teaching the pupils the English language, as large numbers of them cannot speak a word of English on entering school. . . . It is worthy of special study and attention." In 1898 Parker devoted much of his report on ungraded classes to the problem of English instruction. After noting the large numbers of immigrant children and their widely varied backgrounds, Parker stated that these children differed greatly among themselves in terms of education level and learning abilities. He recommended that class size be strictly limited to thirty-five to facilitate individualized instruction, that a flexible course of study responsive to individual needs be used, and that "the greater part of the work at first must necessarily be on language." He lamented the fact that there existed no provision for giving "proper material for teaching our language to foreigners" and suggested a form of object teaching using materials and activities "common to all created beings" as an effective method to begin the process of instruction. Parker pleaded that the schools make available appropriate materials for this work. He did not recommend abandoning the traditional basic ungraded class curriculum entirely, only to depart from it "whenever and wherever the exigencies of the case require or the needs of the pupils demand."[27]

Just how closely teachers or administrators followed Parker's suggestions is unclear. What had become clear was that by the turn of the century ungraded classes were expected to teach English to immigrant children whose lack of English skills qualified them for an ungraded class. Superintendent Seaver commented in 1899 that "in certain districts . . . the large number of the children of recent immigrants who needed to learn the English language before they could be received into the regular classes made it necessary to establish additional ungraded classes." Three years later Seaver differentiated between the ungraded classes, that served mostly "dull and backward but otherwise normal" students, and those "which are used for the instruction of recently arrived foreign children. The children in these classes are as bright as as (*sic*) any others, and only need to learn enough English language to be put upon the regular work of the grades." This important function continued for the ungraded classes until the full development of the "special English" classes during the 1910s.[28]

## Teachers

Successful implementation of this vaguely defined, eclectic, and challenging curriculum in classes of such great diversity certainly proved to be an enormously challenging task. During the history of the ungraded classes the recruitment, selection, and ability of ungraded class teachers generated considerable concern and debate. While constantly stating their belief that only the best teachers should conduct ungraded classes, school officials found that the often poor quality of such teaching remained a persistent thorn in their sides.

Administrators agreed almost unanimously that the nature of the ungraded classroom demanded a highly qualified instructor who could identify and address the varied needs of its students. John Philbrick's position that the "arduous and important" work in the intermediate schools necessitated "special encouragement and assistance" for the teacher foreshadowed similar statements from school leaders in the late nineteenth century. In 1887 the board of supervisors answered its own question, "What sort of teachers should be given charge of these classes?" with "The answer may well be, The very best that can be obtained." The board dismissed the notion that teachers who have shown themselves incapable of handling a regular classroom should be assigned to an ungraded one. It went on to say:

> The different conditions of the various pupils, the peculiar obstacles
> to be overcome in the case of each, the arousing the sluggish, winning
> an interest in worthy things, training to habits of sustained effort and
> carefulness of behavior, awakening the moral consciousness, demand
> the best efforts of the brightest, the most skilled and devoted teachers.
>
> The improvement in the character of the ungraded classes, and
> the increase of their worth to the schools, must depend on the im-
> provement in the spirit, the methods, and the ability of the teachers.

The board concluded that teaching an ungraded class required a selfless,
positive attitude, insisting that those teachers "who are by nature adapted
to these positions . . . will occupy a high place in any just scale of values,
and be worthy of the highest rewards." In 1890 the board, still searching
for ideal ungraded class instructors, proclaimed that "the teachers of ungraded classes should be selected because of their superior qualifications
for the work required. . . . [Ungraded children] are in need of teachers who
are not only apt to teach, but who, from superior mental and moral gifts,
are kind, gentle, patient, industrious, and long-suffering." The school
committee, Supervisor George Conley, and Superintendent Seaver all
heartily agreed with the board's assessment.[29]

On several occasions those who supported the idea of highly skilled
teachers for the ungraded classes proposed higher pay as incentives to at-
tract them. As noted earlier, the Primary School Board contemplated
higher pay for intermediate school instructors. The board of supervisors
similarly suggested higher pay for ungraded class instructors in 1890, asserting that "in no other way can our ungraded classes be lifted to the
position which they should occupy in the estimation of teachers, of pupils,
and of the community." In 1894 the board submitted a recommendation
to the school committee that "teachers of ungraded classes should be specially well qualified for the work, and should receive additional compensation while in charge of such classes."[30]

Nevertheless, such requests were never honored. In a definitive statement on the matter, the committee on rules and regulations of the BSC
decided the following:

> [W]e see no need for special legislation on this point, as we assume
> that our masters would naturally assign to such classes only such of
> their teachers as are fitted to fill such positions. We do not feel con-
> vinced of the expediency of providing that the teachers of these classes

should receive additional compensation while in charge of such classes. As at present informed, we do not favor the principle of providing special salaries for teachers outside of the regular salary schedule. The adoption of such a practice, in our opinion, would be unwise, and would abound in opportunities for dissatisfaction and unjust discrimination. . . . The Board has, we believe, adopted a wise policy in establishing certain ranks of the teachers, and in providing a salary for each rank, and this policy should be adhered to.

The BSC also argued that it should not give special consideration to certain ungraded class teachers because it was not convinced that such work was significantly different from or any "harder or more discouraging" than that in the regular classroom.[31]

In calling for better pay for ungraded class teachers the board of supervisors indicated that the quality of such instructors was not satisfactory. Indeed, the BSC subcommittee's assumption that well-qualified teachers were routinely receiving appointments to ungraded classes was by and large inaccurate. According to Supervisor Conley, "Special qualifications are required for this work, which many teachers do not possess." Echoing the BSC's assertion that "the less than usual care" had been exercised in selecting intermediate school teachers, Conley wrote that "in some schools great care has been taken in the selection of these teachers; in others the material at hand has been used." In 1890 the board of supervisors complained, "too frequently . . . the teachers assigned to these classes have been such as, for various reasons, were not considered fit for the graded classes; and thus a stigma has been placed upon all teachers in the ungraded schools." Twelve years later Edwin Seaver bemoaned the fact that "instead of being assigned to the most skilful teachers, some of these classes have been used as places of refuge for teachers who have failed to do good work in the regular grades, or for teachers who . . . have become supernumerary." Seaver expressed his support for "a higher salary for teachers of ungraded classes if, at the same time, it were made impossible for any but very superior teachers to be promoted to those classes, or to remain in them." Apparently, some well-qualified ungraded class teachers had reason to fear that the school administration would be so desperate to keep them there as to pass the teacher over for promotion to a higher position in the teacher ranks. While some attempts did occur to adjust the official rank of ungraded class teachers within the teacher corps—such teachers were considered low on a hierarchy which scaled teachers on the basis of grade level taught, with primary teachers on the low end—ungraded class instructors never received any special salary compensation.[32]

## The Ungraded Class Image

The problem of recruiting and keeping qualified teachers for the ungraded classes reflected the generally negative image of the classes themselves. Despite the hopes of the 1879 reorganization, the ungraded class continued to suffer from a systemwide reputation as difficult and undesirable places in which to teach and learn. This was so even though school officials did their best to put the classes in a positive light. In 1885 the board of supervisors labeled them "a most important aid to the classification of a school, and a real benefit" to students. In its 1887 report the board again tried to bolster the support and morale for those involved in ungraded class instruction, saying rather defensively that the classes were "taking a somewhat better position than was once accorded" them. The report continued by stating that "the purpose for which the ungraded class was established was purely beneficent, and there is no more disgrace attaching to membership of that class, when it has its right place in the school organization, than to membership of any other class. Pupils are sent to it as a favor, and not as a punishment." Superintendent Seaver joined the defense, arguing in 1902 that the ungraded classes'

> unfortunate reputation is not universally deserved. There are well managed ungraded classes, carried on according to the true intent; and there are ideal teachers of such classes. What needs to be done is to bring the management of every ungraded class back to the true original purpose, and to provide it with the most skilful teacher obtainable. The work of the ungraded class, instead of being looked down upon, as it now is quite generally, should be highly esteemed; for, surely, the production of even moderate results with very dull children is proof of higher teaching skill than is shown by the production of much better results with bright children.[33]

Despite these words of support, the board of supervisors had to admit that "the class is not viewed in the spirit of this purpose in all schools. The teachers of graded classes are too much influenced by the old idea of it as a 'Botany Bay' class, or a class for the 'feeble-minded.'" The board then revealed that teachers "sometimes sarcastically suggest to laggards and the ill-behaved that they should be sent to the ungraded class. Their tone and manner give the class a bad character in the estimation of their pupils." The situation had not improved any three years later: the board reaffirmed the classes' "Botany Bay" reputation, and it again emphasized that teachers banished misbehaving students to them. "For certain reasons," understated the board, "these ungraded classes have never been popular either with teachers or pupils." In 1895 George Conley verified that "from the regular classes [to the ungraded] are removed the slow and backward children as well as those who are troublesome and hinder the progress of others by robbing them of their time and opportunities." In brief yet evocative language he concluded: "Even the most capable teachers shrink from assuming a charge which makes such large demands upon their patience, strength, and skill."[34]

The ungraded classes' image also suffered from their use as a means to circumvent school regulations. Some Boston grammar school principals attempted to secure additional teachers for their schools by exaggerating the need for ungraded classes. Principals would claim an unrealistically high number of students eligible for the classes; ungraded class teachers would then be assigned to the schools and used either to reduce the student/teacher ratio in regular classes or to serve as a "floating" teacher of specialized subjects. Principals also would claim eligibility for more ungraded classes in order to prevent current teachers on their staff from being dropped as a result of any decrease in school enrollment. Concern over these practices grew throughout the 1890s as the number of ungraded classes and students jumped amid a greater concern for efficiency and economy in school operations. As early as 1895 the BSC recommended and eventually passed an order stipulating that the superintendent had to approve all additional requests for ungraded classes. While acknowledging the legitimate need throughout the system for more teachers, Seaver claimed "it is not the money that will be saved by cutting off all unnecessary ungraded classes that is so important; but it is of the highest moment that all schools should be treated fairly and alike. Good administration can permit nothing else." Even so, it was still a problem in 1902 when Seaver reported that the practice of abusing the regulations regarding the creation of ungraded classes had "given [them] a bad name."[35]

## The Early Twentieth Century

In spite of their serious problems, the ungraded classes continued to maintain essential support from school officials who hoped for much better but still realized the need for such classes in the highly regimented Boston public school system. The board of supervisors, and especially Walter Parker, fought for the improvement of ungraded classes and for their equitable treatment from the school bureaucracy. The need for settings that could accommodate atypical students not only persisted but increased, and the classes were not in danger of elimination at the turn of the century. However, by 1902 Superintendent Seaver realized, much as the school committee had in 1879, that this part of the public schools required more efficient supervision and management, to return the classes to, as Seaver had said, their "true original purpose." To school officials such management involved identifying specific needs of ungraded class students and providing more specialized learning environments for those needs. During the early twentieth century, the ungraded classes were joined by several other programs designed to educate disadvantaged or disabled students more efficiently.

Efforts did continue to improve the ungraded classes themselves. In 1910, for example, the BSC tried to strengthen teaching in the classes by requiring a three-day training period for new ungraded teachers as well as by offering occasional exchange visits and in-service programs. Even so, the ungraded class became increasingly less important as Boston's public schools embraced the concept of greater differentiation among its students. Having realized that the tremendous differences among students severely hindered effective management and instruction, school officials took action over the course of several years. "To make progress with such a miscellaneous group is hardly possible," wrote Superintendent Franklin Dyer in 1914. "The chief value [of the ungraded class] is to relieve the regular teachers of the children who do not fit. If the policy of attempting to meet the needs of the children themselves is to be followed it is necessary that these classes should be very carefully reorganized."[36]

That same year Assistant Superintendent Maurice White mentioned one already successful attempt at such reorganization: the establishment of special classes "for the feeble-minded" in 1898. These classes recently had been "greatly increased" in number, White said, "relieving the ungraded classes of a great burden and at the same time giving to these unfortunates a much better training." White commented that the two broad categories of ungraded students, "backward children and non-English speaking children . . . have been differentiated to a considerable extent, although this work is not completed." He noted the meetings of ungraded class teachers in 1910 and 1911; one important result of these meetings was a 1912 experiment in the Hancock School that had a teacher come and discuss English and citizenship exclusively with ungraded class students "in a conversational way" on a regular basis, an approach White considered a "marked success." During the 1910s the most critical differentiation of former ungraded students involved these non-English speakers. After the Hancock experiment the idea of "special English" classes gained quick and eager acceptance. By 1914 thirty-six special classes were in place (some of which were "steamer" classes for children just arrived), with a total of 1,327 pupils enrolled. Further, these classes had earned their own classification in the annual statistical summaries of the school committee. Consequently, many of the newly arrived students who needed to learn the language of instruction attended special English rather than ungraded classes, relieving the latter of a major responsibility as well as large numbers of students. In addition, Franklin Dyer implied that the then-popular prevocational centers siphoned away older, "motor"-oriented potential ungraded pupils as part of this general effort to develop more efficient reclassification of students "who vary from the normal type." It is not clear how many students the other specialized programs of the early 1900s, especially those with chronic illness or physical disabilities, drew away from the ungraded classes. What is clear is that by 1920 the ungraded class had become a much different entity than it had been at the turn of the century. Special classes, special English classes, and prevocational programs offered more specialized learning environments for students who previously had been placed in the ungraded class for lack of a better option.[37]

The changes in ungraded class enrollment naturally reflected these developments. Between 1900 and 1904 the number of schools with ungraded classes went from thirty-five to thirty although the number of students actually increased by thirty-three. This drop probably resulted from closer scrutiny of ungraded class establishment. In 1905 the number of students and schools with classes rose again, to thirty-seven classes with 2,704 pupils. By 1908 there were just over 3,000 ungraded class students, but these children represented just 3.7 percent of the total grammar school population of almost 81,000. According to one source, the school system operated as many as eighty ungraded classes during the last two years of the decade; another lists at least sixty-three in 1911 and forty-seven in

1914. After 1910, however, school officials rapidly accelerated their efforts to provide more specialized classroom settings; these efforts clearly had a dramatic impact on the nature as well as number of ungraded class students. In 1911 there were 1,611 male and 1,165 female ungraded pupils, a total of 2,776 that proved to be the high for any year after 1910. Between 1913 and 1914 the number of these students plummeted from 2,686 to 1,437, a decrease of more than 46 percent. The next year saw an additional decrease of 52 percent to 686 students. From 1915 ungraded enrollment dropped steadily: 443 in 1920, 255 in 1925, 191 in 1930. By 1935 only thirty-one students attended ungraded classes; in 1938 all twenty pupils were promoted out of the one remaining class, and 1939 saw no ungraded students at all.[38]

Thus the importance of the classes had lessened dramatically over time. Superintendent Dyer wrote proudly that this "vigorous reorganization" had reduced their number and changed their character so that "few of the classes are now of the 'omnium gatherum' type." From 1920 until their discontinuation, the ungraded classes served mainly as, in Dyer's words, "'clearing houses' for irregular children who with a short term of individual attention may be classified into the grades." Such children most likely were newly arrived and older; they attended an ungraded class until sufficient information or accomplishment could determine the proper place for them within the massive, highly stratified and specialized Boston public school system. Created to ease the fears and suspicions about a certain class of the city's children, the intermediate schools never pretended to do more than make the system run more smoothly and soothe the anxieties of the city's leadership and elite. Even as the few calls arose for greater, more sympathetic attention to the educational needs of their students, the ungraded classes' fundamental function remained that of an efficiency-driven element of the city's public school machinery, providing a place for students who seriously disrupted the operation of the system or who otherwise were considered unfit for normal participation in the life of the schools. Once the system established other settings to serve the same purpose, the days of the ungraded class were numbered. The ungraded classes—once virtually the only placement option for a system lacking the ability to specify or address effectively the wide range of mental, physical, and behavioral diversity that has always characterized public school children—simply faded away as they were no longer truly needed.[39]

# 6

# THE HORACE MANN SCHOOL
# FOR THE DEAF

Until the late 1860s, severely or totally deaf children in Boston had few opportunities for elementary education. Their disability prevented any substantive participation in public schools, and attendance at the closest residential institutions for deaf education (at Hartford, Connecticut and Northampton, Massachusetts) proved difficult for many, impossible for others. Opportunities for private instruction existed but were extremely limited. Thus, the Boston School Committee's establishment of a School for Deaf-Mutes in late 1869 generated considerable interest and excitement from parents and friends of the city's deaf children. It also earned the attention of national and international educators involved with public schooling and deaf education. Recognized as the first permanent public day school for deaf children in the United States, Boston's "School for Deaf-Mutes"—renamed the Horace Mann School for the Deaf in 1877— had by the early twentieth century become a source of great pride for Boston school authorities as well as a centerpiece of the oral method for education of the deaf.

## Founding of the School for Deaf-Mutes

In September 1864 the Boston School Committee's Committee on Rules and Regulations filed a report on the status of the schooling of the city's deaf children. The report responded to a petition from Philo W. Packard, a private tutor for deaf children, which requested that the school committee "make an appropriation for the instruction of deaf mutes in the city, who are incapacitated, either by age or circumstances, from attending"

Connecticut's state residential school for deaf individuals at Hartford, about 100 miles from Boston. Packard had been providing instruction voluntarily to about twenty deaf-mute boys and girls who were too young (under nine years old) to gain admission to the Hartford institution. He believed that many more such children could benefit from formal schooling.[1]

The Committee on Rules and Regulations, while appreciative of the lack of educational opportunities for the deaf, expressed its reluctance to accede to Packard's request. It noted that one-third of the children to whom Packard referred lived outside the city limits, that the Hartford school had lowered its admission age to eight, and that the significant debate over the advisability of educating any child under the age of eight rendered offering such instruction inappropriate, at least for the time being. The subcommittee also reminded the general school committee that the state, rather than localities, traditionally had provided for the "instruction of this unfortunate class" and that Massachusetts had in fact made "ample and satisfactory provision in this matter." The report then stated that should the time arrive for a school for deaf children in Boston it would be the state's responsibility, not the city's, to "accomplish the desired result." The subcommittee recommended denying Packard's petition, and the general committee agreed.[2]

Nevertheless, in 1868 the idea of a school for deaf children in Boston resurfaced. The Reverend Dexter S. King, a member of both the state legislature and the Boston School Committee, took an interest in deaf education and suggested the establishment of a public day school, rather than a residential school, for this purpose. King presented this idea to the full school committee, which then appointed a subcommittee to consider it. Although the idea was researched, the subcommittee did not issue a report. In January 1869 the same subcommittee, this time with King as chair, reconsidered the proposal, and in April it recommended establishing such a school. The following month the state legislature authorized the governor to send, with parental permission, deaf children to either Hartford, the Clarke Institution for Deaf Mutes in Northampton, "or any other school for deaf mutes in the Commonwealth" and to have the state pay the tuition of children whose parents or guardians could not afford it.[3]

With the state now offering to support indigent deaf children in any school in the state, a day school for the deaf appeared a sound economic as well as educational endeavor. School officials calculated that sending its deaf children to other designated deaf schools would cost the city, in terms of its portion of state aid for such children, four times the amount of opening its own school, which conversely would receive aid. They also argued for the school on the grounds that there were in fact "enough deaf-mute children in the city entirely destitute of the means of education to form such a school, and whose friends would joyfully improve the opportunity of sending them to school." According to a 1927 report issued by then Superintendent Jeremiah Burke, Reverend King convinced the committee that a day school was far more preferable than a residential institution because deaf children should enjoy the opportunity to live at home "where they belonged" instead of in an institution "where their defects were emphasized and their likeness to the rest of the world minimized." Due primarily to King's efforts, the Boston School for Deaf-Mutes opened on November 10, 1869, with twenty-five students (selected from thirty-eight applicants), a principal, Sarah Fuller, and two assistant teachers experienced in deaf education. It originally consisted of two separate locations but was soon consolidated at 11 Pemberton Square.[4]

## Growth of the School, 1869–1900

The school thrived from the beginning. In its early years it received from the state one hundred dollars for each resident student and one hundred and fifty dollars for nonresident students who came to Boston to enroll. In 1871 there were thirty-eight students; by 1874 sixty-three received instruction from Sarah Fuller and six assistants. In 1877 the BSC changed the school's name to the Horace Mann School for the Deaf (HMSD) in honor of the famous Massachusetts educator who had done much to inform Americans about deaf education, especially the oral method of instruction as it existed in Europe. By 1884 the number of students had risen to eighty-two, two-thirds of whom were from Boston. As of 1900 the school boasted fourteen teachers and an enrollment of one hundred and eighteen students, yielding a student-teacher ratio of about 8.5 to 1.[5]

During this period of expansion, the state continued to contribute heavily to the school's financial support. In 1886 Boston received about $7,600 from the state to help offset the school's cost of almost $12,000. In 1887 the state enacted legislation stipulating that the cost of educating such students should be borne by the state and not the city, a policy which to the Boston school system's Committee on Accounts meant that the state would assume "the entire expense of this school." In 1898, however, the BSC complained that Massachusetts still was not paying the entire bill despite the law. It also asserted that per pupil costs had risen from about $120 in 1878 to more than $200 in 1898 and noted that nonresident tuition had been reduced from $150 to $105 during the 1878–79 school year. Accordingly, the state increased the nonresident tuition to $150 again, thus providing an additional $2,000–3,000 for the city. The state continued to supply most of the funding for the school well into the twentieth century, in part to assure that HMSD students would be more "on a par with other children, by furnishing them an education at the public expense."[6]

The almost fivefold increase in the number of students by 1900 contributed to, but was not solely responsible for, persistent complaints about the school's accommodations. Within five years of its founding a report labeled the school's rooms at Pemberton Square "wholly inadequate." In 1874 the BSC declared that the "rapid increase in numbers in this school since its organization" necessitated better housing, noting the "cramped and limited room for classification and other necessary conveniences." The school committee therefore requested the city "to furnish more and better accommodation." In 1875 the school relocated to a different building that quickly proved inadequate as well. The BSC's 1884 report characterized that structure as "unsuitable . . . besides being utterly inconvenient in all its interior arrangements, it is unwholesome, owing to defective drainage, and the high walls around it shut out the light. This is a serious hindrance to the education of its pupils, who must be trained by quick and accurate sight to supply the want of the absent sense." In 1885 the state granted the city a lot on Newbury Street for construction of a new home for the school. By the next year the new building had reached the planning stage. Finally, on November 10, 1890, twenty-one years to the day after its opening, the Horace Mann School for the Deaf moved into its new accommodations in the fashionable Back Bay, thus temporarily solving the pressing problem of inadequate facilities.[7]

## Sources of Success

By the time the Horace Mann School relocated to its new quarters, it had become a source of great pride to school authorities despite its inadequate

In June 1890, the Horace Mann School for the Deaf moved into a new building on Newbury Street, where it stayed until 1929.

facilities. In 1891 the board of supervisors declared, "No Boston public school, whether established for a general or for a specific purpose, accomplishes its objects with more skill and thoroughness than the Horace Mann School for the Deaf." Superintendent Edwin Seaver called it "verily our most precious educational gem." Despite its lengthy search for adequate housing, the school had obviously captured the strong support of those who sponsored and administered it. The reasons for such support included a liberal admissions policy as well as a sympathetic view of deaf children coupled with an optimistic perception of their educability. Perhaps most important to its renown was its effective, pacesetting curriculum emphasizing the oral method of instruction in a day school setting; this put the school at the forefront of deaf education worldwide and at the heart of the oralism-manualism controversy.[8]

Admission to the HMSD depended primarily on the extent of a child's hearing loss, which at the time was typically (and rather crudely) determined by such methods as clapping hands, slamming doors, placing ticking watches in proximity to the ear, or putting tuning forks on the forehead (the first audiometer, invented by Alexander Graham Bell, would not be available until 1886). The public school regulations for 1881 specified that "pupils over five years of age are admitted in accordance with an act passed by the Legislature in 1869." That same act guaranteed all deaf children of the state, regardless of ability to pay, an education at any school for the deaf in Massachusetts (as well as the institution at Hartford). According to this act the governor could "send such deaf-mutes or deat (*sic*) children as he may deem fit subjects for instruction." HMSD regulations specifically stated:

> Any deaf child over five years of age, residing in Boston, not mentally or physically disqualified, is entitled to admission. Children residing out of Boston will be admitted, subject to the preceding conditions, and will be charged the average cost per pupil for tuition, unless received as State beneficiaries. No pupil will be admitted without a certificate of vaccination, signed by a physician. . . .
>
> Children from other States will be received, subject to the above conditions, on the payment of tuition, or upon warrants from the executives of such States.[9]

Because the school was a part of the state network for deaf education, potential students entered an application process that other such schools in the state shared. This process consisted first of a letter to the governor requesting state support for their child and certifying that he or she was "a DEAF-MUTE, and cannot be properly instructed in the Public Schools of this Commonwealth." Second, this claim required verification by a town selectman as well as a doctor's statement assuring the governor that the child was "free from all contagious diseases, and . . . from all immoralities of conduct; is neither sickly nor mentally weak, and is a fit subject for instruction at the expense of the Commonwealth." The process also included a questionnaire, addressed to the parent or guardian, that asked about the physical condition of the parents, the parents' school preference, the history and nature of the child's deafness, and the child's educational background as well as speaking ability. Once satisfied that the child was an eligible candidate, the governor granted admission to a school as well as state assistance if necessary. To ensure that all eligible children in the state knew of their educational opportunities, the state board of education asked every school committee in the state to report to the board the names of any students whom the local committee believed deserved such instruction. Officials associated with the HMSD proudly proclaimed that until 1921 the school never denied placement to a worthy applicant regardless of the child's status.[10]

The school also benefited from a generally humanitarian and optimistic attitude toward young deaf students and their capabilities for formal education. Deaf children attracted considerable sympathy and concern from civic and educational leaders. The state's shouldering of the costs for their education in an era when government involvement in schooling still drew extensive criticism suggests that citizens cared about these children and believed education would help them, attitudes shared by others across the nation. The dedication ceremonies for the new school building in 1890 offered a series of speakers who commented on the "unfortunate" nature of these children yet who saw the school bringing young ones "from darkness into light." One speaker assured the principal of the school that "you will always have my cordial sympathy in the good work which I trust you may long be spared to carry forward." At that ceremony Edwin Seaver summarized such views by saying that "from the humanitarian point of view, [the school] wins our sympathy by its purpose to relieve, as far as possible, a most unfortunate class of children from the inconveniences of their misfortune." Seaver also revealed that officials had strong faith in the effectiveness of educating the deaf: "We can and do rejoice in the increasing skill and success with which the peculiar work of this school is accomplished. . . . [W]e should remember that the mind of a non-hearing child may be, and usually is, as sound and as capable of improvement as the minds of other children."[11]

The early experience of the HMSD confirmed in the minds of school officials the correctness of Seaver's positive attitude. The BSC expressed regret in 1874 that so many people associated deaf-muteness with mental deficiency, observing that intelligence is only slightly affected by deafness; therefore, deaf children were quite capable of extensive instruction. In 1879 Superintendent Samuel Eliot wrote that although many felt that "an asylum was the only practicable provision" for deaf-mutes, the Horace Mann School in fact demonstrated that it could instruct its students "in such a way as to bring them nearer and nearer to the condition of those who hear." Boston thus publicly proclaimed that deaf children both deserved and made good use of a public day school education adapted to their needs.[12]

## Oralism and the HMSD Curriculum

From its beginning, the Horace Mann School anchored its curriculum in oralism, the approach to communication and instruction briefly summarized in chapter 4. Oralism initially gained wide recognition among educators of the deaf as the German method, developed by Samuel Heinicke in the eighteenth century. Heinicke's approach focused on lipreading and using other senses, including taste, to help a student learn and remember proper sounds. Officials of the Horace Mann School described this method as best suited for congenital deaf-mutes with properly formed vocal organs but also stated that it could benefit children who were partially deaf as well. The decision to champion an oral approach fundamentally shaped the school's direction and reputation over the next sixty years and became one of the school's most stable characteristics.

The attraction of oralism to the school's leadership was rooted in the presence and easy access of several key supporters in the Boston area who believed strongly in its value. Horace Mann and Samuel Gridley Howe, two prominent Bostonians, had first proclaimed the advantages of oralism in the 1840s, giving the movement a strong foothold in the city. The Reverend Dexter King, the school committee member and citizen most responsible for realizing the vision of a public day school for the deaf in Boston, had long been a staunch advocate of fully integrating deaf people into the world of the hearing—a fundamental corollary of oralism and a potent rationale for founding a day school. The daughter of prominent Boston attorney Gardiner Greene Hubbard was, according to one source, one of the school's earliest students. Mabel's success under Sarah Fuller's tutelage deeply impressed her father, who was a friend and business partner of Alexander Graham Bell and advocated on behalf of the school during the late 1800s. In addition, the school's oral approach and its role as a day school in facilitating the integration of deaf individuals into the hearing community was praised and reinforced time and again by the members of the Boston School Committee and other school officials, demonstrating their consistent belief that this approach was best for the school and the city.[13]

Even so, Sarah Fuller and Alexander Graham Bell proved most responsible for making the Horace Mann School and the city of Boston a bastion of oralism. Fuller was a Boston public school teacher who developed a strong interest in the education of the deaf before being appointed the first principal of the Horace Mann School. Early in her tenure, she attended a lecture given by Alexander Melville Bell, Alexander Graham Bell's father, on an oral method of instruction he had developed known as Visible Speech. Fuller was so impressed that in the spring of 1871 she convinced the school committee to appropriate five hundred dollars to have Alexander Graham Bell train her staff in the principles and methods

Sarah Fuller served as principal of HMSD from its founding in 1869 until 1910. She was instrumental in bringing Alexander Graham Bell to the school to train the staff. Due largely to Bell's advocacy, the oral method dominated the field of deaf education for nearly a century.

of Visible Speech and then to teach at the school. Bell spent April and May there; he was impressed with the students' lipreading abilities, and Fuller and her staff in turn were impressed with Visible Speech. Fuller's strong leadership of the school for over forty years was grounded in her firm conviction that oralism was by far the best method for teaching children who were deaf. Alexander Graham Bell, meanwhile, was becoming oralism's most famous and effective advocate, and his ties to Boston were many. In addition to his work with Fuller's teachers, Bell tutored several deaf individuals in the area, and his students gave a noteworthy exhibition of their oral skills in late 1871 that greatly impressed many of Boston's elite. Soon after, he became a professor of vocal physiology and elocution at Boston University and eventually married Mabel Hubbard, Sarah Fuller's stellar pupil. Even after reaching national prominence, Bell maintained his Boston ties, even contributing money to the Horace Mann School.[14]

These intricate connections among the school committee, the Horace Mann staff, and the leaders of the oral movement secured the Horace Mann School's commitment to oral instruction, and school officials proved quite open in expressing to the public their rationale for using oralism. The BSC subcommittee in charge of the HMSD argued that "a day school like ours . . . appears particularly adapted for instruction in articulation, on account of the advantage enjoyed by children who live at home, where they are surrounded by hearing persons, and are thus incited to use the power of speech as they acquire it in school." Almost twenty years later the board of supervisors echoed those sentiments:

> It is, indeed, a great feat for a child who has never heard a sound, to communicate orally his thoughts and feelings to members of his family and to read responses from their lips. The deaf child, with this accomplishment, goes out into the world's stir and activity and 'gets on' fairly well; he follows his calling and enjoys his life far better than if he had never learned to talk and to read the lips.

Edwin Seaver agreed, claiming that lack of speech or lipreading skills isolated the deaf child, narrowing his or her possibilities and limiting him or her to "deaf" friendships and associations. "To make their world a broader one, they must have the power of articulate speech and the power of reading articulate speech from the lips of others," Seaver maintained. "This is one reason for undertaking to put deaf persons in the fullest possible communication with hearing and speaking people." Seaver also expressed grave concern that if the deaf-mute did not integrate more fully with normal society, then "a dumb variety of the human race may ultimately become established" through excessive intermarriage. This viewpoint, a key element in arguments for using the oral method, strongly agreed with then-current beliefs held by many in the United States and expounded fervently and frequently by Alexander Graham Bell.[15] The HMSD thus assumed a high profile as an oral day school dedicated to greater assimilation and acculturation—some would say subjugation—of the deaf community to that of the hearing.

Visible Speech instruction involved the use of symbols to represent and identify particular sounds. The symbols were essentially "pictorial abbreviation[s] of the fundamental positions of the speech organs in giving utterance to sounds." Symbols indicated a variety of mechanisms and formations, including tongue placement, control of breath, and directional movements of the nasal passage, lips, and glottis. According to John Philbrick's 1871 report, "The fundamental principle of the system is, that all relations of sound are symbolized by relations of form. Each organ, and each mode of organic action concerned in the production or modification of sound, has its appropriate symbol." Introductory instruction at the school thus involved teaching the symbols through their demonstration, practicing the sound associated with each symbol, and then putting a series of sounds together to form a phrase or sentence. Basic daily drill polished these skills. "The deaf child," commented the subcommittee on the Horace Mann School in 1881, "on entering school, must be taught the words, phrases, and simple sentences, which are used in daily speech, through the constant association of their written forms with the objects and ideas they symbolize." In this way students were able to use the voice for communication instead of the traditional hand signs, which were not used at the school except to facilitate initial instruction of a new student. After observing the method in action Superintendent Philbrick labeled it "a new and powerful instrumentality in the instruction of deaf-mutes."[16]

To execute this program the Horace Mann School was divided into two sections, the second (lower) and the first (higher). The second section concentrated on basic Visible Speech instruction and other general school subjects taught through writing. Second section pupils were those children, usually the younger ones, who "possessed no knowledge of language, written or spoken, before entering school. All were either born deaf, or lost hearing in infancy." An hour each day was spent on Visible Speech, with the remainder of the nine-to-two school day spent on "the acquirement of written language." No lesson lasted more than thirty minutes, and articulation exercises were limited to fifteen minutes. During Visible Speech practice, children used mirrors to gain control of tongue movements. According to one report, most of the children learned to "vary the voice in respect to pitch, force, and duration" as well as speak simple syllables. Written instruction was taught much as it was in the regular classroom; Alexander Graham Bell believed that as much normal instruction as possible should take place in a school for the deaf. In the first section, teachers administered oral instructions, so students were required to read lips. In this section there occurred "daily drill in articulating elementary sounds and combinations, and also exercises for the improvement of the voice."[17]

Included in the daily class schedule was extensive work covering the course of study used in the regular schools. The second section worked on basic primary school subjects, while the first section undertook the study of arithmetic, grammar, geography, physiology, and drawing. By the 1890s, several teachers had added other standard subjects to the curriculum, particularly in the area of manual training: printing, sewing, cooking, woodworking, "free-study movements," and the more traditional subject of history. The older children proved capable of using regular-school text-books for some of their studies. Around 1880 the school set up its own kitchen to instruct girls in cooking and general homemaking. HMSD students also gained entrance to some of the local industrial schools, including the North End Industrial School and the Tennyson Street Cooking School, to receive basic vocational training.[18]

Through the 1880s, Sarah Fuller continued efforts to expand vocational opportunities for her students. School officials acknowledged that Horace Mann students required more time to master regular course work but also observed that their aptitude and retention equaled those of typical students. Some HMSD pupils in fact began enrolling in regular schoolrooms after finishing their program, performing quite well. "The evidence thus far . . . shows that the presence and instruction of deaf pupils cause but slight, if any, inconvenience to teachers, and that the deaf reach at least as high a standard of scholarship as hearing pupils," claimed the board of supervisors in 1891. During the 1890s, Horace Mann students began receiving special graduation diplomas upon satisfactory completion of their work.[19]

## The Horace Mann School Teacher

This complex curriculum placed great demands on the teacher, a fact often noted by school officials. Those who selected instructors for the Horace Mann School realized the challenging task presented by students and subject matter in the classroom. In 1891 the board of supervisors explained that the Horace Mann teachers were "carefully selected from the best teachers in the other public schools. They must be gentle, sympathetic, patient, firm, self-sacrificing, and devoted to their work; they must possess good sense, tact, and skill; they must know the principles of education and the best methods of teaching." Once selected, a new Horace Mann teacher became a pupil herself under Sarah Fuller, who would train her "in the special art of teaching the deaf. After years of experience, they become expert in this art; and, were they to resign their places, it would be difficult, if not impossible, to fill the vacancies." Henry Washburn, one of the founders of the school, exclaimed at the dedication ceremony for the Newbury Street building in 1890 that "the progress made in this institution . . . is due to the patient and persevering toil of a band of teachers, who merit our warmest commendation." The Boston School Committee discussed at length the problems teachers faced in the school, noting that Visible Speech demanded much more of a teacher's energy than did the signing method. They had to pay extremely close attention to mistakes of students and work very hard to form their own sounds perfectly. They needed to have both "great patience and enthusiasm" in often repetitious work and a thorough knowledge of "Vocal Physiology." Teaching the deaf also required an "accurate ear" and "tact . . . to keep up the interest of the children in what to them is too often mere drudgery."[20]

The greatest praise went to the principal, Sarah Fuller, who administered the school in addition to providing training for new staff. Fuller held the principalship until 1910 and displayed an obvious love for her work and her students. She was active not only in the school but also in the formation of the Convention of American Instructors of the Deaf and the American Association to Promote the Teaching of Speech to the Deaf. Fuller also proved instrumental in the education of Helen Keller, describing her work with that internationally known deaf-blind individual in a report to the Boston School Committee in 1903. As early as 1874 the school committee lauded Fuller, saying she had "labored with great faithfulness and earnestness" while exhibiting "great executive ability in the management of the school." The committee revealed that she had won their "entire confidence." Henry Washburn hyperbolically related her work to that of Jesus: "[M]ust she not have heard His voice again and again who once took little children in His arms and blessed them ?"[21]

## The Early Twentieth Century

Through the early 1900s, the Horace Mann School for the Deaf continued to grow. The enrollment of 118 in 1900 increased to 137 in 1905 and 153 in 1910. Between 1910 and 1929, attendance fluctuated between 145 and 160, with 1930 seeing a jump to more than 170. The student/teacher ratio was established at a maximum of ten to one, with some classes occasionally as small as five or less. Sarah Fuller eventually retired in 1910 after forty-one years of service; the BSC replaced her with Ella Jordan, who served until poor health forced her to resign effective on the school's fiftieth anniversary, November 10, 1919. Mabel Adams, the assistant principal, succeeded her. By 1927 the school employed a principal, an assistant principal, fourteen teachers, and five special teachers in the areas of cookery, sewing, manual training, printing, and millinery.[22]

A wide variety of ages, backgrounds, and extent of hearing loss characterized attendees of the school in the early twentieth century. They ranged in age from five to twenty-four and by the 1920s came from dozens of different towns and cities as well as from all sections of Boston. Principal Mabel Adams's report for 1921 stated, "Roughly speaking, the pupils who attend the Horace Mann School may be divided into three classes: The hard of hearing, the totally deaf who have acquired speech before losing their hearing, and the totally or almost totally deaf who have never heard spoken language and therefore possess no thought medium." Of these students about 80 percent had never heard speech. Three years later Adams reported that of the students "not all are totally deaf; many have some slight perception of sound; some have enough hearing to distinguish vowels; others can distinguish words but not sentences; and yet others are just too hard of hearing to make progress in the ordinary schools." Thus the school had extended its services to students who were only partially deaf. Even so, inability to function in a regular classroom remained the essential criterion for admission.[23]

Adams lamented the fact that it was no "easy matter to determine where border-line cases belong, whether in a school for the deaf, a special class, or an institution giving custodial care." Regulations still prohibited attendance by any student judged to be "mentally weak." To help determine such placement and more correctly identify Boston schoolchildren in need of deaf education, the BSC appointed an Advisory Council for Deaf Children in 1920 and an otologist/advisor for the school, Dr. Harry Cahill. Cahill gave lectures to teachers, examined prospective pupils, and attempted to identify any disabilities other than hearing that might have had an effect on a child's performance at school. It is not clear how long Cahill served: Adams's 1924 report suggested that the school lacked such expert advice, but the 1927 report mentioned that "the school is unusually fortunate in having . . . an otologist of repute who gives special attention to health problems concerned with deafness, and also tests the hearing." At any rate, by the 1920s more precise audiometers were available to facilitate the process of determining the extent of a child's hearing loss.[24]

## Curricular Developments, 1900–1930

While identification of needy students gradually became more sophisticated, the curriculum continued to incorporate as many features of the regular school curriculum as possible. The school term and vacations matched those of the regular schools. The school day lasted from nine to two, as it had for decades, to accommodate students who had to travel considerable distances. In 1900 the school adopted the regular course of study, except for the omission of singing and, of course, the addition of vocal training and speechreading. Regulations also permitted more than one year to finish the work of a grade; first grade work often took three or four years to master in the HMSD due to the severe lack of communication skills on the part of entering students.[25]

After completing the equivalent of first grade work, pupils followed a daily program based upon the departmental plan, where groups of children would move from room to room and receive instruction in various subjects from different teachers. The school developed this approach to provide children with opportunities to read the speech of several teachers as well as to permit a teacher to take children through the entire course of a subject. (The school's removal into the greater space on Newbury Street facilitated the change to departmental work, which took effect soon after relocation.) A Horace Mann student would then progress through the regular schools' course of study for each grade, completing the HMSD program when mastering eighth grade subject matter. Most students required eleven or twelve years to finish the eight grades, although a few managed to do so in a shorter time. The rate of progress depended largely "upon health, constant attendance, and mental endowment," according to the school committee.[26]

The school's methodology also continued to employ the oral method of deaf education almost exclusively. "No change in this respect has ever been contemplated," wrote Superintendent Jeremiah Burke in 1927. "Speech and lipreading, supplemented by writing, pictured illustration, and natural gestures in the earliest years . . . build up a sufficient body of language to permit the pupils to proceed in the acquirement of an elementary education approximating that of normal children." The nature of the first year of the Visible Speech curriculum was explained in Edwin Seaver's report for 1903: detailed instruction in positioning the mouth and other vocal organs, explorations into sound vibrations and tentative formations,

A geography lesson at the Horace Mann School, c. 1892.

introduction of Visible Speech symbols, practice in forming vowel and consonant sounds, use of pictures to build vocabulary, and the development of the other senses. Students moved on after demonstrating ability to emit and recognize all "elementary English sounds," recognize a basic vocabulary, and use that vocabulary to form sentences and questions. Practice in lipreading was considered particularly beneficial to students struggling to cope with a sudden loss of hearing and its concomitant anxieties. Emphasis continued on writing, as did the almost complete prohibition of signing or fingerspelling. The BSC assured the public that the oral method had proven quite effective in teaching deaf children to speak intelligibly: "most deaf children can learn to talk so as to be readily understood by their families and intimate friends, and painstaking strangers can understand them with no more difficulty than attaches to the comprehension of English spoken with a strong foreign accent." To enhance oral education, students other than beginners were regraded according to their "speech, lipreading, and auricular" needs for the first "period" in the departmental plan.[27]

In the early 1920s the HMSD introduced instruction in what it called "residual hearing" and "rhythm." Residual hearing training involved "systematic stimulation" of the hearing of those students not totally deaf. Such stimulation came from bells, the victrola, a variety of musical instruments, and the teacher's singing voice in an attempt to train "any remnant of hearing which pupils may possess." Jeremiah Burke argued that this work improved comprehension of "close range" conversation and enabled children to hear their own voices better, leading to better speech. Training in rhythm consisted of rhythmic exercise done to music. According to Mabel Adams, the purpose was to offset the effect of a malfunctioning "organ of balance" in the auditory canal by developing in students "a sense of rhythm and a capability for smooth rhythmic motion, resulting in great improvement to their posture and carriage." Adams reported that the school had always taught the Palmer system of penmanship using rhythmic motion "not for the penmanship but for the rhythmic value."[28]

## Preparation for Life beyond School

As it had done in the late 1800s, the HMSD used manual training extensively to hone students' skills and prepare them for employment after their education. Edwin Seaver revealed in 1903 that woodworking, type-setting and printing, cookery, and other branches of manual training still formed part of the curriculum. He stressed that many of the school's graduates had found jobs as a result of skills acquired in school. While some of this training occurred during the regular school day, a significant portion took place after the end of the school day at two. By 1912 many students were partaking of after-school training in a variety of skills: cooking, sewing, sloyd (a Swedish form of manual training emphasizing woodcarving), silversmithing, dressmaking, millinery, and embroidery were taught to Horace Mann students "outside of school hours, by friends of the school." One such friend was Lillian Brooks, who operated a trade school for the deaf at a Boylston Street address close to the school at no charge to the city. When Brooks closed her school in 1914, Superintendent Franklin Dyer termed it a "serious loss" and strongly urged that the work somehow be continued. The nearby Prince School permitted Horace Mann students to use woodworking and printing equipment which the HMSD lacked. "They simply eat up the work," asserted the instructor in 1920. "I have to jump to keep them busy and my greatest trouble is obtaining lumber enough." In 1912 the school committee attempted to establish a prevocational center attached to the HMSD, but after having rented quarters and hired staff the opening was first postponed and then canceled, perhaps due to the resignation of the superintendent.[29]

By the early 1910s, students who graduated from the Horace Mann School had several options. The first was to enroll as a pupil in one of the city's high schools. Many students had done so even before 1903, when Edwin Seaver disclosed the case of a female graduate who had made remarkable achievements in studying Latin and French. In late 1912 the BSC authorized the superintendent to assign a Horace Mann teacher to provide assistance for HMSD graduates in the high schools. Superintendent Dyer called this program "an open question," stating that it had not been fully effective because "the children have been scattered in schools remote," making it difficult for the teacher to address their needs adequately. Nevertheless, HMSD graduates frequently pursued successful high school studies, both academic and vocational.[30]

A second option was to enroll in the HMSD's own one-year secondary program that concentrated on developing vocational skills. This program of "advanced study" commenced in 1911 and included only a limited number of students (twelve in 1914, for example). During the two years in which no pupils graduated from the school there was no "advanced study" class at all. By 1920 the HMSD faced an increasing demand by parents for a second year of such study; in 1921 a "tenth" grade was consequently established. "The aim will be, first of all, to meet the individual needs and aims of the pupils in such manner as will further their vocational plans; and secondly, to introduce them to such cultural courses as will help their use of language and their understanding of the life and institutions about them." This tenth grade, however, never truly caught on, primarily because there existed "no provision for secondary education for the deaf in Massachusetts." State funding of deaf education had become an accepted practice, and without it the BSC resisted implementing an expensive secondary program on its own. The 1927 superintendent's report mentioned only the nine grades in the school and indicated that Horace Mann graduates desiring extensive secondary education were looking for it elsewhere in the system.[31]

The third option for Horace Mann students was to leave the school system either to seek further schooling at some other institution or, most likely, to find employment. Officials stressed that they provided as much vocational training as possible because it was crucial to any student wishing to find work. "The deaf need intensive vocational training even more than the normal," wrote Mabel Adams in 1924. "All of them must earn their living in competition with the hearing world and the odds are heavy against them. Their only hope is to be able to do some one kind of work so well that their handicap will not matter." Jeremiah Burke was more optimistic, stating that "it is difficult to place the deaf in occupations, but after the adjustment is once made they usually make good. The concentration and habits of attention learned at school make them valuable workmen." To assist its graduates in finding jobs the school continued to offer extensive industrial education. Furthermore, by the 1920s the school was sending older students to classes operated by the Boston school system's Department of Manual Training. Adams indicated that "the school usually obtains employment for its pupils and keeps a card catalogue of their whereabouts," but several years later Burke mentioned only that "the school and the department of vocational guidance work together for placement."[32]

Overall there existed a distinct lack of specificity regarding the success or failure of HMSD students or graduates. Although official reports and other records of the school commented frequently on the school's successes, very little was mentioned or even implied regarding students who were unable to succeed either during or after their school experience. Since Horace Mann students by definition were those for whom regular public school attendance proved impossible, those who could not master the HMSD curriculum presumably left the school system and furthered their education either privately or at another day school or residential institution. Unfortunately, the Boston Public Schools did not provide any specific data in this regard. The same is true with respect to exact figures on post-school activity or employment. A number of reports offer various individual success stories of students who had moved on to notable accomplishments in other schools or the working world, but only the vaguest references to less than satisfactory results and to the need for better follow-up and aftercare programs hinted at the existence of students who failed in or beyond school. Clearly the goal was to put a widely respected, generally quite successful school in the best possible light.[33]

## The HMSD and the Community

While the Horace Mann School's ability to actually place students in jobs was limited, the school did engage, especially during the 1920s, in extensive interaction with the local community by visiting homes of students and dispensing information on deafness. Teachers initiated home visits to develop "cordial and friendly relations between the home and the school" as well as to give "the parents actual instruction in methods of teaching the deaf." In cooperation with the Boston Education Association for Deaf Children—the parents association for the school—and in consultation with the retired Sarah Fuller, teachers visited homes on late afternoons in addition to weekends and vacations, demonstrating lessons and methods of instruction as well as listening to parent concerns. Such visits benefited all concerned, according to Jeremiah Burke: the "home folk" learned "what they ought to expect of the deaf child, and how they may help him," and the teacher brought "back to the school a picture of the child's social background which is of infinite future value."[34]

The community also came to the school: the HMSD became "a bureau of information for all matters pertaining to the handicapped of every kind." Inquirers included "adults interested in lip reading, parents of mentally defective or crippled children, [and] deaf strangers seeking employment." They came not only from Boston but also from all over the United States and from other countries. Requests came on the telephone, through the mail, and in person. "Every city school for the deaf finds itself functioning as an information bureau, a social service clearing-house, and an employment office," wrote Burke. Mabel Adams accepted this responsibility happily, asserting that her school existed "for the service it can render and every teacher holds herself in readiness to spend herself for the good of the children and the public."[35]

The school also offered an additional service: lipreading classes on Wednesday afternoons. These classes were designed for students with deteriorating hearing who did not currently require attendance at a school for the deaf but did need lipreading instruction "both for present needs and to provide for a future in which their deafness is very likely to increase." Begun in 1920, the classes enrolled eighth graders and high schoolers, focusing on training students to concentrate on a speaker's lips with their eyes to relieve strain on the ears. Interestingly, teachers had to overcome fears of some parents that lip reading itself injured hearing. Mabel Adams wrote that "certain curious misapprehensions and prejudices were encountered" which expressed such a belief: "It was found that the parents had received this impression from doctors and social workers." Such fears proved not to be serious, for three lipreading classes existed by 1925, and the program soon thereafter took the form of separate reading centers.[36]

## Problems for the School

Despite these many and varied accomplishments, the Horace Mann School for the Deaf encountered a number of difficulties in executing its program. One of these, securing competent teachers, frustrated principal Mabel Adams in the mid-1920s. "The school's greatest problem at the present time is where to turn for trained teachers," she stated in 1924. Noting some unexpected vacancies and the looming threat of a number of retirements, Adams maintained that the past approach of taking good teachers from the elementary ranks and giving them on-the-job training was no longer succeeding due to limited pay incentives and better opportunities elsewhere in the schools. (Even though HMSD teachers during the 1910s had received slightly higher pay than elementary teachers of comparable rank, teachers in secondary programs were better paid.) Too, the system of examination and certification initiated by the BSC had produced "few tangible results." Adams argued that the lack of competitive compensation forced teachers of the deaf to seek better job opportunities at other schools for the deaf. One response to this shortage was to use teachers untrained in deaf education as instructors in the subject areas of manual arts and household science.[37]

Effective transportation of students to and from school constituted another serious concern for school officials. As a day institution serving students from all over metropolitan Boston, the Horace Mann School did as much as possible to accommodate the needs of those students coming from great distances. A few students came from well beyond the metropolitan Boston area, some of these even from different states. Presumably such children boarded in private homes in or near the city, although the available records are silent on how such arrangements might have been made. Many other students did not live in Boston proper but in surrounding towns and suburbs; these children made the laborious daily commute to and from school using public transportation in the form of trains, elevated railways, or streetcars. Some pupils also most likely commuted to school by private transportation or on foot. As early as 1874, the school committee marveled at the ability of deaf children to travel to the school "with nearly the same freedom from danger that their *hearing* brothers and sisters enjoy." At that time, the committee proudly announced that "during the five years since the establishment of this school accidents to the pupils have been almost unknown." Almost fifty years later, Mabel Adams reported that many parents made great sacrifices to ensure their child's safe round-trip transportation. However, she also acknowledged that other parents kept their child out of the school because of objections to him or her traveling on the public streetcars. Adams dismissed the idea of substituting smaller neighborhood classes for a central school in order to ease the transportation problem, claiming that such schools "have been found to be most unsatisfactory wherever they have been tried in other states." Instead she continued the school's tradition of making the commute as easy as possible for students. The state had always provided transit or "car" fares to the school's pupils, and the HMSD held shorter hours than did the regular schools. In addition, HMSD administrators assisted attendees and parents, especially those who had "but scanty English," by arranging ticket purchases, assigning older students to accompany younger ones, meeting commuters at different public transit stops, and arranging half-day sessions and return travel for sick children when necessary. Such efforts involved considerable planning, but the school believed that the students had a right to and a need for education regardless of the complications involved in assuring it.[38]

By far the most significant problem the school faced in the 1920s was the lack of suitable accommodations. Poor housing and equipment had plagued the school until the opening of the Newbury Street structure in 1890. This new location solved most of the problems leading to its construction and proved quite suitable for a number of years. Nevertheless increasing attendance, the aging of the facility, and new curricular demands led to overcrowded, substandard conditions by 1920. In that year enrollment stood at 148, which according to Mabel Adams was too large for the school's home: "The present building was intended for only a hundred pupils, and consequently it is necessary to use for class rooms attics which are too hot in summer and too cold in winter. There is no proper hall for physical exercises or assembly purposes. The lunches have to be eaten in small scattered rooms." Adams insisted that because so many students came from so far away "physical conditions should be made comfortable and hygienic for them to alleviate this strain to the utmost."[39]

But by the next year those conditions had only worsened. For the first time, overcrowding forced the school to deny admission to eligible applicants. Rooms often had to seat fifty percent or more beyond capacity, while the departmental plan made it impossible to avoid scheduling classes in rooms far too small. Lighting was also insufficient, a critical drawback in a school needing to give its pupils "a chance to see every face in the room in a good light." The lack of a playground or interior halls for exercise "add to the fatigue of the day for the pupils." These poor conditions apparently led to "restless and fractious" behavior by children "often weakened from illness, unable to hear anything, and partially shut off by their position from seeing fully." Controlling these boys and girls at times created unfortunate "nervous strain" among teachers.[40]

By 1924 Adams was insisting that temporary accommodations for younger students at other schools were far too inadequate to ease the crisis. "A building with proper lunch room and gymnasium facilities, a playground and work shop, and rooms enough to accommodate all the pupils who properly belong in a school for the deaf, is much needed," she declared. In time the school committee heeded her advice: the 1927 *Annual Report of the Superintendent* included a drawing of the proposed new building for the Horace Mann School for the Deaf. Mabel Adams and Assistant Superintendent Augustine L. Rafter had persuaded the school committee to grant appropriations for a new structure containing twenty-five classrooms; an assembly hall and gymnasium; separate art, science, printing, manual arts, sewing, cooking, and rhythm rooms; a health unit; and a housekeeping unit. Built on Kearsarge Avenue in the Roxbury section of the city, the new structure was dedicated on November 10, 1929, the sixtieth anniversary of the school's opening. The Horace Mann School thus entered the 1930s with newfound wherewithal and continued optimism.[41]

## A Reputation for Quality

The city of Boston shared its pride in the Horace Mann School for the Deaf with large numbers of other professionals and interested parties. One constant theme running through all the documents, reports, and evaluations of the school was that its work was unique, advanced, and productive and therefore worthy of national and international attention. From its beginning, the HMSD welcomed visitors and observers from within as well as outside the school system who expressed almost unanimous approval, and often outright amazement, at the school's success. After June 1871, when Horace Mann students put on a public exhibition of their speaking skills, praise came in at a steady clip. The BSC reported "excellent progress" by students and disclosed that "parents and friends express their surprise and pleasure that the pupils accomplish so much. Such reactions pleased a school committee which was "at first inclined to regard [the school's] establishment as a doubtful experiment." That same report informed its readers that "letters of commendation are constantly received from prominent educators who have visited the school and examined the plan pursued." Support for the school included deeds as well as words, with "donations of money and clothing . . . for the benefit of pupils whose parents are in indigent circumstances" coming from enthusiasts wishing to help. The BSC applauded such efforts but interjected a note of caution in 1874, saying that "without this education and the mental discipline attendant upon it, there is danger that some of [the students] may become, not simply burdensome, but dangerous members of the community." The school was thus not just a successful educational curiosity; it was also a crucial social necessity.[42]

Visitation and praise of the school continued as it gained a more pronounced reputation in the school system and in American efforts to educate the deaf. The school committee reported in 1884 that the HMSD "has now been in successful operation so long that it must be counted as one of our regular departments of instruction." In 1888 the committee suggested that the school's "high degree of excellence" should have been receiving even more publicity than it had so far. By 1890 Edwin Seaver believed so strongly in the school's importance that he stated, "results have here been achieved that may well challenge the admiration of the whole world. The educational processes here carried on constitute a practical psychology of the highest value for teachers everywhere." Almost forty years later Superintendent Jeremiah Burke boasted that the highly trained HMSD teachers continued to demonstrate "sympathy and devotion and a true missionary spirit; and these qualities the Horace Mann teachers seem to possess to a remarkable degree." Meanwhile, the school continued to draw attention and praise from outside observers. Professors from nearby colleges often sent their students to visit the school and study its methods in the hope of improving the instruction of normal as well as deaf children. Mabel Adams declared in 1921: "There are many other visitors to the school—foreign educators, doctors from all over the country . . . and teachers and parents of children suffering from every imaginable affliction." Even allowing for potential tendency toward defensive or self-congratulatory rhetoric, it is clear that the Horace Mann School impressed a great many people for many years.[43]

The effect the school's success had on the day school movement for deaf children is unclear. Erie, Pennsylvania, apparently opened a school similar to the Horace Mann School in 1874, and Wisconsin established a system of public day schools in the 1880s; several other day schools existed by 1890. Bell himself became actively involved in extensive lobbying efforts in favor of day schools. However, his efforts met with mixed results, and the day school movement experienced much the same intense controversy and acrimony as that found in the communications debate. But the ultimate effect of the school's renown—at least as viewed by Boston school officials—was summed up by Supervisor Ellis Peterson in a statement issued in 1898:

> The Horace Mann School has proved to America and Europe (1) that a "day school for the deaf" is at least as good as an "institution for the deaf;" and (2) that the oral method of teaching the deaf is more natural, educates more, develops the brain more, and results in more happiness at home and in society than either the sign method or the combined method. . . . This is a remarkable school, both for its simple methods and for its application of sound pedagogical principles.[44]

As a separate instructional setting, the HMSD certainly contributed to a more economical and smooth functioning of the school system, serving also as a source of income for the city's schools. Nevertheless, the school's primary purpose—and sterling reputation—was grounded solidly in a specialized pedagogy for the city's deaf school-age population. Consequently, with its status as an original and for a time unique attempt to incorporate the oral-based instruction of deaf students into the realm of public elementary education, the Horace Mann School for the Deaf generated a strong sense of accomplishment among Boston educators who turned a "doubtful experiment" into a respected and influential example of oral deaf education and of public special education in the United States.

# 7

## DISCIPLINARY PROGRAMS FOR THE BOSTON SCHOOLS

The axiom that public schools represented a fundamental weapon in the battle against poverty and crime remained strong in Boston through the nineteenth century and into the twentieth. One result of this powerful and durable belief was the continued effort to bring into the public schools children whose public behavior and/or private life style allegedly threatened the stability and security of the city. Because supporters of public education deemed regular school attendance essential, truancy—especially of impoverished children—became a primary concern, particularly after the passage of compulsory education laws. Attendance alone, however, was not sufficient for the schools to do their job. The axiom also suggested that appropriate classroom behavior by all students was of crucial importance if they were to benefit from public education. Students who failed to attend school lacked critical exposure to school training; misbehavers in the classroom disrupted effective dissemination of that training to themselves and others.

This double-barreled problem of school discipline greatly worried educational as well as civic authorities. As the school system grew larger and more complex, the need for effective measures to cope with truancy and classroom misbehavior increased. Until the 1890s the problem of truancy received most of the official attention, leading to the opening of the Boston Parental School in 1895. Most of the chronic misbehavers were either tolerated, sent to an intermediate school or ungraded class, or permitted to leave school. Only those convicted by the courts of violating school regulations were sent to the Parental School.

However, with the increased specialization of the system and evolving interpretation of some of the conditions leading to misbehavior, Boston developed programs within its system for students who continually disrupted their classes. The first of these were the disciplinary classes begun in 1906. Eventually, school officials merged responses to truants and misbehavers into a single program designed to address the problem of students who seriously challenged the public schools' authority: the Boston Disciplinary Day School, started in 1915. The founding of each of these programs represented definitive steps to move control of truants and other poorly disciplined pupils from judicial to educational authorities. These efforts also constituted a remarkable exhibition of perpetual optimism that was fueled by faith in the power of schooling and rarely tempered by the frustration and disappointment that so often resulted from their implementation.

## The Boston Parental School, 1895–1914

Once Massachusetts's compulsory education law took effect in 1852, Boston children convicted of truancy were typically sent to the House of Reformation, located on Deer Island in Massachusetts Bay. By the 1860s the House of Reformation had acquired a firm reputation for harboring some of the state's most dangerous youth, and the Boston School Committee joined other educators and officials in claiming that sending "neglected" children convicted of the minor crime of truancy to Deer Island was ill-advised and counterproductive. The BSC, supported by Superintendent Edwin Seaver, consequently urged the Boston City Council to establish a separate truant school. After several years of delays and negotiations among the BSC, the city council, and the state legislature, the city of Boston finally appropriated $125,000 to establish a Parental School for Boys designed specifically for truants. The Parental School commenced in 1895 with accommodations for about eighty students.[1]

The Boston Parental School existed for nineteen years, operating under a partnership of the school committee and the city council. It opened amid considerable optimism. Edwin Seaver was greatly relieved to have an alternative to the infamous "Deer Island," and he advocated for the school an approach to education and discipline, known as "intelligent self-control," which he believed reflected the most modern theory and practice in the treatment of "delinquent" or "incorrigible" children.[2] The school committee described the new school in glowing terms:

The Deer Island institution for "incorrigible" youth had a notorious reputation, which led to the eventual establishment of a "safer" school for truants, the Boston Parental School, in 1895.

Admirably situated, its physical surroundings alone exert a most wholesome influence. The boys committed to the school will be removed from every suggestion of crime and criminals, and while under constant surveillance, they will be cared for in a manner which will show them that the restraint they are under is not punitive. . . . If the Board of Directors of Public Institutions place the management of the school in the hands of men and women of high moral character, sound judgement, strict, but not severe, in discipline, and with special fitness for the work expected of them, no boy will be the worse for commitment to the school.[3]

Using a program that combined manual labor and academic instruction, the Parental School tried to instill habits of discipline and hard work in its students in order to prepare them for a successful return to the public schools. The school also employed a policy of early release as an incentive for students who had demonstrated good behavior and progress and as a way to ease overcrowding. Daily attendance figures grew to more than two hundred by the 1901–2 school year and remained in that range for the rest of the decade. The average number of students on probation from the school also typically surpassed two hundred. Most children attended the school for a period of twelve to eighteen months. Well over 60 percent of the students had at least one foreign-born parent, the majority being from Ireland, Italy, or Russia.[4]

Although the school's primary visiting supervisor, Walter S. Parker, praised its accomplishments in a detailed report in 1903, the school experienced constant problems of overcrowding and inadequate facilities. It quickly outgrew its original campus and, according to its overseers, constantly struggled with a lack of satisfactory resources and personnel. Eventually the state legislature, which had ultimate authority over such schools in Massachusetts, grew dissatisfied with the policies and high rates of recidivism among all of the state's "detention" schools. It consequently ordered the Boston Parental School to cease operation in 1914. The legislature's action reflected then-current beliefs that home-based day programs for "incorrigibles" were far preferable to residential institutions in deterring truancy and other crimes committed by youth.[5]

## Disciplinary Classes

During the years of the Parental School's operation, Boston school authorities relied on that institution to reform and educate the habitual truant. However, the Parental School only rarely took in another kind of student whose behavior supposedly demanded a special educational setting: the chronic misbehaver in the regular classroom. Because commitment to the Parental School required court action, only the most severe misbehavers—those who were convicted of "persistently violating the reasonable regulations of the common schools"—could be sentenced to a truant or reform school. The number of such children was quite small; consequently school officials developed other alternatives to address the problem posed by misbehavers. The ungraded class had served for decades as a primary intrasystem solution to this problem, despite regulations to the contrary. But by the 1890s other possible solutions arose, and by 1906 the school committee had arrived at a concrete but, as it turned out, limited and short-lived answer: the disciplinary class.[6]

In June 1906 the Boston School Committee ordered the establishment of a limited number of "special classes intended for boys requiring special attention and discipline." A pupil was to be recommended by the assistant superintendent in charge of that district. Teachers were recruited from the regular ranks and given an additional eight dollars a month over their regular salary. In December of that year, teachers and students associated with the discipline classes received free tickets for travel on public transit. The BSC authorized these classes "as an experiment, the success or failure of which can be determined better after trial." Once taken, these actions generated much optimism. By providing for boys "who have not proved amenable to ordinary school discipline and have been a disturbing element to the classes which they attend," the committee hoped "that by wise, judicious, and kindly influences they may be prevented from being sent to the Parental School and retained in the public school system without the necessity of recourse to court proceedings."[7]

The superintendent named six districts (Bigelow, Eliot, Harvard, Lyman, Rice, and Lewis) as likely locations for these classes. The first class began on December 12, 1906, and it numbered eleven students sent from eight districts. The BSC praised the often long commuting time for many students as a way to keep a boy from unsavory companions as well as to reorganize his life and bring a "fresh, fair start." That first year attendance averaged 98 percent. In addition to the regular academic program, the students received extensive manual training (clay, cardboard, and woodworking as well as weaving and basketry) and physical exercise "affording an excellent opportunity to work off that vim and go which are quite certain to be found in their physical make-up." Discipline was "firm and exact" but did not employ corporal punishment, or so the BSC claimed. In addition, teachers and students lunched together, giving the boys a chance to associate with successful role models. Due to the "marked" success of this first class, a second was opened in the Rice district in early 1908. The students in these classes generally ranged in age from eleven to fifteen. Superintendent Stratton Brooks boasted that "in both classes the deportment of the pupils has been excellent, the attendance regular, the interest in the work great, and the progress of the pupils satisfactory." The only problem seemed to lie in getting the children to return to their home district school after satisfactory performance in the disciplinary class. Brooks added that "the most important lesson to be gained from the disciplinary class is that superior teachers with fewer pupils would work an almost incomprehensible improvement in school work of all grades."[8]

Once again, however, initial promise and enthusiasm for a disciplinary program dissipated, this one especially quickly. School officials never created any additional disciplinary classes, although the Rice district class was replaced by one in the Lincoln district in 1911. The number of disciplinary class students went from seventeen in 1907 to thirty-three in 1908, back to twenty in 1909, up to twenty-seven in 1910, but back to fourteen in 1911. By 1913 there were no such classes—the Lincoln class was discontinued in 1912 due to a lack of pupils, and the Lewis class ceased operation soon after with no official reason given. One report simply said the classes "were not successful for obvious reasons" and implied that the work was just too difficult. Another report, written much later, revealed that the BSC seemed to believe "that some other type of disciplinary control would be preferable." In all likelihood they failed because they proved either unmanageable, too expensive, less favored among teachers and administrators than other specialized programs just then getting under way, or some combination of these factors.[9]

## Founding of the Boston Disciplinary Day School

With the discontinuation of disciplinary classes in 1912 and the Parental School in 1914 the Boston schools once again faced the problems of dealing with truancy and misbehavers in the regular classroom. In response to court demands for a disciplinary school, the school committee established the Boston Disciplinary Day School in January 1915.[10]

The Boston Disciplinary Day School (BDDS) evolved into a viable compromise between city and state interests. The BDDS was, as its name indicated, a day school and remained so. The city therefore had to rely on state institutions for detention of those worst offenders committed in juvenile court. Nevertheless, the Disciplinary Day School did meet two other demands long sought by the school committee. First, the BSC finally had complete control over the curriculum, administration, and financing of school programs for truants and misbehavers. Second, commitment to this school did not require court action, allowing school authorities much more latitude and flexibility in their decisions concerning pupil placement. At the same time, state authorities were pleased that the new school permitted students to live at home, an opportunity that current delinquency theory held to be of great value.

Like the Parental School, the Boston Disciplinary Day School served both primary- and grammar-level pupils; ages typically ranged between nine and fifteen. It began as a small enterprise (two teachers and thirty boys), suffering initially from instability in both student attendance and the quality of instructors. However, in 1919 the school moved into more "suitable" rooms. Enrollment grew steadily from a low of fourteen in 1917 to twenty-nine in 1919, forty in 1920, and fifty-three in 1921. By 1920 that daily attendance had been "remarkably constant" and had grown enough to require a third teacher (the student-teacher ratio had been set at a maximum of 20:1). Over the course of a year between 150 and 200 students would be assigned to the school, but the majority would soon be referred to a state institution, be returned to their home districts, leave school for employment, or would otherwise be sent from the school. Daily attendance during the 1920s averaged in the low fifties.[11]

## Characteristics of the BDDS

While Parental School students generally were viewed as neglected children from broken homes who needed a firm yet sympathetic environment in which to reform, teachers, observers, and administrators offered few specifics about the character of these students. In contrast, adults freely offered detailed characterizations in official records of BDDS pupils. Augustine Rafter, the BDDS's supervisory assistant superintendent during its formative years, offered this description of the school's attendees:

> These boys are not merely truants, practically all have some court record for breaking and entering, larceny, etc. Some are general school offenders not amenable to school discipline. They are generally below grade in mentality. Fully a third are of special class caliber. Many of them appear undernourished and give evidence of lack of sleep. Almost to a boy, they are smokers with the habit apparently fixed. They come, usually, from unintelligent, inefficient, broken homes from which the teachers ask or expect little cooperation.[12]

In 1924 the chief attendance officer of the Boston schools, Joseph W. Hobbs, wrote that "the boys invariably possess well-developed bad habits, such as laziness, inattention, lack of concentration, untruthfulness and untrustworthiness." Three years later Superintendent Jeremiah Burke labeled BDDS boys "morally sick" as well as "lonely and neglected." All three officials stressed the terrible home life of many of the students and expressed hope that the school could provide them with a positive environment for reformation and learning.[13]

In contrast, school officials provided few such details concerning their expectations for teachers. Many of the teachers, who were chosen from the regular grades, had previously taught in all-boy classes. The school's instructors were considered regular Boston schoolteachers and did not draw any special compensation for their work. School records do indicate that observers publicly expressed satisfaction with teacher performance at the school; for example, Rafter maintained that "the outstanding cause of the success of the school is, of course, the genuine, virile force and character of the teachers."[14]

The guiding philosophy of the school reflected a dual perception of its attendees. On the one hand, school officials expressed their desire to protect well-behaved students from the influence of those in the disciplinary school. On the other hand, these officials expressed great sympathy for "habitual truants" and "incorrigibles," frequently noting that as victims of poor homes they needed support, understanding, and compassion and that the school should act as a "hospital" for these "morally sick" boys.[15]

To realize this philosophy, the school employed a curriculum combining academic work with manual and practical training as well as physical exercise. Academic classes were small, averaging fifteen, in order to facilitate individual or small group instruction. The goal was to "cover the minimum requirements of the course of study for the grades." Beyond those general comments, little was said of the academic component of the curriculum. Burke did note that some students responded well to academic instruction while others resisted it strongly. He asserted, however, that negative reactions to academic study occurred only at first, disappearing after the "storm" had subsided.[16]

The nonacademic side of the curriculum—industrial, vocational, and physical education—was much more popular with the students. Jeremiah Burke described the school's "fully equipped . . . diversified shop" with "complete machine equipment for such various pursuits as woodworking, sheet metal, machine work, printing and electricity." He claimed that the students not only enjoyed this kind of work ("every boy in the school goes to the shop") but also benefited from it: "Here they learn the great lesson of application and the finished product is the reward. They learn what hard work and industry can do." The school also emphasized cooking in order to lead "the boy back again to his own fireside and to arouse his interest around home." The school's program also included extensive gardening, the products of which would be "done-up by the cold-pack process" and used at the school. Finally, the students participated in extensive physical activities: soccer, baseball, croquet, tennis, football, basketball, squash, and "ring-toss" all proved popular. Burke maintained that playground activity taught self-control, sportsmanship, discipline, and the importance of both work and play.[17]

School officials believed that proper execution of this program required creating in the student a sense of self-discipline and self-worth. They hoped that student "wanderlust" would be satisfied by riding long distances every day on public transit to get to the school and that the new surroundings would appeal to them enough to ensure their interest and cooperation. Once enrolled, it was felt, a boy would finally sense that he "fit" somewhere, and thus would remain busy and cooperative in both attendance and behavior. It is important to note, however, that the lack of detailed accounts of actual events or progress in the schools in relation to generalized descriptions of goals and potentialities requires caution and skepticism when considering what daily life in the BDDS was actually like.[18]

By the late 1920s, the Boston public school system thus finally had its own fully functioning and, its officials insisted, effective program to attack the dual problems of habitual truancy and chronic misbehavior in the regular classroom. It had taken city school officials several decades to evolve such a program. In doing so, they had developed optimistic plans; encountered lengthy delays and frustrations; expressed considerable concern over potential dangers to students, families, and the community; and reached solutions which, while sometimes adequate, were never ideal. Repeatedly, optimism turned to disillusionment as original plans proved either inadequate or inappropriate in coping with a particularly challenging, albeit extremely small, segment of the school population. Nevertheless, by 1930 the city's civic and educational leadership had in the Boston Disciplinary Day School a stable and accepted approach to the intrasystem education of the few students who had seriously challenged but not transcended the system's patience. Despite the troubles, closures, failed experiments, and unfulfilled expectations, the disciplinary programs provided a valuable service: segregation of students whose presence in the schools was thought to threaten other students or disrupt the schools' operation. Thus the basic paradigm of a specialized, segregated day program within the public schools for students with severe disciplinary and behavioral problems had become firmly entrenched—the ultimate product of decades of planning, experimentation, and readjustment to the realities of a most difficult task.

# 8

## THE BOSTON SPECIAL CLASSES

Elizabeth A. R. Daniels opened the first class designated specifically for "mentally defective" children in the Boston public school system on January 30, 1899. Between twelve and fifteen boys and girls attended the class held in room 9 of the Rice Schoolhouse on Appleton Street in the South End. Until December of that year, Daniels's class was the only one of its type in the entire school system. In just over twenty years, however, the number of these "special classes" jumped to 77, serving almost twelve hundred students. By 1930 a Department of Special Classes administered the education of around two thousand mentally disabled children attending 135 classes and centers designed specifically for them. Segregated, specialized public education for Boston schoolchildren identified as mentally disabled had come to stay.[1]

Boston was not the first city to implement such classes. In Europe, Prussia had started "auxiliary schools" for mentally disabled children in 1859. In the United States, Providence, Rhode Island, generally receives credit for starting the first class of this type in 1896, although Cleveland, Ohio, had experimented with the idea in a somewhat different form in the mid-1870s. In Massachusetts, Springfield established a special class in 1898. Nevertheless, Boston soon became the leading employer of the special class in the state and along with New York City set the pace in the special education of mentally disabled American public school children during the early twentieth century. For Boston, special classes represented still another attempt by its school officials to differentiate public school students for purposes of educational efficiency and economy. And in antedating by more than a decade similar programs offered in the system for children with a variety of disabilities, the special class constituted a core component of the evolution of specialized instructional settings in the city. The growth of these classes reveals much about the impact of compulsory education on public schooling. However, it also demonstrates the extent to which the understanding of mental retardation had changed during the 1800s and the extent to which beliefs in the importance of bringing every child under the influence of public schooling, and of providing certain groups with specialized instruction, had become ingrained in the minds of educators and other community leaders.[2]

## Origins of the Special Class

Schoolteachers in the United States had long known, of course, that considerable differences in ability existed among pupils in a given classroom or school. The typical response to such differences involved adjusting the instruction of each student to his or her particular capabilities and grouping children of similar abilities whenever possible. This constituted the traditional practice in the ungraded, one-room schoolhouses of the colonial and early national periods that served all ages and educational levels in the same setting. In emergent urban systems such as Boston's, early classification of students depended more on educational attainment than on age. While older students often mixed with younger ones, the level of achievement in each student grouping (often several groups were instructed separately in the same room) was relatively equal. With the advent of grading and classification based on age, however, teachers became more concerned about the wide range of differences of academic performance among their pupils. With the majority of students attending schools on a daily basis and with curricula increasing in complexity and standardization, teachers could identify more easily those students who consistently suffered from observable learning difficulties. They could also see how individual rates of progress could differ over time even among students seemingly similar in ability.[3]

In the late 1860s, the Boston School Committee formally discussed the issue of significant intellectual differences among pupils in the city's graded classrooms. In its annual report of 1867 the committee issued a call for appreciation of the "great differences . . . in the capacities of children" and for compassion in coping with those of "sluggish temperament or organic defect." As noted earlier, the BSC also acknowledged that the basic curriculum had been designed for those of "average ability" and that many students learned at either a slower or faster rate. In dealing with different abilities in the classroom, the school committee of the 1860s recommended only in-class solutions and did not engage in discussion of the advisability of a separate program.[4]

Nevertheless, individual intellectual differences in the classroom created considerable pressure not only on the teachers but also on the system of promotion. By the 1880s, when that system had become entrenched and the pressures acute, the ungraded classes offered some relief. While exact data are unavailable, it is apparent from narrative descriptions of the ungraded classes that they certainly included students whose intellectual ability significantly delayed their progress up the school ladder. Lack of sufficient evidence prevents any thorough understanding of how teachers dealt with such children in the classroom. Those not sent to an ungraded class probably either left school or continued as best they could through the ranks. At any rate, provisions for students with mental disabilities were at best haphazard and generally inadequate well into the 1890s.

The strongest practical impetus to special class development came from the growing numbers of students whose lack of ability created tremendous demands on a teacher's time. The compulsory attendance law of 1889 excluded students whose "physical or mental condition renders attendance inexpedient or impracticable." Even so, large numbers of students with significant mental impairment did attend the public schools, since school officials pushed hard to enroll as many children as possible and no process of screening or ability testing existed at the time. "We must remember," cautioned Edwin Seaver in 1900, "that our schools contain children with all grades of native mental endowment from high genius down through all degrees of talent, capacity or incapacity, to the very verge of idiocy." Seaver said that the public schools should not have to instruct the "extreme cases of mental deficiency," whom he felt belonged in an institution. "But there are cases," he stated, "hardly less than extreme, which are found in our schools, and which need our special care."[5]

Two years earlier the Boston School Committee had come to a similar conclusion—and acted on it. On November 11, 1898, the BSC ordered "as an experiment" the formation of a "special class" in the Franklin school district "or other suitable room" for mentally "deficient" pupils chosen from all areas of the city. The committee hired Elizabeth Daniels as the teacher, fixing her salary at $792 for the school year.[6]

Over the next ten years, several more special classes opened, showing that the BSC considered its "experiment" successful and that the need for such classes persisted. In explaining that need to the public, school officials consistently cited two essential reasons: to provide the unique, individualized attention that mentally disabled children deserved, and to ease the pressure on regular classes and teachers that the presence of such children created. For example, a report on the school system issued in 1911 commented that segregation of "feeble-minded children . . . is essential for good administration, and . . . is also beneficial to the child." The BSC observed in 1912 that "there can be no doubt that the work of a grade teacher is enormously lightened by the removal of children of this description from her large class, and the opportunity for the remaining children to progress is improved." Efficiency and individualized instruction would remain intertwined as rationales for special class instruction.[7]

## The Process of Student Selection

From the initiation of the special class program school officials expressed great concern over the challenges of student selection. Creating the classes was one matter; identifying the students who most needed them was an altogether more difficult one. Although significant changes in beliefs and understandings regarding mental retardation occurred between 1900 and 1930, consequent changes in identifying students who should attend special classes were limited, and the process itself was never clearly defined. The notably diverse levels of cognitive disability among Boston's public school students, and the reluctance of many parents to permit assigning their child to a special class, further complicated the identification and selection of special class children.

By the early 1900s, Boston school officials noted a wide range of cognitive disability among the school system's potential special class population. In discussing this population, Superintendent Edwin Seaver classified students into three broad categories:

> first, the true imbeciles, who ought not to be kept in public schools at all . . . ; second, feeble-minded children, who, without being wholly imbecile, nevertheless show the marks of an abnormal mental condition and have been found nearly or quite unimprovable under ordinary class-room instruction; and third, normal but very dull children who are nevertheless not beyond the reach of class-room instruction skilfully administered.

Edwin P. Seaver, superintendent of the Boston public schools from 1880 to 1904, supported the continuation of ungraded classes and HMSD, as well as the establishment of the Parental School and special classes for "feeble-minded" children, all before 1900.

Seaver argued that special classes should target the second group of students, leaving the responsibility for the first group to the residential institutions and for the third group to the general classroom teachers. However, severe institutional overcrowding necessitated accommodating at least some children of the first group. And while significant discussion did take place regarding the viability of returning a few special class students to the regular grades during the early 1900s, school officials ultimately determined that this was an ill-advised and unsuccessful policy given what was by then seen as the permanent, fixed nature of intelligence. Consequently, the process of selecting special class students emphasized finding those children who, it was believed, were clearly incapable of making any progress in the regular classroom—those fitting Seaver's first two categories.[8]

Even within these parameters, special class student selection remained a subjective and inexact process. For the first several years of special class operation, the Boston Public Schools used a referral system to locate appropriate students. The first special class teacher, Elizabeth Daniels, and Superintendent Edwin Seaver solicited recommendations from the various grammar school principals to choose the dozen or so children for that first class. Students were selected for the second special class, taught by Harriet

Lyman, on the basis of a student's assumed need for special class instruction, the likelihood of his or her regular attendance, and the benefit of "the relief afforded various school districts" rather than on any particular similarity of the students' conditions or abilities. The children chosen for these two classes exhibited a variety of disabilities in addition to obvious mental retardation. As special class instruction began to grow, Seaver consulted with the teachers to determine which children should attend. In addition, Seaver began using a local physician, Dr. Arthur Jelly, as consultant for identifying special class students in 1903. Following Seaver's intense lobbying, Jelly became the paid medical inspector in charge of special class selection in 1906; thereafter all referrals of potential students went to him.[9]

In the years following Jelly's appointment the most significant change in the selection process involved the introduction of intelligence testing and other forms of mental measurement. The Boston schools eagerly adopted mental testing as a way to differentiate "scientifically" among students; by the early 1920s thousands of Boston pupils were being tested annually, and the results of that testing were used to place students in special classes. Even with the advent of testing, however, the selection process for special class students remained quite mysterious, at least to the general public; only the most general descriptions of that process appeared in official school records.[10]

An important feature of the selection process was the requirement that parental approval be obtained prior to a child's enrollment in a special class. According to official records, parents often objected to such placement. In her report on the first special class, Elizabeth Daniels wrote that on her visits to homes she "found parents uniformly interested and willing to admit the unfortunate condition of their offspring . . . and seemed much pleased at the interest of an outside person who could make helpful suggestions." As time passed, however, parents apparently stepped up their resistance to the idea of their child becoming a special class student. Edwin Seaver cautioned in 1903 that "there is need of some care and delicacy in dealing with parents of these unfortunate children." A more blunt report complained that "the greatest difficulty to the success of the work is the frequent unwillingness of parents to allow children to attend special classes." The report argued in favor of legislation forcing parents to send "pupils who have been by competent medical authority judged to be fit subjects" to special classes in either public or private schools. One report did say that in 1910 teachers visiting families "in most cases find friendly support from the parents," but this was among families who had already permitted their child to attend. That same report claimed that "neighborhoods are gradually learning the truth about the special classes, and public sentiment is thus being educated"—suggesting that parental reluctance was grounded in either negative information or misinformation about the nature of the classes, perhaps reinforced by the then-growing fears and suspicions and consequent stigmatization of the "feeble-minded."[11]

In 1920 Ada Fitts, the director of special classes, explained that principals had prepared letters for parents encouraging them to take advantage of the special class. One letter assured parents that "our object is to give these pupils an opportunity to advance more rapidly than they would in regular grade work." Another mailing included examples of special class assignments packaged as proof that such work "is exactly the same as the work that the other children are doing in the other grades"—in other words, selling the idea of a special class by denying that its curriculum was substantively special. That letter also told parents that special class children enjoyed every opportunity for promotion, and a boy or girl was in fact "very fortunate to be selected to enjoy the advantages offered in the special class." The letter closed by inviting parents to visit the class to "see the splendid work that Miss _____ is doing with the children." To Fitts, proper communication with parents was crucial: "In order to overcome the natural reluctance of parents to place their children in such classes it is necessary to use the utmost tact and consideration."[12]

## Administrative Growth and Program Expansion

Between 1899 and 1912, the school committee proceeded cautiously in increasing the number of special classes. The second class opened in late 1899 in Roxbury under Harriet Lyman, the third in late 1901 in East Boston. By 1904 seven special classes existed, including one held in a room of a West End church provided by "a clergyman who is interested in the special work." The number of classes grew to eight in 1908 and to nine in 1910; in 1911 those nine classes enrolled 133 children. From that year on, boys constituted the majority of special class students. During this period, control of special classes passed from the superintendent to the supervisor of kindergartens to the principals of the grammar school districts.[13]

For the first few years of this formative period the BSC exercised considerable discretion in informing the public about special class development. No individual or group outside the schools took part in organizing or directing the classes although some charity groups did contribute money or classroom space. Confirming a critic's observation that the schools considered publicizing special classes unwise for fear of alienating parents and the public, Edwin Seaver claimed that such "publicity—too much of it—is likely to interfere with their success."[14]

By 1912 the special class had demonstrated its value to the satisfaction of school officials, who then moved to strengthen its base and expand its scope. In November 1911 the BSC ordered the board of superintendents to find the number of public school pupils "below the standard for special classes, including pupils already enrolled in such classes." The board reported a total of 812 "mentally deficient children" in the schools but noted that only 154 were at that time special class students, thus leaving 658 "possible candidates" for the classes. In 1912 the committee authorized an additional seventeen classes in an attempt to reach the hundreds of children identified in the survey. Even so, complaints that the number of special classes was inadequate continued through the 1910s and 1920s.[15]

In response to such concerns, special classes underwent a period of explosive growth well into the next decade. From 1911 to 1917 the number of classes went up almost 700 percent and the number of pupils over 730 percent. After that year, the rate of increase dropped, but the numbers continued upward. Table 3 indicates how rapidly the number of special classes and special class students increased from 1917 to 1931.[16]

To cope with this tremendous growth the school committee reorganized special class administration. In April of 1912 the position of supervisor (later director) of special classes was established. The committee named Ada M. Fitts, who had been appointed teacher of the special class organized in November 1902, to the post. According to school regulations, the special class supervisor had "general supervision and control of such classes, and should perform such duties . . . as may be assigned by the Director of School Hygiene" (a position created a few years earlier). By 1928 the Department of Special Classes had expanded enough to require an assistant director. The administration of special classes thus had emerged as a noteworthy arm of the school bureaucracy.[17]

**TABLE 3**
**Growth in Special Classes, 1918–1931**

| Year | Classes | Students |
|------|---------|----------|
| 1918 | 67 | 1,019 |
| 1919 | 71 | 1,123 |
| 1920 | 77 | 1,183 |
| 1921 | 80 | 1,216 |
| 1922 | 85 | 1,313 |
| 1923 | 87 | 1,361 |
| 1924 | 91 | 1,447 |
| 1925 | 96 | 1,534 |
| 1926 | 109 | 1,657 |
| 1927 | 119 | 1,836 |
| 1928 | 126 | 1,941 |
| 1929 | 129 | 1,951 |
| 1930 | 135 | 1,993 |
| 1931 | 133 | 2,089 |

# The Special Class Ladder

The remarkable growth of special classes was reflected not only in enrollment and administrative structure but also in the evolution of an educational ladder distinct from that of the regular schools and classrooms. Prior to 1912, special classes constituted a simple collection of experiments widely dispersed among the school districts "to meet the immediate needs of the locality." Little attention was given to their coordination as the essential purpose was to relieve regular classes of overly burdensome students. As the program expanded, however, greater planning and coordination took place. By 1912 enough classes existed to allow the development of a few special class "centers" for older students, and within a year or two more sufficient numbers of special class children had left the school system to create a demand for "after-care" or "follow up" programs to address students' needs beyond school. This special class/special class center/aftercare system became the fundamental structure of special education for students with identified mental disabilities in the Boston public schools.[18]

Typically, a child would be identified for the special class in the first three grades. The child would continue in the special class until either receiving a promotion to a regular grade (a rare event) or reaching the age of twelve or thirteen, by which time it was assured that the special class had "done all" it could for him or her. The class thus provided as much basic education as possible for its eligible students.[19]

Once they reached twelve or thirteen years of age, many special class students transferred to a special class "center." Before 1912 classes were geographically quite removed from each other, forcing a single class to include students of all ages and levels of ability. In that year, however, the first attempt to differentiate and classify these children occurred in the Eliot district of the North End. Two special classes in that district were combined into a center that divided older from younger students, with a teacher for each group. In 1913 a center opened for girls at the Frances E. Willard School in the South End. In 1914 another center commenced, this one for boys at the George T. Angell School. By then, the experimental Eliot district center had been discontinued. The two surviving centers each had several rooms at their disposal to provide instruction in specific subjects at various levels to children grouped according to sex and mental ability. Students from special classes were sent to these centers to continue their education; as of 1915 the Willard center had seventy-five students, the Angell center eighty-five.[20]

School officials considered the centers the "higher schools" of the special education program for pupils with mental disabilities. One official noted that the need for the centers intensified with the increase in the maximum age of compulsory education from fourteen to sixteen during the 1910s. "Promotion from single classes to such a center is something that corresponds to promotion to a high school from the grades and is a distinction much coveted by the pupils," wrote Ada Fitts in 1920. Superintendent Franklin Dyer claimed that the advantages of the centers included effective separation of young from old, male from female, and "lower grade" from more trainable pupils. It also worked to the teachers' advantage: "The group of teachers can work according to their special aptitudes. . . . By consulting together, a fine *esprit de corps* will be developed."

By the late 1920s there were six centers—in the South End, Dorchester, the West End (2), Roxbury, and East Boston—enrolling several hundred children between the ages of twelve and sixteen.[21]

The curriculum at the centers focused on manual and vocational training. Most school authorities believed that with sufficient training many special class students could find gainful, productive employment after leaving school. In addition, these authorities realized that successful adjustment to the world beyond school also required follow-up activities designed to assist a special class student in adjusting to social and economic realities. As a result, an extensive follow-up, or aftercare, program was established as the final component of the schools' special education for students with mental disabilities. In discussing the aftercare idea in 1913, Superintendent Franklin Dyer noted that some teachers had attempted to provide such care informally and that they held the qualifications and information to do so; however, they lacked the time and resources to do the job adequately. He asserted that due to the typical special class student's lack of "self-direction" he or she earnestly needs "an institution that will provide this oversight, or an officer who will watch the career of each graduate and act as adviser, who will consult with employers, cooperate with court officials and institutions and continue the guidance and control begun by the teachers." Two years later Dyer repeated his call for a full-time follow-up teacher. He cited figures that showed certain special class students had been either out of work for long periods of time or could hold a job for only a short while, and he concluded that effective aftercare would correct this problem and thus serve as "one of the great means of preventing pauperism, crime and racial degeneracy."[22]

In 1917 Superintendent Frank V. Thompson finally was able to report, "Last year one of our highly competent and experienced teachers was assigned to follow-up work." Her duties included locating and assessing potential job positions, helping students obtain positions, educating employees about the students, protecting students from "moral and economic exploitation" and "safeguarding them from criminalistic careers," advising parents on how to ensure their child's "future social and economic welfare," and gathering data on student performance after school in order to help educators offer better training for special class students. In 1920 Ada Fitts reported that this teacher, Helen M. Mead, had done a splendid job of guiding students to employment, informing employees about what to expect from special class workers, getting to know the families of the students, and earning the respect of court officials and social workers. Fitts concluded by saying that "probably no other phase of special class work is of more importance than this social and after-care work."[23]

In 1921 Fitts presented information gathered by Mead on the activities of over two hundred girls who had left the Willard center since 1916. Fifty-seven had gainful employment (in factories, stores, laundries, restaurants, and houses); twenty-five were at home and six of these were married; forty-seven were in other grades of the public schools, private schools, parochial schools, or back in a special class; thirty-five were in schools outside of Boston; twenty-eight were under the care of the state as residents of institutions for the feeble-minded, prisons, houses of detention, or "boarded out"; eight had either disappeared or been "excluded"; one was sick at home, and one was deceased. The superintendent's report for 1927 said that most of the special class students worked in menial jobs but, unlike twelve years before, many managed to keep them for long periods of time. "This indicates," said the report, "that the industrial efficiency of many special class boys and girls may be made available if the right conditions are maintained, and that by understanding these pupils and their limitations it is possible to train them to meet the problems of life with a fair degree of success."[24]

## The Special Class Curriculum

The earliest detailed description of curriculum appears in Elizabeth Daniels's report on her first class. After explaining the process of student selection, Daniels focused her remaining commentary on intraclassroom activities. Essentially, she said, "There is little class work . . . the teaching is almost wholly individual." Her basic philosophy was:

> Book learning is the most difficult of all learning for these children, and certainly will be of the least use to them in after years. The time and energy that would be spent over books would far better be used in manual, sensorial and physical training, that the training of their latent functions into faculties may lead them to useful and happy lives and self support.

Consequently, Daniels emphasized physical and manual tasks over academic work. She employed "kindergarten work adapted to their needs" in

An example of "nature work" found in a kindergarten class in the Rice School. The Rice School served as the home of the first special class in January 1899.

addition to sewing, weaving, braiding, drawing, pencil and paint coloring, clay modeling, block-building, and nailing. Physical training included "competitive games with ring-toss, bean-bags, and balls, work with dumb-bells, wands, marching forwards and backwards, running, jumping, dancing together." She also noted that "when a child appears deficient along any line I take that opportunity to teach a lesson." Daniels did teach basic reading, writing, and arithmetic skills (including money-changing), along with simple work in language, botany, geography, and natural history to "those who are capable." Numerous visitors came to her class to witness these early endeavors. The second special class teacher, Harriet Lyman, followed much the same program, writing that of her students "all have learned to enjoy and profit by easy hand work."[25]

It soon became obvious to early instructors and others that a rigid, preset curriculum would not function well in the special class. Daniels's comment that she individualized most of her work indicated the wide range of abilities and interests found among her students. Such diversity was vividly described by her colleague Harriet Lyman:

> The children can be graded together in very few subjects, and show a great diversity in their various small attainments. One can read readily, but cares nothing for a book, has little language of his own, and no idea of number. Others, who have been years under instruction, can copy

a little writing, but cannot read a word. Some are fond of drawing, but of the present class all are extremely deficient in the simplest number work, relying upon memory without any exercise of reason. Some are garrulous, others strangely silent as if from years of repression. One is heavy and inert, another never motionless.[26]

David Lincoln, a recognized expert on mental retardation who twice wrote articles examining the Boston special classes, also argued for a flexible curriculum. In describing notable differences among the city's special class students in physical ability, intellect, and ages, Lincoln stated his belief that:

> It is impossible to fix a uniform program of study for these irregular fluctuating classes. This is obvious, if we consider the differences between them. . . .
> There can be no universal rules for governing exceptional children. A teacher who relies on cut and dried methods will surely fail; tact and sympathy are absolutely indispensable, and a readiness in resources to meet new exigencies.[27]

Diverse student ability remained a fundamental fact of life in the special class, and school officials did take steps to ease some of the resultant pressures. Class size was limited to fifteen, and unlike those for ungraded or regular classes, the limit was respected. As of 1905 if logistics necessitated more than fifteen students per class, an assistant was assigned. The 15:1 ratio continued for special classes into the 1930s and was significantly less than half the average for regular classes. In the centers, class size stood at a 20:1 ratio. In responding to Dr. Weir Mitchell, a nationally prominent physician who said special classes should have twenty to twenty-five students per teacher, Boston special class instructor Mary Burkhardt poignantly explained the need to keep such classes small: "Although I am not naturally vindictive, I wish that he would be forced to teach a Special Class of that number for a few months. That would be punishment enough for saying such a thing. Any one who has had practical experience in teaching a Special Class knows that at the end of a month even fifteen would be considered by Mitchell too large a number to deal with properly."[28]

Limiting class size enabled special class teachers to implement more easily a curriculum requiring extensive individualized instruction. As it had in the first special class, the curriculum continued to concentrate on manual rather than academic tasks. Lincoln's 1903 report stated that in addition to the subjects Daniels mentioned, basketry and woodworking became components of the curriculum, resulting in finished products such as baskets, stools, doll furniture, and boxes. Lincoln also noted that "singing is carried on in spite of the partial lack of pianos." Judging from his article, it appears that teachers would instruct groups of children whenever possible (such as in singing), but the article also emphasizes that the wide diversity demanded constant one-on-one teaching. Lincoln's follow-up report in 1910 indicated that the curriculum had changed little, with the numerous forms of manual training still dominating the special class program—an approach, he argued in his earlier review, quite similar to "those in vogue in all modern schools for the feeble-minded in America."[29]

Between 1912 and 1916, the development of special class centers significantly altered the structure of special class education in Boston. However, this structural change altered the special class curriculum only a little. Until the centers became large and numerous enough to include most of the older children with mental disabilities in the city, many special classes kept those older boys and girls until they left school. In these classes the curriculum remained the same. However, in special classes that fed students to the centers, the curriculum was shifted away from specific vocational tasks and adapted to the younger clientele, generally students of the first three or four grades.[30]

In the centers, academics covered reading, writing, arithmetic, language, spelling, history, and geography. Physical activities included games, drills with various objects, folk dancing, and gymnastics. Manual work was assigned according to gender: girls learned "domestic science, millinery, sewing, embroidery, crocheting, knitting, mending and preserving," whereas boys engaged in "brush making, boot blacking, wood working, serving of lunches, dish washing, simple tailoring, gardening, assistant janitor work, and other forms of comparatively unskilled labor." The primary goal of special class center curriculum was to teach any and all skills that special class students could put to good use in the world of work, thus reducing the likelihood of their "criminal" activity and enhancing their contributions to the economy and society.[31]

To provide information about special class instruction to school officials and the general public, supervisors and other interested parties filed formal reports offering some detail on daily life in special classrooms. Although a few of these reports revealed problems ranging from classroom overcrowding to negative treatment of special class children by their general education peers, most are almost completely (and rather suspiciously) devoid of negative comments or critique, indicating through the words of teachers, observers, students, and parents virtually complete satisfaction with special class instruction. Elizabeth Daniels, Harriet Lyman, and David Lincoln produced fairly detailed descriptions of students who had overcome their disabilities and proven to be "happy," "industrious," "docile," and accomplished both academically and socially as a result of special class attendance. Ada Fitts and others had particular praise for the special class centers, hailing the boys' accomplishments in shop and other industrial work as well as the girls' successes in cooking, sewing, and other domestic arts. One teacher maintained that special class students were in some ways better students and better people than students in the regular high schools tended to be. An article prepared by special class teachers but attributed to Ada Fitts expressed such optimism succinctly: "The attitude of children entering the Special Class is often sullen, resentful and discouraged. These children gradually become happy, helpful units in humanity's whole. No miracle has been performed! The very name Special Class explains the reason for this seemingly miraculous change."[32]

## The Boston Way

In 1914 special class teachers in Boston collaborated in producing a detailed explanation of the city's special class curriculum. The product of these efforts was a manual entitled *The Boston Way: Plans for the Development of the Individual Child.* The basis for this manual was a seventy-nine-page *Syllabus for Special Classes,* first published in 1914. That syllabus listed thirty different areas of special class work covering a wide range of topics, projects, materials, games, and assorted other activities. The fourth edition of *The Boston Way,* published by the Special Class Teachers Club in 1928, listed over forty subject headings from academics to manual training to recreation activities, all of which were discussed in minute detail. With each new edition "in great demand," *The Boston Way* gained a national reputation as a thorough and useful guide for special class teachers throughout the country and even overseas. While this work did not represent a single, unified curriculum, it was "an attempt to show the lines of work which may be followed." Thus the special class curriculum remained flexible even as it became more complex and sophisticated.[33]

## Training Special Class Teachers

To staff the special classes and centers effectively, school officials in Boston strongly emphasized careful selection and training of qualified special class teachers. Whereas teachers for the ungraded classes and disciplinary schools were often less than adequately trained, paid, or otherwise supported, special class instructors received certain unique considerations from the outset. Generally speaking, pay for special class work was much the same as that for teachers of the elementary schools; more importantly, special class teachers received concrete support in the form of thorough training programs and support services that distinguished them from their colleagues.

As viewed by administrators and observers, the requisite qualities of a special class teacher represented the best that professional teaching could offer. Ada Fitts believed that an instructor "must be one who is quick to perceive, able to adapt, whose sympathies are keen and whose outlook is broad, but who combines with these gifts, steadiness of purpose and the power to raise and hold her pupil to his best. A sense of humor will help out in many a situation." Fitts maintained that the teacher was the "most important factor" in the success or failure of the special class. Professionally, special class teachers needed to be "wise and accomplished," with a sound knowledge of kindergarten teaching methods. They should not only know "how much freedom can safely be given the child," but also his or her limitations, and they should have training "along universal lines of pedagogy" as well as an awareness of "the heart of the child." Teachers also had to be able to act independently and use their best judgment consistently. Fitts added that the teacher had to have skill "in the recognition of remedial mental defect." According to a special class curriculum manual, "the supreme need of one who would teach or train a little child is the power to put oneself in his place—to go as far as the actual point of meeting with his actual need . . . [to] link her strength to her pupil's weakness, her knowledge to his ignorance, her skill to his lack of skill."[34]

To ensure a sufficient supply of competent special class teachers, the school committee and the various superintendents initiated a variety of teacher training programs. Elizabeth Daniels had participated in training exercises for teachers of the mentally deficient, either at Hervey Wilbur's private institution in Barre, Massachusetts, or at the Seguin School operated by the widow of Eduoard Seguin, Elsie Mead Seguin. In March 1902 the BSC approved a general leave of absence, for a maximum of a year with pay and travel expenses, to five grammar and primary schoolteachers for training in teaching "mentally defective, or backward children" at the School for Feeble-Minded Children in Elwyn, Pennsylvania. Two months later, the committee approved Edwin Seaver's visit to that same institution to evaluate the program and meet with its director, Dr. Martin Barr. Although he was at first "appalled" at Seaver's request to send teachers to train at Elwyn, Barr accepted "on condition that I could have them under my absolute control and could have women of cultivation and refinement." He then noted that Seaver "sent me most delightful women in every way, earnest, thoughtful, capable, hard workers." Barr gave them "clinics" and taught them sloyd (a type of woodworking) as well as other kinds of manual training over a period of three months. Other teachers were sent to the Seguin School, the private school at Barre, or the Massachusetts state school at Waverley. The last not only provided training but also assisted in the development of the early special classes. Teachers of the first eight special classes in Boston received such training. The purpose, according to Seaver, was to guarantee the "steady success of the special classes" by offering specialized instruction to "some of the ablest young teachers now in the city's service" who would then "be *promoted* to the special classes" (emphasis in the original).[35]

　　Certificates specifically created for special class teaching were awarded in 1904. By 1913 school regulations specified certificate requirements as "one year's successful experience in teaching a class of mentally defective children," or a year's experience assisting in a Boston special class, or two years experience teaching regular classes together with the "successful completion of a course for teachers of mentally defective children, approved by the board of superintendents." By 1915 teachers at the special class centers needed "three years successful experience in teaching and governing a class of mentally defective children." Later requirements included possession of a high school diploma or its equivalent. Certification also involved examinations in a variety of subjects including special class philosophy and methodology as well as knowledge of other elements of the special class curriculum. As the number of special classes grew, so did the number of certificates awarded. These were valid for one to six years depending on the examinee's performance.[36]

　　For its practicing special class teachers, the Boston schools also implemented a number of in-service programs designed to enhance teacher skills as well as create forums for discussion and mutual support. In 1912 the BSC budgeted two hundred dollars for "a course of lectures to teachers of special classes on 'The Teaching of Backward Children,'" leading to a series of talks by Yale psychologist Arnold L. Gesell. Late in 1914 the school committee passed an order requesting "the Superintendent to prepare and submit a plan for the training of teachers for classes of mentally defective children." The result was a course begun in January 1915 consisting of a clinic at the state institution at Waverley, lectures by Waverley superintendent and renowned expert Dr. Walter E. Fernald on the "problem of the special class child and the methods to be used for his development," additional course work on manual and household arts, and in-service practice and evaluation offered by veteran Boston special class teachers and the supervisor for the Department of Special Classes. The extensive course also included visits to the homes of special class children. An additional program, budgeted at one hundred dollars by the BSC in September 1916, supplied short courses on "The Diagnosis and Treatment of Individual Differences" and "Problems of Individual Adjustments in Child Life" given by Drs. William Healy and Augusta Bronner. The superintendent lauded this program as "highly beneficial." It should be noted that not until the early 1930s did the city's normal school, the Teachers College of the City of Boston, offer any course work in special class instruction.[37]

In addition to courses and lectures, the school committee encouraged special class teachers to participate in professional conferences and associations on local, regional, and national levels. Teachers would on occasion visit each others' classrooms to observe and advise. Certain Friday afternoons were set aside for not only lectures but also informal conferences and other group discussions. Usually led by the special class supervisor, these conferences covered a wide range of subjects, including career placement for special class children; academic vs. manual work; home visits; after-school and follow-up care; physical, manual, and sense training; and reports on special class work in other cities and countries. Superintendent Franklin Dyer wrote that "for teachers engaged in what would otherwise seem to be discouraging work such conferences are of great value," helping to give Boston's special class teachers a "very high order of professional spirit." One participant related her experience: "The benefit derived by the teachers from these conferences is immeasurable and the reactions upon their pupils are equally important. As the reservoir of our inspiration, enthusiasm, and vitality becomes dry towards the end of the week, these Friday afternoon conferences fill up anew this reservoir with these qualities which our children require of us."[38]

These conferences proved quite popular in the mid 1910s although it is not clear from the records how long they continued. Nevertheless, discussion among the city's special class teachers remained vibrant, leading to collaboration on the nationally popular curriculum manual *The Boston Way* and the formation of a Special Class Teachers Club by the mid-1920s. In addition, the school committee facilitated participation in national conferences. It approved leaves of absence for several teachers to attend the 1911 National Conference of Charities and Correction, and it financed Ada Fitts's presentation before that same organization in 1916. Finally, in the late 1920s, Massachusetts began sponsoring regional conferences for all the state's special class teachers. Programs included lectures by professionals, demonstrations by special class students, and reports from teachers. By the early 1930s, attendance at these conferences, which Boston often hosted, numbered in the several hundreds.[39]

Clearly, school authorities in Boston believed from the beginning that the work of the special class was sufficiently important and unique to deserve a structure and a training system that recognized the legitimacy and distinctiveness of a special education for students with mental disabilities in the public schools. The school committee expressed the hope that the classes would build up "proper habits of life" and prevent those "shiftless and vicious habits" that led to "moral obliquities" at a great cost to the community. At the same time, the special class could recognize the individual needs and capacities of each child in order "to help its pupils to progress along the lines of their needs and abilities, and to be of value to the community." Such themes were repeated constantly, indicating the seriousness with which special class educators viewed their work.[40]

# 9

## PROGRAMS FOR CHILDREN WITH OTHER DISABILITIES OR SPECIAL NEEDS, 1908–1930

The first two decades of the twentieth century were times of dramatic change in the Boston public school system. Between 1900 and 1920 that system, like most large urban American school systems, underwent the re-organization of top-level administration and the creation of a multitude of new departments and bureaus. In addition, a fundamental shift in the general curriculum toward vocational preparation of a large portion of the public school population took place, as did an extensive attempt to identify those students who required some form of specialized program. This last group of changes is particularly relevant to a discussion of special education history in the city. The earlier efforts in specialized education programs—special and ungraded classes, disciplinary programs, and the Horace Mann School for the Deaf—were joined during the early 1900s by several more, all of which commenced officially between 1908 and 1913.

One of these programs, that of rapid advancement classes for a small number of pupils deemed superior, arose largely from concerns expressed about the graded system of classification. The others—instruction for children with serious health problems, conservation-of-eyesight classes for students with serious vision impairment, and speech improvement classes treating a variety of speech problems—resulted from the growing desire of public school officials to address any specific characteristic seen as negatively affecting but not necessarily proscribing a child's presence in the classroom. By 1930 these special education programs had combined with the earlier ones to form a sizable and significant effort to serve all Boston public school children whose educational needs transcended the ability of the regular classroom to respond effectively.

## Rapid Advancement Classes

For decades Boston school officials discussed the impact that the graded system had on students, not only on those less capable but also on those with "superior minds." In 1898 the Boston Latin School offered an accelerated program for a few of its pupils, and some students in other Boston high schools participated in a limited "enrichment studies" program. The Latin School program proved short-lived, however, as Superintendent Edwin Seaver argued that an accelerated program hurried students through school too quickly. Then, in April of 1912, the board of superintendents suggested investigating once again the idea of "classes for the definite purpose of accelerating the progress of able pupils, and if so in what schools." The board also requested information on any organized plan to allow students to complete the elementary course of study in less than the prescribed eight years. Two months later the BSC reported it had found no general system or method for such acceleration.[1]

However, with its desire to differentiate among school children growing and its assumed responsibility to educate students as quickly and efficiently as possible, the BSC pressed ahead with plans to organize such a program. In June 1913 the committee requested the superintendent "to establish fast moving classes wherever he finds it expedient." The new superintendent, Franklin Dyer, responded by authorizing two such classes in the Oliver Wendell Holmes district, effective on September 10, 1913. At this time the classes were officially named "rapid advancement" classes. A school in the Lewis district actually had acted sooner, however, organizing the first such class in January of that year. The Holmes district had also formed a class before official authorization to do so, this one in March. These classes were regarded as experiments. Some educators favored the idea, while others admitted to "some slight fears . . . because of the immaturity and the possible effect on the health of some of the children."[2]

"Rapid advancement" succinctly described the classes' concept: they offered substantially the same curriculum as the regular grades but covered it in a shorter period of time. Generally, rapid advancement students completed the work of the highest three elementary grades in two years. The first rapid advancement class enrolled thirty students, half from the fifth grade, half from the sixth. Another class admitted students from the fourth and fifth grades with the intention of having them finish grammar school a year sooner. Students were drawn from the middle or upper elementary grades and were apparently selected on the basis of previous academic performance and teacher recommendation. As with special classes, the exact nature of student selection was never specified in school reports or documents.[3]

Educators had originally feared that overwork might affect the pupils' mental and physical health, but reports from the classes indicated that no cause for worry existed. Vigorous outdoor activities and restraint in pushing students too hard academically prevented ill health among them, at least according to observers and teachers. "Every precaution has been taken against overstudy on the part of the pupil," said one 1913 teacher's report, "and one hour a day of outside study is the standard. The pupils find time to enjoy a baseball team and a band of mercy and the parents are satisfied that their children's health is unimpaired by this opportunity to advance as rapidly as they are able." That same year the superintendent had registered concern about the attitude of the children, some of whom at first "showed evidence of lack of effort and attention. They had not shown the need of such previously in order to keep up with their work." But the stimulation that the class offered reputedly corrected their behavior, "so that now their self-mastery, self-reliance and studious habits are matters of remark by their teachers." Assistant superintendent Augustine L. Rafter commented on the large number of books each pupil read, saying that such was "tangible proof of the love of literature which has been inculcated." Within two years of the classes' founding, the students, he claimed, had shown excellent attendance, good health, cooperation, studious resolve, and an ability to work quickly and efficiently. Other indicators of the program's success included superior performance by rapid advancement students on citywide achievement tests as well as in high schools. Rafter wrote that "a searching survey . . . revealed not only that the experiment was a success, but that the status of the classes was far better than the most sanguine advocates had hoped."[4]

Between 1913 and 1918 the number of rapid advancement classes increased. During the 1913–14 academic year, school officials called for more such classes, suggesting at least one in every district large enough to sustain it. Total enrollment grew from thirty children in each of the first two classes in 1913 to more than four hundred children in thirteen classes by the end of 1917. The established teacher/student ratio was 30:1. Such growth proved short-lived, however, as the classes encountered a new development: the introduction of the intermediate or junior high school. In a 1918 document delineating the organization of intermediate schools, the board of superintendents announced its "unqualified approval of the idea underlying the establishment of rapid advancement classes," saying that they "have fully demonstrated the possibility of selected pupils completing successfully the prescribed courses of study in a shorter time than the majority of pupils can." However, the board also contended that the classes did not "readily find a place in a school organized as the intermediate school is organized; i.e., with departmental teaching, promotion by subject, and differentiation of work." It recommended the development of a plan which would allow rapid advancement by qualified pupils in order to complete the six years before high school graduation in five while fitting the intermediate school structure more closely.[5]

Within a year, school officials had devised such a plan. Introduced into the intermediate schools probably during the 1918–19 school term, it permitted qualified pupils to take a foreign language for extra credit, thereby earning within five years a sufficient number of credits to graduate. The assistant superintendent in charge promised to give the plan a fair trial although he admitted that courses other than foreign languages should also qualify students for extra credit. Consequently, rapid advancement classes were phased out: seven classes for 192 students in 1918, five for 136 in 1919, and only one class for 28 children in 1920. Between 1921 and 1923 there existed two such classes serving between 55 and 60 students, but by 1924 they had been disbanded completely.[6]

Between 1924 and 1928 there were no classes designed exclusively for superior students as the schools experimented with advancing them on an individual basis through the intermediate and high school levels. Nevertheless, during the latter year the BSC authorized "the acceleration of pupils in a small group of Boston schools of various types." This reintroduction indicates that the experiment with individual promotion was deemed unsatisfactory in achieving the acknowledged purposes and preferable conditions of sound rapid advancement as set forth by a survey committee of the Boston public schools: "A pupil should advance at a rate commensurate with his ability. . . . Waste may be prevented and excellent salvage work accomplished by a prudent selection of groups of the best students and by providing proper facilities for their rapid advancement." In 1928 three rapid advancement classes for 119 primary grade children were in operation. The next year a survey committee released the results of a questionnaire researching rapid advancement programs in other cities. They showed that the responding cities paid "little attention to the development of systematic schemes for accelerating the bright child." The survey committee then outlined a program for reestablishing rapid advancement classes for children who would complete the third, fourth, and fifth grades in two years. For intermediate and high schools, the committee recommended the continuation of advanced students taking extra subjects for extra credit. As of 1930, nine rapid advancement classes offered instruction to 282 children from grades three through five, and the program for academically superior students had started anew.[7]

## Programs for the Chronically Ill

While rapid advancement classes focused on academic differences, a much larger specialized program concentrated on treating the significant number of public school children who suffered from serious ill health, particularly tuberculosis. Health had always been a concern of school officials, especially as it affected efficiency and student performance in the classroom. In 1897 Edwin Seaver discussed the struggle that physically weakened children experienced in keeping up with the pace of study. He suggested that reduced course loads and a longer time permitted to meet requirements for graduation would benefit the "ailing," who otherwise would be forced to "turn a deaf ear to the warnings of parents and physician, and ask teachers for no relief . . . until . . . the necessity comes for leaving school altogether." During the first decade of the twentieth century, school authorities began efforts to reduce the number of ailing children in the schools and to ensure the education of even those for whom school attendance proved impossible. The result of these efforts was a three-step plan that consisted of making classroom environments more healthful, establishing open-air classes for children too sick for normal academic progress but not ill enough to require hospitalization, and providing hospital classes for children, especially those with tuberculosis, whose illness prevented school attendance entirely.[8]

According to school officials in Boston and throughout the United States, tuberculosis represented a tremendous threat to the health of school children. Awareness of and concern over the seriousness of this highly contagious and deadly disease grew significantly in the first decade of the twentieth century, especially in the years 1904 to 1908. At the Sixth International Conference on Tuberculosis, held in Washington, D.C., in September 1908, sentiments were repeatedly expressed regarding the need to protect school children from exposure to TB. The National Tuberculosis Association then began a "health crusade" on behalf of school children all over the United States. The city of Boston was extensively involved in such efforts, hosting a number of committees dedicated to TB's eradication as well as serving as a "pioneer center" for its study and cure. The Boston School Committee's efforts to combat tuberculosis through generalized health improvements as well as the establishment of open-air classes were thus very much part of widespread reform aimed at improving the health and living conditions of urban residents all over the country.[9]

To enhance the general health of all students, the school committee ordered that improved temperature control and ventilation of classrooms become a priority of teachers, administrators, and maintenance workers. In January 1912 the BSC adopted a lengthy document prepared the previous year, specifying in detail how to guarantee a healthful environment in the city's schools. "Getting fresh air into the schools is an object that can only be accomplished by the cooperation of the whole School Department, including the principals, teachers and janitors, as well as the Board of Superintendents and the School Committee itself." The document acknowledged that some steps had already been taken to improve ventilation and reduce the often stifling, close conditions found in many of the classrooms. The document called for more windows in new buildings; more frequent window washing, especially on the inside; and leaving windows in an open position whenever possible given weather and security requirements. The committee was quite serious about such efforts, and school officials were encouraged by the results of this program. In 1913 Superintendent Dyer reported that new buildings could be "flushed with fresh air conveniently," that all classrooms held the temperature at 67 degrees "weather permitting," and that windows were remaining open enough for "abundant ventilation" in most schools. The following year Assistant Superintendent Walter S. Parker commented, "One cannot visit the schools of our city at the present time without being conscious of the fact that nearly every building is abundantly supplied with fresh air. . . . If a comparison could be made of the state affairs to-day in regard to . . . five or ten years ago, the difference would be extremely great."[10]

Such efforts apparently improved the environmental quality of the classrooms and contributed to the general health of most school children. Even so, the BSC had recognized earlier that it needed to provide for a large number of students who were constantly in poor health and thus required a specialized learning environment. In 1908 Dr. James Minot, president of the Boston Association for the Relief and Control of Tuberculosis (BARCT), suggested establishing several "open-air" rooms to serve the needs of children suffering from tuberculosis, malnutrition, anemia, and other debilitating illnesses. The committee appointed a subcommittee with Minot as chair to advise on the matter. "It seems desirable," resolved the BSC, "that the subject of tuberculosis and the more or less allied subject of malnutrition among the children attending the public schools be investigated with a view to safeguarding the health of the children and checking the progress of disease."[11]

The subcommittee's report offered a comprehensive analysis of student illness in the schools. First, it decided that children with advanced tuberculosis should not attend school at all. The report also recommended that for "less advanced, but definitely tubercular" children "out-door schools" should be established under the care of a hospital or other health facility, with the school department "merely keeping school for them." (An example of this approach was a class conducted by the schools in cooperation with BARCT and authorized by the committee in the fall of 1908.) For a third group of children "where the tubercular process is not so evident nor so advanced as to give rise to definite symptoms," the report suggested "open-air" rooms or classes, where provisions could be made to improve a student's health while keeping him or her as current as possible in the regular course of study. The report also cautioned that "5,000 is a conservative estimate of the total number of tuberculous children in the public schools of Boston." In response to the subcommittee's report and recommendations, a Franklin Park School for the second group of children was established in December 1909. Also in that year the first open-air class began in the Oliver Wendell Holmes district in order to address the needs of the third group.[12]

In developing open-air classes, the school committee was simply following the logic of the subcommittee report. It had said,

A child spends a large part of its life in a schoolroom. Strong and healthy children are those that have spent the most time in the open air. Life in the open air is the best investment one who is not strong can make. The nearer the schoolroom can approximate to the open air the larger will be the return to the city on its investment in the schools. [13]

The BSC targeted for open-air classes students who seemed to have insufficient constitutions for regular class work. Final selection decisions for the classes belonged to teachers, school nurses, and medical inspectors, who would then recommend a child to the district principal. Attendance required final approval from the director of school hygiene. It was decided from the start that students with advanced tuberculosis would not be assigned to the open-air classes but instead would receive treatment in a city hospital; neither did the classes accept students with identified mental retardation. Particularly targeted afflictions were malnutrition and nervous disorders. Also included were those "undersized and below normal weight for their height; those showing evidence of glandular enlargement and those who return to school after a long convalescence." The ultimate objective was to "better the health of the pupils" while keeping them up with the regular course of study.[14]

The open-air classes essentially tried to provide a learning environment as much like the outdoors as possible. Classroom temperature was limited to 67 degrees, outside weather permitting, and at least some windows remained open at all times. "Flushing" of the classroom took place daily. Each child received blankets to help ward off the cold, and wherever possible classes used movable, reclining furniture to provide optimal seating and rest in sunlight. Most open-air classrooms faced south to take advantage of the sun and were situated in the upper floors of larger school buildings whenever possible. Children brought their lunches from home or paid a fee (two cents) for school lunches that included milk, soup, and hot beverages. School authorities attempted to provide "whatever conduces to conditions that make for a more vigorous, healthful life."[15]

By 1914 open-air classes had implemented a specialized curriculum which covered the basic course of study but also accommodated the medical needs of the students. Regulations set class size at thirty-six students, and the pupils came from all elementary grades, with usually two or three grades represented in a single class. According to the superintendent's report for 1913, its "underlying principle" was that alternating work with rest "gives to both the mental and physical development every possible growth." The school work included reading and literature, speaking, writing, arithmetic, drawing, geography, music, and science. But this curriculum, developed by a Dr. Harrington, also featured work on personal hygiene, daily sessions of physical training and exercise, and several designated periods of rest or recess. Teachers felt that arithmetic demanded great mental energy, so it was always taught "at periods following rest." Students also practiced writing and drawing on a blackboard. Exercises stressed stretching and breathing as well as games that did not "drive children into a state of over-excitability or over-exertion." The school day lasted from nine to three-thirty, with a ninety-minute lunch break. A 1921 report asserted that the open-air students were "kept up to grade in academic work. Their attendance is higher than that of corresponding grades, and an education is provided for children who, owing to their poor physical condition, would otherwise be deprived of one. . . . [T]he happy, smiling faces of the little ones must repay the teachers for their untiring efforts."[16]

Open-air pupils also received considerable medical attention. The daily schedule incorporated medical inspection during the first thirty minutes. Regular measurements of height and weight took place, and if a child experienced any weight loss the causes were "carefully investigated and remedied." School nurses attempted to visit the home of every open-air class member "to give the necessary instruction relative to the home care of the child." Children also benefited from dental examination and treatment as well as general physical exams twice every academic year. One report indicated that "all physical defects receive early treatment and are followed up by the school nurses during the school year." Teachers supposedly tried to ensure that students ate a healthy lunch every day.[17]

Open-air instruction stayed strong for almost twenty years (see table 4). The open-air program's final year was 1928. School officials had mentioned as early as 1914 and 1915 that in all likelihood the movement to improve the quality of the atmospheric environment would eventually eliminate the need for separate open-air instruction. Franklin Dyer surmised in 1915 that "except for markedly defective children the so-called open-air room is unnecessary." A combination of improved environmental control as well as better health and medical inspection of children in general probably led school officials to conclude that the open-air classes had become obsolete. In addition, efforts to fight TB comprehensively had apparently begun to pay off. Although a cure was still decades away, the death

**TABLE 4**
**Trends in Enrollment Figures for Open-Air Classes, 1916–1928**

| Year | Number of Classes | Number of Students |
|------|-------------------|--------------------|
| 1916 | 15 | 470 |
| 1921 | 25 | 678 |
| 1922 | 24 | 690 |
| 1926 | 19 | 525 |
| 1928 | 12 | 339 |

rate from TB had been reduced by half in the United States between 1908 and 1923. The president of the National Tuberculosis Association claimed that between 1921 and 1924 alone, over one hundred thousand lives had been saved as a result of coordinated efforts to improve sanitation and living conditions and thus reduce the debilitating effects of the disease as well as the number of public school children who contracted it. The increased segregation of tuberculous individuals in the steadily growing number of isolated "sanatoriums" and hospitals clearly contributed to these developments as well.[18]

In Boston, the open-air classes catered to children with health problems who could attend school, whereas the school system's "hospital" classes brought instruction to those who could not. In essence, hospital classes took public education to children confined to various health-oriented institutions such as hospitals and sanatoriums. These classes began as a service for children afflicted with tuberculosis for whom school attendance was denied. The Franklin Park School, established for children in immediate danger of developing a fully involved case of the disease, was essentially the first such class. Although consisting basically of one room in a Franklin Park building, this school held a close association with the Boston Consumptives Hospital. As of 1914, the BCH, located in the city's Mattapan section, hosted a hospital class using Boston public school teachers. This class initially enrolled about fifty children and employed two teachers. Superintendent Dyer assured the public that "suitable precautions" to prevent the infection of instructors would be taken. The hospital supplied the accommodations, food, blankets, rest chairs, and couches for the children and lunch for the teachers. The schools provided classroom furniture, books, and various other school supplies. Unfortunately, teachers and equipment proved difficult to secure due to the hospital's distance from most other public schools.[19]

The number of hospital classes grew slowly but steadily over the next fifteen years. Between 1914 and 1920 there were three, all apparently located at the Mattapan facility. However, by 1927 the number of institutions with public school classes had grown to seven: the Consumptives Hospital, Boston City Hospital, Long Island Hospital, Prendergast Preventorium, House of the Good Samaritan, Clinic for Epileptic Children, and the Temporary Home conducted by the Massachusetts Society for the Prevention of Cruelty to Children. In the seven years before 1930, several hundred children were served annually, but actual enrollment at any given time was considerably less. In 1930 there existed six hospital classes with a year-end total attendance of 151. All grades were included; average daily attendance was less than 75 percent of those enrolled because of recurring medical problems, surgery, quarantine, or other factors. The curriculum probably closely resembled that of the open-air classes, that is, the regular course of study interspersed with appropriate exercise and ample time for rest. A 1927 report revealed that community organizations such as the Red Cross, Girl Scouts, and the Women's Municipal League, as well as children from the regular grades, contributed supplies and entertainment to hospitalized students. Assistant Superintendent Augustine L. Rafter declared that "any modern Scrooge would be converted from cynicism to an ardent belief in a fellow feeling among all for all if he could observe the widespread interest manifested for children in hospital classes."[20]

## Conservation-of-Eyesight Classes

The growing expertise in detecting physical disabilities, as seen in the more sophisticated assessment of hearing loss among potential students for the Horace Mann School for the Deaf, also affected the education of children with poor eyesight. Totally blind children had been educated at the Perkins Institution and Massachusetts School for the Blind in South Boston (removed to suburban Watertown in 1912) since 1832. Its proximity had precluded the development of a public day school for the blind. As a spokesman for the institution said in 1901, "It was incorporated solely and specifically for the purpose of instructing and training such boys and girls as are excluded from the common schools for lack of sufficient sight. Therefore it is a valuable link in the magnificent chain of the public school system. . . ." However, the Perkins curriculum was designed exclusively for totally blind children, and the school found it difficult to accommodate those pupils with only partial, albeit significant, vision loss who were being diagnosed more efficiently by the early 1900s. Furthermore, Perkins officials were concerned about what they termed certain unspecified "types of behavior" among semiblind Perkins students "which increase their difficulties on leaving school." Consequently, Edward E. Allen, director of the Perkins Institution and also a member of the Massachusetts Commission for the Blind, urged the Boston School Committee to establish a class that would provide the necessary schooling for partially blind children in the city.[21]

Allen apparently made a convincing argument, for shortly after his request the school committee in March 1913 established a class for "semiblind" pupils. It opened in the schoolhouse on Thornton Street in Roxbury's Dillaway district on April 3, 1913. The BSC hired Helen L. Smith, who had been trained at Perkins and also had taught there, on Allen's recommendation. Smith spent two months at the new Perkins campus in Watertown "making special appliances" for the class, "for her appeal was to be the eyes rather than the fingers of her pupils." The committee set her salary at $4.75 per day, and she and the pupils received free tickets on the streetcars. It was the first public school class in the United States for "children with defects of vision too serious to admit of their education in regular graded classes." In March 1915 the BSC officially changed the name of the course to "class for Conservation of Eyesight."[22]

Students entered the class after a referral and examination process that determined the extent of their vision loss. Such students had a variety of optical impairments, but mostly cataracts or severe near- or farsightedness. More sophisticated diagnoses in the 1920s revealed that conservation-of-eyesight children suffered primarily from myopia, cataracts, and astigmatism, with vision losses from 33 to 90 percent. The children varied in their visual capabilities: Franklin Dyer said in 1913 that "every case is different. . . . [S]ome . . . use large magnifying glasses, others are endangered by so doing. Some are allowed to read ordinary type, others are in danger of misusing their ability to read so as to injure their sight.

The school attempts to train each child according to its defect." Most also experienced serious academic difficulties resulting from their disability.[23]

As the classes evolved, two basic purposes of instruction emerged: "first, to prevent further deterioration of vision, and second, to educate these children, as far as possible, along the same lines as the normal sighted children." Nevertheless, during the formative years of the classes, teachers apparently did not follow any prescribed methodology in executing the purpose and substance of the curriculum. The Perkins Institution continued its strong interest in the classes and provided as much practical advice as it could, but again its work focused on the completely sightless. Edward Allen conceded that, in Rafter's words, "teaching the pupils in these classes is more difficult . . . than . . . teaching the totally blind." One certainty was that instruction had to be as carefully tailored to each child's individual needs as possible; therefore, the student/teacher ratio was set at 12:1. Helen Smith's earliest classes were even smaller: her first enrollment totaled nine, with daily attendance averaging between five and seven. In 1914 Smith and her Perkins-trained assistant, Sarah Lilley, together taught a total of just nineteen children coming from all grade levels.[24]

With small class size and an uncertain methodology, conservation-of-eyesight classes attempted to follow the regular course of study. As much of the subject matter as possible was taught orally. Teachers also used textbooks printed in extra large type, wrote in large letters on the blackboards, and occasionally provided students with "large pencils and specially ruled paper." By 1927 teachers did not need to use the blackboard so much because "adequate texts in geography, history, arithmetic, and reading" were available. School officials installed special lighting in some of the rooms and tried to assign the classes to rooms with north and/or east exposures to reduce glare; even the furniture and school supplies were in special shapes and soft colors to prevent eye strain. The classes also used certain forms of manual training requiring "the minimum of eye guidance . . . knitting by both boys and girls, crocheting, weaving on small and large looms." The goal was to permit normal progress through the grades, and Jeremiah Burke noted in 1927 that "a score of pupils from these classes" had enrolled in the city's high schools.[25]

The demands of the curriculum necessitated hiring specially qualified teachers. The first two had been hired on the recommendation of the Perkins Institution, but gradually school officials drew instructors from the ranks of the city's regular teacher corps. By 1927 all the classes' teachers had regular classroom experience. To keep them abreast of developments in the treatment and education of partially sighted children, the conservation-of-eyesight instructors took outside courses, read professional literature (some published by members of their ranks), and joined the Massachusetts Conservation of Eyesight Society. This organization worked to promote "a fine, professional, cooperative spirit among the teachers." Moreover, by 1917 the teachers had begun "a series of meetings designed to place at the disposal of all what each individual may have learned." Like other teachers of special programs for students with disabilities, conservation-of-eyesight instructors seem to have taken pride in their work and strove for cooperation and mutual support.[26]

One concern facing some supporters of these classes was the fear that segregating the partially blind child from normal classmates might have an adverse impact on his or her development. A. L. Rafter revealed that parents proved reluctant to permit enrollment not only because of travel distances but also because of resistance to having their child undertake an unusual course of study in a segregated setting. Rafter declared that students with poor vision were "ultranervous and supersensitive" and should accordingly receive as much instruction under normal conditions as was feasible, thus avoiding any overt attempt to identify them as abnormal. He noted that to integrate such a child would be to "normalize" him: "when he mingles with other children and recites in their class rooms such nicknames as 'blinky' and 'blindy' disappear." Franklin Dyer complained in 1915 that the one extant conservation-of-eyesight class was "isolated from any regular grade rooms." To address these concerns, school officials encouraged merging the classes' instruction with that of a regular graded class. This approach took place in 1920 in the Williams district, where a conservation-of-eyesight class composed of primary children joined regular grade rooms for "oral work in language, number, music, physical training, etc." but returned "to their own room for technical work requiring special and intensive instruction." The records do not disclose the extent to which such integration was practiced in other schools.[27]

While generally praising the work of these classes, school officials moved slowly to establish them, and they remained an extremely limited program in the by-then massive public school system. A second class did not commence until 1917, and by 1920 five classes served only 60 students. By 1925 the number of classes had jumped to nine and the student total had doubled to 120. In 1927 eleven classes served 167 pupils, but by 1930, 10 fewer children attended thirteen classes. The classes were well distributed throughout the city—Charlestown, East Boston, the North End, Roxbury, the South End, South Boston, and the West End as of 1927. School authorities hoped that the wide distribution would reduce travel distance to and from school. Nevertheless the classes' numbers remained small, perhaps a reflection of the reluctance to segregate such children, perhaps only a function of the possibly limited number of students eligible for such instruction who could obtain parental permission to attend.[28]

## Speech Improvement Classes

While the number of students treated for severely impaired vision grew but slowly, remaining under two hundred each year into the 1930s, children with identified speech difficulties existed in much larger numbers throughout the school system. The result was the development of an extensive program for speech improvement. This program began as two separate classes serving children with a range of speech defects in 1912. By 1930 it consisted of over one hundred classes with more than two thousand students. Eventually it would become the largest single program in the Boston public school system for the special education of students with disabilities.

The first recorded attempt to address speech problems among school children in Boston took place in the fall of 1895. The director of physical training established an "experimental class or clinic . . . for a few stutterers and stammerers" taken from two grammar schools and two high schools. The director, who was assisted by four teachers from the Boston Normal School, reported "marked improvement by most of the members of the class in gaining control over their organs of speech." Designed essentially as a laboratory for students at the Normal School, the class did not immediately lead to any program for speech correction in the public schools. However, its success did cause its director, Dr. Edward Hartwell, to state that "stuttering is a pedagogical nuisance which can be readily abated by the school authorities if they should happen to care to abate it." In 1904 and 1905 the Horace Mann School also experimented with classes for a small group of children with speech defects, but this program also proved only temporary.[29]

In 1912 the school committee finally addressed the problem of speech disability among students, doing so in two different ways. First, the BSC permitted Professor O. H. Ennis of New York to conduct experimental classes for "stammerers" from April to June of that year. Ennis had met with "stammering" children and their parents in March to explain the program. His initial experimental class of two weeks proved successful, leading to the addition of three more such classes to last until the end of the school year. That fall classes were established on a permanent basis in two separate districts under the supervision of Theresa Dacey, a Boston grade schoolteacher who had spent the summer in New York City studying speech improvement techniques with Dr. Edward Scripture of Columbia University. Meanwhile, a special class "for the instruction of dumb children" connected with the Horace Mann School for the Deaf commenced in January 1913 to provide speech instruction for mute hearing children. This class was soon superseded by another, known as a "class for hearing mutes," which Franklin Dyer had organized with the approval of the BSC. The school committee initiated this shift because, according to the superintendent, hearing mutes belonged "properly with the group of speech defectives," not with a school for the deaf. The class thus began anew under Dacey's supervision with Katherine M. Binkley as temporary teacher. A few months later, in March 1914, the class for hearing mutes officially merged with those for stammerers, giving the speech improvement classes a unified base on which to build.[30]

Speech improvement classes proved quite popular from their inception. By the end of 1914 about 350 children attended the "classes for stammerers," located in the West End, Roxbury, the South End, and East Boston, with an additional 250 on a waiting list. High schools and evening schools also explored the possibility of opening such classes. Assistant Superintendent Walter S. Parker wrote, "From the results that have been accomplished thus far, and the urgent needs of many not yet reached, it would seem imperative that more [classes] be established and more assistants appointed to assist the director in the work." Parker's call was answered. Over the next fifteen years the number of speech improvement classes and students increased remarkably. As the program evolved, the classes became known as "groups." Teachers instructed these groups in the numerous speech improvement "centers" which arose in convenient locations throughout the city. Between 1916 and 1930, the number of classes rose from 28 to 123; the number of centers from 4 to 26; and the number of students from 374 to 2,361.[31]

School authorities consistently indicated that the children who attended the speech improvement centers exhibited not only a variety of speech defects but also a number of other conditions that hindered their progress in the regular grades. Since the classes were occasionally called "classes for stammerers" during their first few years, stammering or stuttering obviously constituted a significant problem among the student population. However, the classes soon enrolled children with a variety of other conditions: lisping, mutism, aphonia, "slovenliness or negligent speech," "defective voice and undeveloped speech due to partial deafness," and "backwardness in all oral work." Speech teachers also observed that mental disturbances, including "discouragement, fear, diffidence, nervousness, stubbornness, and decided retardation in school," frequently accompanied speech disorders. As in other special education programs, the process of student selection was never clearly described or defined, raising legitimate questions regarding the methods of diagnosis and the effect of cultural differences on the determination of speech "defectives."[32]

The speech improvement program was unlike others geared to the city's disabled students in that it did not require total segregation from regular students or full-time participation. Instead of attending a speech center all day, a student would leave his or her regular class for sessions that were held two days a week for about ninety minutes to two hours each. Franklin Dyer's 1915 report stated that teachers tried to arrange schedules that would disrupt the child's regular class work as little as possible and that special provisions were made for speech students to make up work missed. Nevertheless, scheduling problems did occur. In 1920 Augustine Rafter announced that he had "not been entirely satisfied with the manner in which certain pupils who attended the Speech Improvement Classes have been considered in their parent schools." Some children, he reported, were denied credit in certain subjects because they had absented themselves at particular times to visit a speech center. Rafter asked Superintendent Thompson for his cooperation in instructing regular grade teachers to cooperate with the efforts of the speech classes, "to the end that no pupil may be dissuaded from attending" one.[33]

Once inside a speech center classroom, a student encountered a curriculum designed to attack specific conditions while improving her or his mental outlook. In 1915 a typical ninety-minute program consisted of the following:

> 15 minutes, exercises for breath control and voice development; 15 minutes, exercises in applied phonetic work, word building, oral expression, etc.; 5–10 minutes, exercises for physical correction and speech exercises of a recreative kind; 15 minutes, exercises for free oral expression in language, arithmetic, geography, history, physiology and hygiene; 10 minutes, exercises for free conversation, story-telling, joke or puzzle periods, speech games; 30 minutes, exercises for free intensive practice by reading poetry or prose, reading and acting children's plays, and by debates.[34]

In later years children were grouped according to the specific nature of their disorder. Instructors tried to treat "systematically" more specific "minor or allied" physiological problems, such as involuntary muscular twitching, through the exercises described above as well as through follow-up work by the Department of School Hygiene. Teachers generally claimed a large success rate in dramatically improving and often eliminating speech "defects." Figures as high as 85 percent were cited as the proportion of students either cured or greatly improved. Others claimed in more general terms that most students had their problems reduced considerably.[35]

Also recognized and addressed were the psychological and behavioral difficulties that teachers believed accompanied speech problems. "Modern medicine claims to have demonstrated that defective speech is at bottom a pathological condition," declared Augustine Rafter. "The pupils in speech improvement classes are oversensitive and so constricted in their speech cramps and spasms that liberation must be secured. They must be made to feel at home and at their ease. The very first and an indispensable element in any course . . . is the establishment of confidence between teacher and pupils." Supervisor of speech classes Theresa Dacey agreed, noting that speech teachers "must deal with grave causes, deep-rooted and far-reaching" that affected these "sensitive, fretful, backward, ill-tempered, struggling candidates." In the 1920s Superintendent Jeremiah Burke advocated an all-encompassing speech improvement curriculum that would free these children "from the bugbear of isolation, ridicule, and retardation."[36]

School officials asserted that speech improvement work demanded highly skilled teachers. They looked for individuals who were thought to have the experience and temperament for such work. Dacey's ideal speech teacher possessed "geniality, sympathy, patience and ingenuity to deal with the sensitive, discouraged, or fearful type." She argued that the successful teacher would employ "art and tact" in coping with the individual requirements of every child. Above all, instructors had to have sufficient energy to handle a demanding schedule as well as large numbers of children. In 1914 each teacher worked with about 80 students; ten years later a speech teacher on the average provided weekly instruction in small groups to 134 children with a range of identified disorders. Almost every teacher in the program came from the ranks of the Boston teacher corps. This was as true in 1930 as in 1914.[37]

Once recruited, the novice instructor trained in the mechanics and treatment of speech disabilities at one of the centers under the tutelage of other teachers or the speech supervisor. After training, the teacher benefited from occasional in-service and mutual support programs much like those enjoyed by special class teachers. By 1917 speech instructors had organized a "round table . . . for the furtherance of speech correction." Meetings took place monthly and included discussion on such items as the waiting list for classes, follow-up information on discharged students, transfers and adjustments of teaching positions, and "discussions on problems of common interest." Courses also were offered to improve particular skills, for example in oral and dramatic art. An extended twenty-lesson course was offered on Friday afternoons in 1917 by the president of the College of the Spoken Word, Delbert Staley. Boston's speech instructors also passed along some of their knowledge by giving "very freely of their time and experience to the teachers of suburban towns." The effect of this training and support was, in the words of Superintendent Frank V. Thompson, "a remarkable spirit and enthusiasm" among the corps.[38]

## Purpose and Rationale

The special education programs initiated between 1908 and 1913 reflected not only the willingness and ability of school officials to differentiate students with greater precision but also to take advantage of emergent understandings and technologies related to the identification and treatment of specific exceptionalities. The rapid advancement classes were unique among these programs in that they found purpose more in serving the machinery of the schools than in addressing individual needs of gifted students. These children were moved quickly through the system to reduce their boredom and thus minimize their misbehavior, and to save time and money by producing the desired results in less time. But the other programs all represented specific attempts to address specific disabilities by providing specialized instructional settings and employing recent advances in diagnosis and technology.

As in the case of the special class and the Horace Mann School, the segregation of these students on the basis of their identified specific disability certainly smoothed the operation of the schools. But it also demonstrated a serious belief that the public schools should provide a viable education to every child under their charge, an education that would serve not only the student but also the needs of the school system—and ultimately those of society. By the late 1910s each of these programs manifested the ways in which special education had come to justify its work: through an ultimately convincing combination of those rationales which for decades had been used to various degrees and in various ways to promote and explain the segregation of children with formally or informally identified disabilities.

# 10

# THE LEGACY OF SPECIAL EDUCATION IN BOSTON, 1838–1930

A primary purpose of this study has been to examine some of the early history of special education as a means to better understand the potential obstacles and opportunities inherent in a more inclusive approach to the education of public school students with disabilities. Looking at the origins of special education in Boston is a valuable process for two reasons: Boston's story reveals a wide range of theory and practice related to the segregation and integration of exceptional students, and the movement toward inclusion in the United States at this point seems inexorable.

In the last twenty-five years legislation, school regulations, and school practice have all moved clearly toward the principle that students with disabilities should be integrated much more fully into regular education classrooms. The mainstreaming model of the late 1970s and early 1980s rejected the belief that segregation of exceptional children in the public schools should be considered normal and acceptable. Instead, it called for placing students with disabilities in general classrooms whenever those students could demonstrate their ability to participate successfully in standard activities. Although the general education classroom is not expected to make significant adaptations to accommodate an exceptional child under the mainstreaming model, the notion that special education students belonged in and could contribute to the life of the general classroom was a dramatic shift from the mostly segregationist practices used before the passage of the Education for All Handicapped Children Act (PL 94-142) in 1975.

The inclusion model differs significantly from mainstreaming in that it expects the general education classroom to make substantive and significant accommodations to its structure, curriculum, and activities in order to include greater numbers of exceptional children for much longer periods of time. The burden of adaptation thus falls not on the student with a disability but rather on the staff and students who plan and carry out the work of the general classroom. Under the mainstreaming model, then, initial placement of an exceptional student is typically located outside of the general classroom, whereas under an inclusive model the initial placement clearly should be in the general classroom. Despite this crucial distinction, both mainstreaming and inclusion assume that integration of students with special needs is a positive and necessary goal. Federal and state legislation, as well as the regulations of thousands of school districts across the country, now support the spirit and intent of the inclusion model. Thus, authentic and extensive integration of special education within regular education is still a hotly debated topic but seems to represent the current general will. And to proponents of full inclusion, nothing less than 100 percent student participation in the general classroom 100 percent of the school day should be considered satisfactory.

Nevertheless, the early history of special education in the Boston public schools suggests for several reasons that the widely applauded movement toward inclusion will not take place without considerable dissent or struggle. If anything, this history demonstrates how strong the pressures and impulses have been in special education to segregate children with special needs from their nondisabled peers. The segregation of these students began because special education was indeed seen as being of and for exceptional children whose segregated placement and instruction in the public schools was deemed necessary for a variety of reasons. In fact, the origins of special education are deeply rooted in a series of social, pedagogical, and practical assumptions that render the integration of special and general education highly problematic.

## Pressures toward Segregation

Marvin Lazerson's summary of developments in the origins of public school special education in the United States clearly articulates the tensions shaping its growth:

> Special education . . . like so much else in the progressive era . . . com-
> bined both optimism and fear, humanitarian concerns for children
> and the deprived and coercive practices to control deviant behav-
> ior. . . . The two concerns . . . were always in tension with one an-
> other, but because they were so often class-based, the latter tended to
> overwhelm the former, as the humanitarian concerns of special educa-
> tion became secondary to the desire to segregate all those the educa-
> tional system found disruptive.[1]

While Boston's efforts in this area strongly suggest that humanitarian
and child-centered concerns played a more powerful role than Lazerson
asserts, his comment still accurately portrays the struggle and intensity of
the segregationist impulse in accommodating children with identified disabilities in the public schools.

The patterns of segregation seen in public school special education
followed naturally from traditional efforts to educate individuals with obvious disabilities, especially as manifested in the institutions designed to
house, treat, and educate them. While certainly seen by their founders and
benefactors as benevolent and sympathetic creations, the "schools" and
"asylums" developed for the deaf, the blind, and the mentally retarded nevertheless isolated and stigmatized their clientele by placing them behind
intimidating walls and keeping them from the mainstream of society. Doctors, educators, and other researchers associated with these institutions emphasized the unique nature and requirements of teaching institutionalized
students. Even as Samuel Gridley Howe argued that a school for "feeble-
minded" children could serve as the "last link in the great chain of common schools," the notion that such children actually belonged in the public schools themselves never gained credence until the late nineteenth
century at the earliest. By the early 1900s, public school officials in Boston
and elsewhere often remarked, especially in the case of mentally "deficient"
or "defective" children, that a considerable number of the boys and girls
found in the public schools should be institutionalized, but due to overcrowding at those institutions the public schools "had no choice" but to
do what they could with them—namely, segregate them from the general
school population in ungraded classes, special classes, or some other program. At the insistence of the state government the Boston public schools
assumed greater responsibility for the education of many children whom
educators and doctors may have considered appropriate for an institutional
placement; consequently, the segregation of these children simply took

place on the grounds of the city's public schools instead. At this time a public school education for many students with disabilities—particularly those in the special classes—represented but a minor situational step removed from segregated instruction in an institution.

Historically, the impulse to segregate and isolate school attendees who manifested some significant abnormal characteristic or condition has always been strong in public school systems seeking economy and efficiency while responding to fears and suspicions of the general public. Misunderstandings of and contempt for "foreigners" or "minorities," for students with various and often mysterious disabilities, or for children demonstrating attitudes or behavior considered bizarre or dangerous began shaping public school ideology and practice in Boston in the early nineteenth century and lost little if any momentum or influence over the next hundred years. Sociocultural differences among Boston school children—and between many of those children and the teachers and administrators who ran the schools—increased as the years passed. Although "scientific" notions regarding cultural background and other forms of "abnormality" led some to form more sympathetic considerations of such children, they led others to harbor harsher views (as manifested in the eugenics movement and in more negative constructs of mental retardation and incorrigibility) by the early 1900s. Isolating those whose physical, intellectual, and/or behavioral characteristics were seen as seriously and obviously different from the norm continued as the accepted practice even as beliefs and knowledge regarding those differences shifted over time.

Thus the question of "what to do" with children whose disabilities allegedly prohibited their participation in mainstream public schooling was almost always answered with, "Segregate them." The belief held strong for decades that the presence of such children in the regular classroom was inefficient and ill-advised. Teachers and administrators constantly observed that these children took too much of a teacher's time and energy, posed a threat to the smooth functioning of classrooms and schools, and represented a troubling if not dangerous influence on the "normal" children who made up the vast majority of the student population. On a practical level, as early as the 1840s and 1850s teachers opportunistically recognized the value of an isolated setting in which to "place" students who, for whatever reason "were giving them more than ordinary trouble." The intermediate schools, ungraded classes, disciplinary classes, the Disciplinary Day School, and to a certain extent special classes all served as convenient dumping grounds for such children: if they were too much trouble, they were put somewhere else. Even as the expressed, and to a large degree genuine, concern for an appropriate pedagogy for these "difficult" children grew stronger, segregation was still seen as necessary. With the exception of the speech improvement program, all of the special education programs in Boston required that a student be isolated from her or his peers for virtually the entire school day. In other words, special education was just that: special, different, unique, something to conduct in a cloistered world, at a tangible philosophical and practical distance from the regular classroom.

Issues of separation and segregation played out specifically in decisions regarding proper curriculum for children with identified disabilities. By the late 1800s, the issue of whether or not individuals with disabilities were at all educable had for the most part been settled. The work in American institutions and the progress made in Europe regarding the instruction of the deaf, the blind, and the mentally retarded had convinced most educators that such students could benefit at least to some extent from formal instruction. The remarkable stories of Laura Bridgman and Helen Keller had shown a skeptical audience that even those with seemingly insurmountable disabilities could learn effectively. Rather, the question centered on how much such students were capable of learning, what subjects were of greatest interest or value to them, and what constituted the best way to help them contribute to society. Teachers in the intermediate schools, ungraded classes, the Horace Mann School, rapid advancement classes, conservation of eyesight classes, open-air classes, and speech improvement centers all attempted to use the standard curriculum as much as possible. By the early 1900s, the belief that deaf children, mute children, partially sighted or chronically ill children, or children with serious speech disorders could master much of the standard curriculum if given a certain latitude went virtually unchallenged. As a result, the potential for significant integration of students with disabilities with their general education peers certainly existed.

However, for students in the various disciplinary programs and the special classes—and to some extent the ungraded classes—curricular beliefs focused on the value of manual, physical, industrial, and moral education at the expense of academic "bookwork." The students in these programs carried the ethnic and/or alleged intellectual make-up that caused school authorities to presuppose their expected roles in society as well as their expected interests and capabilities. For these children, physical, manual, and industrial work was considered to be most appropriate: it would hold their interest, suit their presumed limited capabilities, provide some useful skills, and above all strengthen their moral fiber. Academic work, it was assumed, could do little to bolster these efforts. These beliefs reflected attitudes and practices found nationwide: fear and contempt of the immigrant and the "mental defective," limited expectations for "morons" or "dullards" or "incorrigibles," the certainty that intellectual disability could not be "cured" but that children with it could be "improved" in certain ways. These children were seen as educable, but only in certain ways and only to certain ends. In addition, each special education program possessed a significant body of content and/or methodology that differentiated it significantly from the regular curriculum. Hence, regardless of the extent of their commonalities with the standard curriculum, each special education program was considered sufficiently different to demand segregation in the multiple ways that education is constructed—through objectives, curricula, methodology, and teacher training. For many, special education required distinctive consideration, planning, and implementation.

As Lazerson notes the desire to segregate and isolate did not originate from solely negative beliefs about the character and educability of students with identified disabilities. Much was learned about such children from decades of observing and instructing them in Boston's classrooms. For many of the teachers who worked in these segregated settings, their daily interactions with exceptional students helped to construct and reaffirm a belief that their students were capable and deserving of, even entitled to, an individualized education. Teachers in most of Boston's special education programs—especially those of the Horace Mann School and the special classes—developed solid convictions that special education for their students was a waste of neither time nor money, that society would indeed benefit both practically and spiritually from significant efforts to provide appropriate segregated instruction to "those who vary from the normal type." Administrators such as Edwin Seaver, Sarah Arnold, Walter Parker, and Augustine Rafter repeatedly articulated the position that individual children did count in the massive public school system, even those who created grave problems for the school machinery.

Student-centered rationales for segregated instruction arose initially with the Horace Mann School in the 1870s but intensified dramatically during the three decades following the creation of the special classes for students with mental retardation. Although segregation continued to constitute the instructional model for most special education programs, the needs of the children did serve as an important factor in special education's early development. It is also true that notions which we refer to today as deinstitutionalization, normalization, regular education initiative, or other efforts to integrate children with disabilities more fully into the school community also generated some support in the public schools of Boston. Debates over the wisdom of maintaining intermediate schools and un-graded classes arose when a few officials argued that "inferior" children would benefit from close, or at least closer, proximity to positive peer role models, an argument made in support of the discontinuation of intermedi-ate schools and their reorganization into ungraded classes. By the early 1900s, Augustine Rafter was commenting on how greater integration of conservation of eyesight students with their regular class peers would re-duce the stigmatization of the former. The speech improvement program, of course, provided a special education but did so on a "pull-out" basis, so that speech improvement students received most of their instruction in regular classrooms.

The best example of attempts to normalize a population of students with disabilities is found in the Horace Mann School for the Deaf. One of the primary factors cited in this school's founding was the belief that the American School for the Deaf in Hartford did not provide a "normal" enough environment for its students; supporters of a day school for the deaf asserted that Boston's deaf children would benefit greatly from at-tending a day school and living at home. The oral method of instruction, which served as the cornerstone of the Horace Mann School curriculum, emphasized the importance of learning skills that would facilitate the deaf child's participation and integration in the much larger world of the hear-ing. The school followed the regular school curriculum as closely as pos-sible, and students enjoyed opportunities to acquire work skills alongside their hearing peers. Although the school was housed in quarters separate from the other Boston schoolhouses, the goal of the school—indeed, the very essence of a day school—was to permit a special education in a much more normalized environment than institutions for the deaf, with their typically isolated grounds and insular approaches to education and com-munication, could ever permit. (It must be noted that such "normaliza-tion" was and is considered by many among the deaf community as an assault on their culture and community.)

Along with the protoresource room model of the speech improve-ment program, the Horace Mann School exemplified the possibilities for greater integration with the normal world for students with serious disabilities: the former in the schools themselves, the latter in the wider community. Nevertheless, the belief held strong that for most disabled students—especially those with the less understood and more greatly feared conditions of mental retardation or "incorrigibility"—total segregation was the only accepted practice. The goal was to produce "happy helpful units to society's whole" without clogging the educational machinery or endangering the instruction—and the character—of either the "normal" or the "special" student population. For those reasons, normalized or integrated learning environments were considered highly inappropriate.

## The Right to an Education

Current pressures to maximize integration of students with disabilities are to some extent driven by the rise of the disability rights movement. This movement, which dates at least to the late 1970s, argues that individuals with disabilities constitute an oppressed minority and thus need to fight vigorously for their right not only to an inclusive education but also to enjoy fairness and access in terms of housing, transportation, medical care, employment training and opportunities, and communication aids. Disability rights advocates bring to the public's attention all aspects of society and culture that they claim limit the potential and/or the basic human and civil rights of any individual with disabilities. To them, a fair and acceptable education is one that eliminates any form of segregation or any sense of inferiority among children identified as disabled.[2]

In Boston, such direct advocacy for the full rights of individuals with disabilities neither occurred nor became an issue before 1930, certainly not to the extent we witness today. The question of whether all students have a right to a public school education is inextricably linked to the rise of state-mandated compulsory education and the emergence of government-operated free public schooling. Current conceptions of the right of all children to a "free and appropriate education in the least restrictive environment" are anachronistic when applied to children with disabilities during the origins of special education in the nineteenth and early twentieth centuries. Most compulsory education laws did not mandate universal attendance until the 1900s; Massachusetts law did not compel school attendance for students with identified disabilities until 1919. Institutions were routinely considered appropriate places for the education of students who could not succeed in the public schools without special accommodation; as the "last link" in educating the public, such institutions clearly were seen as an appropriate and justifiable educational placement.

Thus the greater concern at the time was not the student's right to an appropriate education but rather the state's perceived need to have as many children as possible brought under the influence of the public schools. By the mid-1800s public schools in Boston were seen as vitally important resources in the maintenance of civic order and social prosperity. Boston families were constantly advised, cajoled, or threatened by civic and school authorities to send their children to school, although even minimal attendance wasn't required until 1852. The perceived need to "Americanize" immigrant children and to inculcate all young Americans with the norms and values of the dominant culture, as embodied in common school ideology, subsumed the right of children to attend school to the need of the state to have them do so. With the steady strengthening of compulsory education laws, the state's right to compel school attendance, whether in public school or elsewhere, solidified. Students with identified disabilities (however vaguely or specifically defined) were in fact encouraged to obtain whatever education they could, in part because many such children came from backgrounds and homes which were presumed to need the controlling influence of public education the most.

As the state strengthened its claim to the right to compel attendance, discussion and debate intensified concerning the right of children with identified disabilities to obtain not just an education but one that suited them individually. One description of ungraded classes praised them as being a place where certain students could obtain instruction more suited to their "peculiar" needs. In the 1890s, Supervisors Sarah Arnold and Walter Parker had argued that the schools should accommodate individual needs of both struggling regular class students as well as those with special needs in the ungraded classes. The extensive discussions and justification of the emerging special education programs in the early 1900s frequently cited the right of students with disabilities to receive an individualized education, arguments often grounded in the developmentalist, child-centered rhetoric associated with the advent of progressive education. If the state had a right to compel their attendance, the argument went, then children with special educational needs had a right to an education suited to those needs. Whether there existed legal obligation to deliver an individualized education or to be educated alongside "normal" peers in integrated general classrooms was a much less important issue than whether the public schools had a moral obligation to recognize and respect the needs of each student. By 1930 the argument that disabled children were entitled to a special education went hand-in-hand with arguments that providing an education suited to each child's individual needs met the needs of the schools and of society as well. Even so, the question of whether the rights of individuals with disabilities were being denied through segregated instruction in the public schools never came up in early twentieth century Boston.

Segregation has thus typified both policy and practice in special education in a powerful way for well over a century, and the pressures and concerns which led to segregation in Boston are in fact quite similar to current concerns regarding integration and inclusion expressed by those who openly or even privately question the practice. The source of this broad, at times heated, debate reflects another crucial lesson from the Boston experience: "special education" is by no means monolithic. Each of these programs exhibited characteristics distinguishing them not just from the traditional classrooms but from each other as well. Each program possessed a unique set of originating impetuses, rationales for existence and development, student needs and abilities, and status or prestige within the school system. Although the National Education Association had begun championing special education as a collective entity by the early 1900s— leading eventually to the formation of what would become the Council for Exceptional Children—Boston's programs for students with disabilities remained very much their own educational worlds. Even today, special education manifests significant distinctions between and among programs for specific disabilities in terms of purpose, practice, and support. For example, many advocates of deaf education deplore the loss of opportunity to create singular and unique deaf communities in schools as well as in society that enforced integration and practices of inclusion may help bring about. Others question whether students with disabilities can receive the best possible education in an educational setting that is not constructed specifically for them. Consequently, initiating efforts to integrate special education with general education more fully—efforts which often assume that "special education" can be treated as a single entity—may well invite misunderstanding and conflict. The history of the field, at least as seen in Boston, strongly suggests that the unique characteristics, interests, and needs of students in special education programs carry over to the programs themselves. Like the students involved, the uniqueness of these programs must be respected and accommodated in any long-term planning or reorganization of the special education-general education relationship—including the reality that many special education advocates view some segregated instruction as necessary and beneficial.

## Possibilities for Integrating Special and General Education

To summarize, the evidence from Boston suggests that efforts to achieve such integration will be an uphill struggle for several reasons. First and foremost, the pressures to segregate students with disabilities are old, deep, and multilayered. Attitudes toward abnormality and disability have evolved dramatically since the nineteenth century but still exhibit tendencies toward suspicion, pessimism, ignorance, or outright fear. The belief that the presence of students with disabilities disrupts activities in the regular classroom dates at least to the mid-1800s and remains strong among wide cross-sections of administrators, teachers, and parents. Comments that segregation, because of its ability to deliver more individualized instruction in a setting specifically tailored to the special needs of students with disabilities, is best for large numbers of exceptional children also have persisted for well over one hundred years. Boston's story amply demonstrates that the perception of special education as indeed *special* is potent as well as durable. Special education itself is multifaceted and highly complex and does not lend itself easily to generalized assumptions or universal actions (for example, that the movement to full integration would be best for all children). In Boston are found the traditions of separateness and uniqueness among individual special education programs; therefore, the sense of specialized identity and knowledge which distinguishes special education programs from each other, let alone special education from general education, have existed for decades and have become firmly entrenched.

Yet past experience shapes current practice and future possibilities only to a certain extent; the past is powerful but not all-consuming or inexorable. Despite the strong historical traditions of segregation and separation informing current policy and practice in special education, new assumptions and understandings can work to mitigate those traditions. Definitions and constructions of equality and equity in public education have changed considerably since the early 1900s, dramatically challenging beliefs about the rights of all students regarding their educational placement and instruction. The emergence of cross-categorical approaches to classifying and educating children with disabilities holds a great deal of potential for questioning and reforming traditional compartmentalization in special education. The realization that most disabilities affecting children are mild in nature and can thus be effectively recognized and addressed in the regular classroom through adaptations to a more carefully crafted standard curriculum has altered the views of many concerning the advisability of specialized or segregated placement. This perspective is ironically and indirectly reinforced by Boston's experience, where for generations only students with the most obvious or serious disabilities were identified and removed from the regular classroom.

Boston's development of special education in its public school system offers one final lesson for, and encouragement toward, the process of integrating special education with regular education. There exists in public schools, and has existed for over one hundred years, a demonstrated presence of teachers, administrators, and other interested parties who hold a genuine concern for all students. Throughout the development of special education in Boston, comments on and commitments to the unique needs of individual students and the duty of public education to recognize and address those needs have been voiced and acted upon. At times this discourse has been mere rhetoric, designed to rationalize certain actions or mask certain motives. Nevertheless, the commitment to all children has grown stronger and more accepted, stamping special and general educators alike, in Boston and elsewhere, with a conviction that the requirements of each child in the public school system need not, even must not, be subsumed to those of the system itself, regardless of issues of convenience, economics, or ideology. It is this legacy of true commitment to equitable treatment for each child that has continued in the face of constant change and promises that, ultimately, the best interests of such children will be served. If full integration is indeed beneficial to everyone, then Boston's history suggests that the human and spiritual resources exist in sufficient abundance to implement it.

# NOTES

## Chapter 1: Introduction

1. 20<sup>th</sup> *Annual Report of the Superintendent of the Boston Public Schools,* in *Annual Report of the School Committee of Boston* (Boston, 1900), appendix 80; Individuals with Disabilities Education Act (PL 101-476), 34 C.F.R. 300.550(b).

2. See for example Douglas Biklen, *Schooling Without Labels* (Philadelphia: Temple University Press, 1992); Douglas Biklen, Dianne L. Ferguson, and Alison Ford, eds., *Schooling and Disability* (Chicago: National Society for the Study of Education, 1989); Dorothy K. Lipsky and Alan Gartner, eds., *Beyond Separate Education: Quality Education for All* (Baltimore: Paul H. Brookes, 1983); Thomas Skrtic, *Behind Special Education: A Critical Analysis of Professional Culture and School Organization* (Denver: Love, 1991); Susan Stainback and William Stainback, eds., *Curriculum Considerations in Inclusive Classrooms: Facilitating Learning for All Students* (Baltimore: Paul H. Brookes, 1992); Madeleine Will, "Educating Students with Learning Problems: A Shared Responsibility," *Exceptional Children* 52 (1986): 411–15; M.C. Wang and H.J. Walberg, "Four Fallacies of Segregationism," *Exceptional Children* 55 (1988): 128–37; Laurence Lieberman, *Preserving Special Education . . . For Those Who Need It* (Newtonville, Mass.: Glo Worm Publications, 1988); Douglas Fuchs and Lynn Fuchs, "Inclusive Schools Movement and the Radicalization of Special Education Reform," *Exceptional Children* 60 (1994): 294–309; James M. Kauffman, "How We Might Achieve the Radical Reform of Special Education," *Exceptional Children* 60 (1993): 6–16. A useful collection of arguments presenting multiple perspectives on the issue of special education reform is William Stainback and Susan Stainback, eds., *Controversial Issues Confronting Special Education: Divergent Perspectives* (Boston: Allyn and Bacon, 1992).

3. See for example Joseph L. Tropea, "Bureaucratic Order and Special Children: Urban Schools, 1890s–1940s," *History of Education Quarterly* 27 (spring 1987): 29–53; Barry M. Franklin, "Progressivism and Curriculum Differentiation: Special Classes in the Atlanta Public Schools, 1898–1923," *History of Education Quarterly* 29 (winter 1989): 571–93; Steven A. Gelb, "'Not Simply Bad and Incorrigible': Science, Morality, and Intellectual Deficiency," *History of Education Quarterly* 29 (fall 1989): 359–79; Robert L.

Osgood, "Undermining the Common School Ideal: Intermediate Schools and Ungraded Classes in Boston, 1838–1900," *History of Education Quarterly* 37 (winter 1997): 375–98; Marvin Lazerson, "The Origins of Special Education," in *Special Education Policies: Their History, Implementation, and Finance*, ed. Jay G. Chambers and William T. Hartman (Philadelphia: Temple University Press, 1983), 15–47. Books include Barry M. Franklin, *From 'Backwardness' to 'At-Risk': Childhood Learning Difficulties and the Contradiction of School Reform* (Albany: SUNY Press, 1994); Seymour Sarason and John Doris, *Educational Handicap, Public Policy, and Social History: A Broadened Perspective on Mental Retardation* (New York: Free Press, 1979); R. C. Scheerenberger, *A History of Mental Retardation* (Baltimore: Paul H. Brookes, 1983); James W. Trent, Jr., *Inventing the Feeble Mind: A History of Mental Retardation in the United States* (Berkeley: University of California Press, 1994); John V. Van Cleve and Barry Crouch, *A Place of Their Own: Creating the Deaf Community in America* (Washington, D.C.: Gallaudet University Press, 1989); Margret Winzer, *The History of Special Education: From Isolation to Integration* (Washington, D.C.: Gallaudet University Press, 1993).

## Chapter 2: An Overview

1. Charles Francis Adams, in U.S. Department of Interior, Census Office, *Report on the Social Statistics of Cities, Part I* (Washington, D.C.: Government Printing Office, 1886), 92; quoted in State Street Trust Company, *Boston's Growth: A Bird's-eye View of Boston's Increase in Territory and Population from Its Beginning to the Present* (Boston: State Street Trust Co., 1910), 7–8.

2. Oscar Handlin, *Boston's Immigrants* (Cambridge: Harvard University Press, 1959), 2–11. These developments are also discussed in detail in Michael Katz, *The Irony of Early School Reform* (Cambridge: Harvard University Press, 1968), 5–11.

3. Katz, *Early School Reform*, 5–11; Handlin, *Boston's Immigrants*, 9–13; Robert A. McCaughey, "From Town to City: Boston in the 1820s," *Political Science Quarterly* 88 (1973): 191–213; Marvin Lazerson, *The Origins of the Urban School: Public Education in Massachusetts 1870–1915* (Cambridge: Harvard University Press, 1971), 5–8. For Boston's civic improvements see Walter M. Whitehill, *Boston: A Topographical History* (Cambridge: Harvard University Press, 1959).

4. State Street Trust Co., *Boston's Growth, passim,* especially 22–23; Whitehill, *Topographical History,* 73–94, 141–73.

5. Allen M. Wakstein, "Boston's Search for a Metropolitan Solution," *Journal*

*of the American Institute of Planners* 38 (1972): 287–90; State Street Trust Co., *Boston's Growth, passim;* Boston Tercentenary Committee, *Fifty Years of Boston: A Memorial Volume* (Boston: Boston Tercentenary Committee, 1932), 749.

6. State Street Trust Co., *Boston's Growth,* 46; McCaughey, "From Town to City," 194; Wakstein, "Boston's Search," 287.

7. Van Wyck Brooks, *The Flowering of New England* (New York: Dutton, 1951); Arthur Mann, *Yankee Reformers in the Urban Age* (Cambridge: Harvard University Press, 1954); Henry S. Commager, *Era of Reform, 1830–1860* (Princeton: Van Nostrand, 1960); Ivan D. Steen, "Cleansing the Puritan City: The Reverend Henry Morgan's Antivice Crusade in Boston," *New England Quarterly* 54 (1981): 385–411.

8. Handlin, *Boston's Immigrants,* 1–2; Barbara M. Solomon, *Ancestors and Immigrants: A Changing New England Tradition* (Cambridge: Harvard University Press, 1956), 1–3; Roland M. Stronberg, "Boston in the 1820's and 1830's," *History Today* 11 (1961): 592; James O. Horton, "Blacks in Antebellum Boston: The Migrant and the Community, An Analysis of Adaptation," *Southern Studies* 21 (1982): 278; Stanley K. Schultz, *The Culture Factory: Boston Public Schools, 1789–1860* (New York: Oxford University Press, 1973), 189, 211; Sam B. Warner, *Streetcar Suburbs: The Process of Growth in Boston, 1870–1900* (Cambridge: Harvard University Press and MIT Press, 1962), 5.

9. Handlin, *Boston's Immigrants,* 25–38.

10. Ibid., 242, 244; Schultz, *Boston Public Schools,* 189, 211–15.

11. Stephan Thernstrom, *The Other Bostonians: Poverty and Progress in the American Metropolis, 1880–1970* (Cambridge: Harvard University Press, 1973), 111–14, 179. Other statistics taken from the respective *Federal Census Reports,* 9th–15th Censuses, 1870–1930, volumes on "Population."

12. For thorough discussions of these developments, see Warner, *Process of Growth in Boston, passim,* and Whitehill, *Topographical History, passim.* Neighborhood segregation is analyzed quantitatively in Nathan Kantowitz, "Racial and Ethnic Residential Segregation in Boston 1830–1970," *Annals of the American Academy of Political and Social Science* 44 (1979): 41–54.

13. Solomon, *Ancestors and Immigrants,* 153.

14. Handlin, *Boston's Immigrants, passim,* especially chapters 3, 4, and 5; Schultz, *Boston Public Schools,* 217–24; Mann, *Yankee Reformers,* 24–51. For discussion of the Irish in Boston politics, see for example John T. Galvin, "Patrick J. Maguire: Boston's Last Democratic Boss," *New England*

*Quarterly* 55 (1982): 392–415; Robert A. Silverman, "Nathan Matthews: Politics of Reform in Boston, 1890–1910," *New England Quarterly* 50 (1977): 626–43; and Ronald P. Formisano and Constance K. Burns, eds., *Boston 1700–1980: The Evolution of Urban Politics* (Westport, Conn.: Greenwood Press, 1984).

15. Two vivid and revealing sources of certain perspectives on immigrant living conditions are Frederick A. Bushee, *Ethnic Factors in the Population of Boston* (New York: Macmillan, 1903) and Robert A. Woods, ed., *The City Wilderness: A Settlement Study* (Boston: Houghton, Mifflin and Co., 1898). A more personalized account is Mary Antin, *The Promised Land* (Boston: Houghton, Mifflin and Co., 1912). See also Handlin, *Boston's Immigrants,* 88–123; Arnold A. Wieder, *The Early Jewish Community of Boston's North End* (Waltham, Mass.: Brandeis University, 1962); and Jacob Neusner, "The Impact of Immigration and Philanthropy upon the Boston Jewish Community," *Publications of the American Jewish Historical Society* 46 (1956): 71–85.

16. Solomon, *Ancestors and Immigrants, passim,* especially 152–75, 82–102; Bushee, *Ethnic Factors, passim;* Warner, *Process of Growth in Boston,* 1–14; Mann, *Yankee Reformers,* 3–5. A sound discussion of national attitudes toward immigrants is John Higham, *Strangers in the Land: Patterns of American Nativism* (New Brunswick, N.J.: Rutgers University Press, 1955). For attitudes toward Catholicism see Handlin, *Boston's Immigrants,* 180–89; Schultz, *Boston Public Schools,* 234–36; James W. Sanders, "Boston Catholics and the School Question," in *From Common School to Magnet School: Selected Essays in the History of Boston's Schools,* ed. James W. Fraser, Henry L. Allen, and Sam Barnes (Boston: Trustees of the Public Library, 1979), 43–75.

17. For general histories of urban America, see Charles N. Glaab and A. Theodore Brown, *A History of Urban America,* 2d ed. (New York: Macmillan, 1976), and Blake McKelvey, *The Urbanization of America, 1860–1915* (New Brunswick, N.J.: Rutgers University Press, 1963).

## Chapter 3: Building the Boston Public Schools

1. For background on the creation of the Boston Education Act, see James W. Fraser, "Boston's Colonial and Revolutionary Experience," in *From Common School to Magnet School: Selected Essays in the History of Boston's Schools,* ed. James W. Fraser, Henry L. Allen, and Sam Barnes (Boston: Trustees of the Public Library, 1979), 11–12; Stanley K. Schultz, *The Culture Factory: Boston Public Schools 1789–1860* (New York: Oxford University Press,

1973), 9–21, 105–6; *A Chronology of the Boston Public Schools,* School Document no. 7, 1929 (Boston, 1929), 92; Edward A. Krug, *Salient Dates in American Education 1635–1964* (New York: Harper and Row, 1966), 33–34; Charles K. Dillaway, "Education Past and Present: The Rise of Free Education and Educational Institutions," in *The Memorial History of Boston,* Vol. 4, ed. Justin Winsor (Boston: James R. Osgood and Co., 1883), 235–41.

2. Data on school population is compiled from various sources: 32nd "Annual Report of the Committee on Accounts," in *Annual Report of the School Committee of Boston* (hereafter referred to as *ARSCB*), 1900, appendix 27; *Annual Statistics of the Boston Public Schools,* School Document no. 10, 1920, 38; "Report of the Business Manager," School Document no. 1, 1930, Table 1; Sam Barnes, "Progressivism on the Wane: The Entrenchment of the Bureaucracy, 1900–1945," in Fraser, Allen, and Barnes, *From Common School to Magnet School,* 98.

3. Schultz, *Boston Public Schools,* 30–41; Dillaway, "Education Past and Present," 245–46. An excellent collection of history and documents on the primary schools is Joseph M. Wightman, comp., *Annals of the Boston Primary School Committee, from Its First Establishment in 1818, to Its Dissolution in 1855* (Boston: Rand and Avery, 1860).

4. William Thurston, from a letter to Turner Philips, Chairman of the Boston Board of Selectmen, March 18, 1818, in Wightman, *Annals of the Boston Primary School Committee,* 13; Noah Webster, quoted in Schultz, *Boston Public Schools,* 253; George B. Emerson, quoted in Schultz, *Boston Public Schools,* 257. Schultz offers a thorough analysis of these developments; see especially 25–30, 252–63.

5. The common school movement is explored in literally scores of sources, ranging from specific monographs to more generalized educational histories. Three of the most informative are Lawrence A. Cremin, *The American Common School: An Historic Conception* (New York: Teachers College Press, 1951); Paul Monroe, *Founding of the American Public School System,* Vol. 1 (New York: Macmillan, 1940); and Carl F. Kaestle, *Pillars of the Republic: Common Schools and American Society, 1780–1860* (New York: Hill and Wang, 1983). Studies which are quite critical of the values and intentions of the movement include Michael B. Katz, *The Irony of Early School Reform: Educational Innovation in Mid-Nineteenth Century Massachusetts* (Boston: Beacon Press, 1968); and David Nasaw, *Schooled to Order: A Social History of Public Schooling in the United States* (New York: Oxford University Press, 1979). My brief discussion is based primarily on Kaestle, *Pillars of the Republic,* 75–103. For more on the creation of the State Board of Education,

see James W. Fraser, "Reform, Immigration, and Bureaucracy, 1820–1870," in Fraser, Allen, and Barnes, *From Common School to Magnet School,* 31; George Martin, *Evolution of the Massachusetts Public School System* (New York: D. Appleton and Co., 1904), 154–55; and George B. Emerson, *Education in Massachusetts: Early Legislation and History* (Boston: John Wilson and Son, 1869), 28–34.

6.   Kaestle, *Pillars of the Republic,* 76–77.

7.   *Annual Report of the Superintendent of the Boston Public Schools* (hereafter referred to as *ARSBPS*), 1852 (Boston, 1852), 47; 40ᵗʰ *ARSBPS,* School Document no. 12, 1922 (Boston, 1922), 8; Quarterly Report of John D. Philbrick, in *ARSCB* (1857), 31; J. Porter Crosby, in "Annual School Festival," in *ARSCB* (1904), appendix 154; 42ⁿᵈ *ARSBPS,* School Document no. 17, 1924, 10.

8.   "Report of Walter S. Parker, Supervisor," in *ARSCB* (1898), appendix 133.

9.   "Report of the Committee on Educational Objectives and Achievements in the Public Schools of Boston," in 44ᵗʰ *ARSCB,* School Document no. 10, 1926, appendix 101.

10.  John W. Perrin, *The History of Compulsory Education in New England* (Meadville, Penn.: Flood and Vincent, 1896), 50; Martin, *Massachusetts Public School System,* 216; Schultz, *Boston Public Schools,* 301.

11.  Ibid., 300–1; *Acts and Resolves Passed by the General Court of Massachusetts in the Year 1852* (Boston, 1853), 170–71, in Edgar W. Knight and Clifton L. Hall, *Readings in American Educational History* (New York: Appleton-Century-Crofts, 1951), 365–66 (The law is now identified as chapter 240 of the Massachusetts General Laws of 1852; the passage referred to is from section 4); Krug, *Salient Dates,* 77–78; Perrin, *Compulsory Education in New England,* 57; Martin, *Massachusetts Public School System,* 212–13; Fraser, "Reform, Immigration, and Bureaucracy," 40; Paul Monroe, ed., *A Cyclopedia of Education* (New York: Macmillan, 1915), Vol. 1, 287.

12.  Martin, *Massachusetts Public School System,* 210–13, 217; Perrin, *Compulsory Education in New England,* 43–45, 57; Monroe, *Cyclopedia,* 287–90; U.S. Bureau of Education, *Bulletin, 1914, no. 2 . . . Whole Number 573* (Washington, D.C.: GPO, 1914), 30–31, 64–65, 121. For a discussion of truancy, see for example *ARSCB,* School Document no. 18, 1889, 42–47.

13.  "A Chronology," 95–100, 109–10. For detailed discussions of these developments see Wightman, *Annals of the Boston Primary School Committee, passim;* Fraser, "Reform, Immigration, and Bureaucracy," *passim;* Sam Barnes, "Reform and the Struggle for Control," in Fraser, Allen, and Barnes, *From Common School to Magnet School,* 76–91; Barnes, "Progressivism on the

Wane," 96; Michael B. Katz, "The Emergence of Bureaucracy in Urban Education: The Boston Case, 1850–1884," Part I, *History of Education Quarterly* 8 (1968): 163–76.

14. J. L. Pritchard, "City Management of Public Schools," *Education* 4 (1883): 90; *First Semi-Annual Report of the Superintendent of the Boston Public Schools,* December 30, 1851 (Boston, 1851), 8; *ARSCB,* School Document no. 11, 1905, 8–9. David B. Tyack, *The One Best System: A History of American Education* (Cambridge: Harvard University Press, 1974), 126–76, and Raymond E. Callahan, *Education and the Cult of Efficiency* (Chicago: University of Chicago Press, 1962) offer detailed discussions of the role that the business analogy played in the administration of urban school systems; Barnes, "Progressivism on the Wane," 93–107, describes generally the application of these ideals in Boston.

15. Fraser, "Reform, Immigration, and Bureaucracy," 33; Krug, *Salient Dates,* 72–74; "A Chronology," 94–96.

16. Krug, *Salient Dates,* 72–75; John D. Philbrick, "Seventh Quarterly Report, March 1, 1859," in *ARSCB* (1859), 54; Burke Hinsdale, Charles F. Adams, Jr., and Gail Hamilton, all quoted in Michael B. Katz, "The Emergence of Bureaucracy in Urban Education: The Boston Case, 1850–1884," Part II, *History of Education Quarterly* 8 (1968): 320–21.

17. 12th *Annual Report of the Board of Supervisors* (hereafter referred to as *ARBS*), in *ARSCB* (1890), appendix 138–39.

18. 17th *ARSBPS* (1897), in *ARSCB* (1897), appendix 68–70; 15th *ARSBPS* (1895), in *ARSCB* (1895), appendix 65–66.

19. 12th *ARBS* (1890), appendix 136–39.

20. 17th *ARSBPS* (1897), appendix 69–70; "Report of George H. Conley, Supervisor," in *ARSCB* (1895), appendix 133–34.

21. 15th *ARSBPS* (1895), appendix 67; 12th *ARBS* (1890), appendix 139; 17th *ARSBPS* (1897), appendix 52–55.

22. "Report of Sarah L. Arnold, Supervisor," in *ARSCB* (1897), appendix 136–41.

23. *ARSCB* (1858), 10–11; "Fifth Quarterly Report," 1858, in *ARSCB* (1858), 25.

24. *ARSCB* (1871), 14–15; *ARSCB* (1876), 9, 10–12; Augustine L. Rafter, "Reports of Assistant Superintendents," in 33rd *ARSBPS,* School Document no. 11, 1914, 134.

25. 29th *ARSBPS,* School Document no. 10, 1910, 5; 33rd *ARSBPS* (1914), 30.

26. 40ᵗʰ *ARSBPS,* School Document no. 12, 1922, 10.

27. "Philosophy of Education," 49ᵗʰ *ARSBPS,* School Document no. 7, 1931, 10.

28. *ARSCB* (1871), 20.

## Chapter 4: The Emergence of Special Education

1. For an in-depth examination of European efforts in deaf education and of the founding of the American School for the Deaf, see John V. Van Cleve and Barry A. Crouch, *A Place of Their Own: Creating the Deaf Community in America* (Washington, D.C.: Gallaudet University Press, 1989), 1–46; and Margret Winzer, *The History of Special Education: From Isolation to Integration* (Washington, D.C.: Gallaudet University Press, 1993), chapters 1–3.

2. Richard Winefield, *Never the Twain Shall Meet* (Washington, D.C.: Gallaudet University Press, 1987), 6–8.

3. Ibid., 11–66, and Winzer, *History of Special Education,* 188–206, each offer detailed and clear accounts of the controversy. The most thorough and richly detailed account, however, is Douglas C. Baynton, *Forbidden Signs: American Culture and the Campaign against Sign Language* (Chicago: University of Chicago Press, 1996).

4. Van Cleve and Crouch, *A Place of Their Own,* 71–105, provide specific information on the role of publications, associations, and Gallaudet University in advancing the cause of and providing forums for debate in deaf education.

5. Most of this discussion is based on Winzer, *History of Special Education,* 206–10; the quote is from p. 207.

6. See Ernest Freeberg, "'More Important Than a Rabble of Common Kings': Dr. Howe's Education of Laura Bridgman," *History of Education Quarterly* 34 (fall 1994): 305–27.

7. For an original and controversial perspective on the history of institutions in Europe, see Michel Foucault, *Madness and Civilization: A History of Insanity in the Age of Reason* (New York: Random House, 1965). For more general histories of the care and treatment of the mentally retarded, see Leo Kanner, *A History of the Care and Study of the Mentally Retarded* (Springfield, Ill.: Charles C. Thomas, 1971) and R. C. Scheerenberger, *A History of Mental Retardation* (Baltimore: Paul H. Brookes, 1983).

8. Winzer, *History of Special Education,* 112–15; Anna M. Wallace, "History of the Walter E. Fernald State School," unpublished manuscript (c. 1941), 1–10.

9. Winzer, *History of Special Education,* 211–16.

10. Mabel E. Talbot, *Edouard Seguin: A Study of an Educational Approach to the Treatment of Mentally Defective Children* (New York: Bureau of Publications, Teachers College, Columbia University, 1964), especially chapters 4 and 5; Philip L. Safford and Elizabeth J. Safford, *A History of Childhood and Disability* (New York: Teachers College Press, 1996), 172–74.

11. Steven A. Gelb, "'Not Simply Bad and Incorrigible': Science, Morality, and Intellectual Deficiency," *History of Education Quarterly* 29 (fall 1989): 359–79.

12. James E. Trent, Jr., *Inventing the Feeble Mind: A History of Mental Retardation in the United States* (Berkeley: University of California, 1994), 141; Walter E. Fernald, in appended "Discussion" to Mary C. Greene, "Should the Scope of the Public-School System Be Broadened So As To Take In All Children Capable of Education? If So, How Should This Be Done?" *Addresses and Proceedings of the National Education Association* (1903): 1006–7.

13. Steven Jay Gould, *The Mismeasure of Man* (New York: Norton, 1981), 149–50.

14. A number of sources address the mental testing movements. This discussion is based on Gould, *Mismeasure of Man,* 146–233; Scheerenberger, *History of Mental Retardation,* 139–47; Clarence J. Karier, *Shaping the American Educational State: 1900 to the Present* (New York: Free Press, 1975), 161–65; David B. Tyack, *The One Best System: A History of American Urban Education* (Cambridge: Harvard University Press, 1974), 198–216; Trent, *Inventing the Feeble Mind,* 155–61.

15. Lewis M. Terman, "The Use of Intelligence Tests in the Grading of School Children," *Journal of Educational Research* 1 (1920): 20.

16. Gould, *Mismeasure of Man,* 192–233; Winzer, *History of Special Education,* 276.

17. Francis Galton, quoted in J. E. Wallace Wallin, *The Education of Handicapped Children* (Boston: Houghton Mifflin, 1924), 308; Safford and Safford, *Childhood and Disability,* 382; Gould, *Mismeasure of Man,* 74.

18. Winefield, *Never the Twain Shall Meet,* 82–96; Van Cleve and Crouch, *A Place of Their Own,* 142, 148; Winzer, *History of Special Education,* 283–88.

19. Fernald, in Greene, "Should the Scope of the Public-School System . . . ," 1006.

20.   E. R. Johnstone, "The Function of the Special Class," *Addresses and Proceedings of the National Education Association* (1908): 1115–18.

21.   J. E. Wallace Wallin, *Education of Mentally Handicapped Children* (New York: Harper and Row, 1954), 20; Wallin, 1924, 46; Marvin Lazerson, "The Origins of Special Education," in Jay G. Chambers and William T. Hartman, eds., *Special Education Policies: Their History, Implementation, and Finance* (Philadelphia: Temple University Press, 1983), 15–47.

22.   The classic work on the influence of progressivism on American education is Lawrence A. Cremin, *The Transformation of the School: Progressivism in American Education, 1876–1957* (New York: Vintage, 1964). Another excellent source is Herbert Kliebard, *The Struggle for the American Curriculum 1893–1958* (New York: Routledge, 1987).

23.   Kliebard, *Struggle for the American Curriculum,* 89–90.

24.   See ibid., 41–51 for a concise discussion of these developments.

25.   Ibid., 42, 43.

## Chapter 5: Intermediate Schools and Ungraded Classes

1.   Report of a Subcommittee of the Primary School Board, presented April 25, 1820, in Joseph Wightman, *Annals of the Primary School Committee* (Boston: Rand and Avery, 1860), 54.

2.   Carl F. Kaestle, ed., *Joseph Lancaster and the Monitorial School Movement: A Documentary History* (New York: Teachers College Press, 1973), 34–35. A detailed contemporary description of the system's method and philosophy as it originated in England is found in *Analysis of a New System of General Education; in Which the Lancastrian Principles Are Discussed and Enlarged, . . .* (London: Gale and Curtis, 1811).

3.   Semiannual Report of the Primary School Board, April 1824, in Wightman, *Annals of the Primary School Committee,* 91; City of Boston, "The Committee to whom was referred the consideration of the expediency of introducing (*sic*) the system of monitorial instruction into the Primary Schools, respectfully REPORT:" filed by J. P. Blanchard (City of Boston, 1827), 1–2; Wightman, *Annals of the Primary School Committee,* 103–4; Standing Committee of the Primary School Board, April 21, 1829, in Wightman, *Annals of the Primary School Committee,* 116. See also Stanley K. Schultz, *The Culture Factory: Boston Public Schools 1789–1860* (New York: Oxford University Press, 1973), 263–68. Portions of the Boston School Committee report of 1828 on other cities' monitorial schools are found in

Elwood P. Cubberley, *Readings in the History of Education* (Boston: Houghton Mifflin, 1920), 553–54.

4. Wightman, *Annals of the Primary School Committee,* 107–10; Kaestle, *Joseph Lancaster,* 43–45; Schultz, *Boston Public Schools,* 267–68.

5. Wightman, *Annals of the Primary School Committee,* 129, 145–46, 148, 161–62; Boston Common Council, Doc. 4 (1837), 4–5; Schultz, *Boston Public Schools,* 268.

6. Boston Common Council, Doc. 4 (1837), 4–11.

7. Boston Common Council, Doc. 17 (1837), 2–8.

8. Order of the City Council of Boston, March 22, 1838, in Wightman, *Annals of the Primary School Committee,* 173; "Report of the Subcommittee on Intermediate Schools of the Primary School Board, 1838," in Wightman, *Annals of the Primary School Committee,* 173–74; Schultz, *Boston Public Schools,* 269; Wightman, *Annals of the Primary School Committee,* 173.

9. Wightman, *Annals of the Primary School Committee,* 174, 304; Schultz, *Boston Public Schools,* 269; Boston City Doc. 13 (1843), 6; *Annual Report of the School Committee of Boston* (hereafter referred to as *ARSCB*), 1879 (Boston, 1879), 9–10; *Report of the Committee on the Supervision of Schools for Special Instruction,* City Doc. 43, (1857), 4.

10. Schultz, *Boston Public Schools,* 270; Wightman, *Annals of the Primary School Committee,* 210, 304.

11. John D. Philbrick, "Fifth Quarterly Report," June 1, 1858, in *ARSCB* (1858), 25; "Tenth Semi-Annual Report of the Superintendent," in *ARSCB* (1865), 123; "Ninth Quarterly Report," June 7, 1859, in *ARSCB* (1859), 80–81; "Second Semi-Annual Report," March 11, 1861, in *ARSCB* (1861), 71.

12. City Document no. 13 (1843), 6; *ARSCB* (1857), 45–46.

13. *Report of the Committee on the Supervision of Schools for Special Instruction* (1857), 4–5.

14. *ARSCB* (1879), 9–10.

15. *ARSCB* (1879), 9–10. For a detailed discussion of the restructuring of the Boston schools during this time, see Michael B. Katz, *Class, Bureaucracy, and Schools: The Illusion of Educational Change in America* (New York: Praeger, 1971), 56–104.

16. All data compiled from the statistical appendices to the respective *ARSCB*s of June of the years cited; 10th *Annual Report of the Superintendent of the*

*Boston Public Schools* (hereafter referred to as *ARSBPS*), 1890, in *ARSCB* (1890), appendix 49.

17.  8th *Annual Report of the Board of Supervisors* (hereafter referred to as *ARBS*), 1885, in *ARSCB* (1885), appendix 175.

18.  10th *ARBS* (1887), in *ARSCB* (1887), appendix 151–52; 12th *ARBS* (1889), in *ARSCB* (1889), appendix 135; "Report of George Conley, Supervisor," supplement to *ARSCB* (1895), appendix 134; 13th *ARBS* (1890), in *ARSCB* (1890), appendix 144; 14th *ARBS* (1891), in *ARSCB* (1891), appendix 267–68; *ARSCB* (1890), 12–13; 13th *ARBS,* in *ARSCB* (1890), appendix 143.

19.  8th *ARBS* (1885), in *ARSCB* (1885), appendix 175; 10th *ARBS* (1887), in *ARSCB* (1887), appendix 151–52; *ARSCB,* School Document no. 15 (1911), 12. On overcrowding in ungraded classes, see the reports of Walter S. Parker in *ARSCB* (1895), appendix 166, and *ARSCB* (1898), appendix 131.

20.  19th *ARSBPS* (1899), in *ARSCB* (1899), appendix 64; 32nd *ARSBPS,* School Document no. 10 (1913), 67.

21.  12th *ARBS* (1889), in *ARSCB* (1889), appendix 135–36.

22.  12th *ARBS* (1889), in *ARSCB* (1889), appendix 134–35.

23.  All data taken from the *ARSCB*s of the respective years, especially those reports of 1881, 1890, 1893, 1897, and 1899.

24.  10th *ARBS* (1887), in *ARSCB* (1887), appendix 151; 12th *ARBS* (1889), in *ARSCB* (1889), appendix 134; *ARSCB* (1890), 12.

25.  "Report of Walter S. Parker, Supervisor," in *ARSCB* (1895), appendix 166; "Report of Walter S. Parker, Supervisor," in *ARSCB* (1898), appendix 130–33.

26.  "Report of Walter S. Parker, Supervisor," in *ARSCB* (1895), appendix 166.

27.  "Report of Walter S. Parker, Supervisor," in *ARSCB* (1896), appendix 137; "Report of Walter S. Parker, Supervisor," in *ARSCB* (1898), appendix 130–32.

28.  19th *ARSBPS* (1899), in *ARSCB* (1899), appendix 64–65; 22nd *ARSBPS* (1902), in *ARSCB* (1902), appendix 57.

29.  10th *ARBS* (1887), in *ARSCB* (1887), appendix 152; 13th *ARBS* (1890), in *ARSCB* (1890), appendix 144; *Proceedings of the Boston School Committee* (hereafter referred to as *Proceedings*) (1894), 394; "Report of George Conley, Supervisor," in *ARSCB* (1895), appendix 132; 22nd *ARSBPS* (1902), in *ARSCB* (1902), appendix 57.

30. 13ᵗʰ *ARBS* (1890), in *ARSCB* (1890), appendix 144; *Proceedings* (1894), 394.

31. *Proceedings* (1894), 394–95; *Proceedings* (1896), 140.

32. "Report of George Conley, Supervisor," appendix 132; 13ᵗʰ *ARBS* (1890), in *ARSCB* (1890), appendix 144; 22ⁿᵈ *ARSBPS* (1902), in *ARSCB* (1902), appendix 57–58; *Proceedings* (1896), 139–40.

33. 8ᵗʰ *ARBS* (1885), in *ARSCB* (1885), appendix 175; 10ᵗʰ *ARBS* (1887), in *ARSCB* (1887), appendix 151; 22ⁿᵈ *ARSBPS* (1902), in *ARSCB* (1902), appendix 58.

34. 10ᵗʰ *ARBS* (1887), in *ARSCB* (1887), appendix 151; 13ᵗʰ *ARBS* (1890), in *ARSCB* (1890), appendix 143; "Report of George Conley, Supervisor," appendix 133–34, 132.

35. 20ᵗʰ *ARSBPS* (1900), in *ARSCB* (1900), appendix 90; *Proceedings* (1895), 36–37; 19ᵗʰ *ARSBPS* (1899), in *ARSCB* (1899), appendix 65–66; 22ⁿᵈ *ARSBPS* (1902), in *ARSCB* (1902), appendix 58.

36. *Proceedings* (1910), 35; "Report of Assistant Superintendent Maurice P. White," in 33ʳᵈ *ARSBPS,* School Document no. 11 (1914), appendix 189; 33ʳᵈ *ARSBPS* (1914), 35–36.

37. Maurice P. White, appendix 188–89; *Annual Statistics of the Boston Public Schools* (hereafter referred to as *ASBPS*), School Document no. 6 (1914), 14–15; 33ʳᵈ *ARSBPS* (1914), 30, 36. See also 34ᵗʰ *ARSBPS,* School Document no. 17 (1915), 10–11.

38. Data for the years 1900–1905 is compiled from the appendices of the *ARSCB* for the respective years. For 1907–1909 see "Semi-Annual Statistics of the Boston Public Schools," School Documents no. 12, 6, and 11 respectively. Data from 1910 to 1939 is compiled from the respective years of the *ASBPS* (all on page 6 after 1916) in the bound volumes of the *School Documents* for those years. For information on the number of ungraded classes between 1909 and 1914, see 33ʳᵈ *ARSBPS* (1914), 35; *Reappointments of Teachers and Members of the Supervising Staff,* School Document no. 7 (1911), 6–7; and *ASBPS* (1914), 5.

39. 33ʳᵈ *ARSBPS* (1914), 36.

## Chapter 6: The Horace Mann School for the Deaf

1. *Report of the Committee on Rules and Regulations,* September 13, 1864, in *Annual Report of the School Committee of Boston* (hereafter referred to as *ARSCB*) (1864), 256.

2.  *Report of the Committee on Rules and Regulations*, 256–57.

3.  *Report of the Committee on School for Deaf Mutes*, in *ARSCB* (1873), 275–79. See also *Acts of 1868*, chapter 200, and *Acts of 1869*, chapter 333. For comments on Reverend King's role in the school's founding, see for example 45th *Annual Report of the Superintendent of the Boston Public Schools* (hereafter referred to as *ARSBPS*), School Document no. 12 (1927), 40.

4.  *Report of the Committee on School for Deaf Mutes* (1873), 278–79; 45th *ARSBPS* (1927), 40.

5.  John D. Philbrick, 23rd Semi-Annual Report, September 1871, in *ARSCB* (1871), 205–6; *Reports of the Superintendent of Public Schools*, August 1874, in *ARSCB* (1874), 372; *Proceedings of the Boston School Committee* (hereafter referred to as *Proceedings*) (1877), 58, 73; *Annual Report of the Committee on the Horace Mann School for the Deaf* (hereafter referred to as *ARHMSD*), 1890, in *ARSCB* (1890), appendix 295; *ARSCB* (1884), 22; *ARSCB* (1900), 4.

6.  *ARSCB* (1886), 15–16; Committee on Accounts, "Report of Expenditures," in *ARSCB* (1887), appendix 78–79; "Report of Committee on Accounts," in *ARSCB* (1899), appendix 28–29; *ARSCB* (1887), appendix 79.

7.  *Reports of the Superintendent of Public Schools* (1874), 372; *Report of the Committee on the School for Deaf-Mutes*, in *ARSCB* (1874), 472; *ARSCB* (1884), 23; *ARSCB* (1888), 61; *ARSCB* (1886), 16; *ARSCB* (1890), 17.

8.  *Annual Report of the Board of Supervisors* (hereafter referred to as *ARBS*), 1891, in *ARSCB* (1891), appendix 272.

9.  Margret Winzer, *The History of Special Education: From Isolation to Integration* (Washington, D.C.: Gallaudet University Press, 1993), 151; *ARHMSD* (December 13, 1881), in *ARSCB* (1881), appendix 318–19.

10. *ARHMSD* (1881), appendix 319–21; "Report of the Principal of the Horace Mann School for the Deaf" (hereafter referred to as "RPMSD"), appendix K to 39th *ARSBPS*, School Document no. 11 (1921), 97.

11. *ARHMSD* (1890), in *ARSCB* (1890), appendix 288–92.

12. *Report of the Committee on the School for Deaf-Mutes*, in *ARSCB* (1874), 469–70; 35th *Semi-Annual Report of the Superintendent* (March 1879), in *ARSCB*, School Document no. 2 (1879), 67.

13. Richard Winefield, *Never the Twain Shall Meet: Bell, Gallaudet, and the Communications Debate* (Washington, D.C.: Gallaudet University Press, 1987), 15–17; John V. Van Cleve and Barry A. Crouch, *A Place of Their Own: Creating the Deaf Community in America* (Washington, D.C.: Gallaudet University Press, 1989), 114–17. See also "RPHMSD," Appendix

M to 38ᵗʰ *ARSBPS,* School Document no. 13 (1920), 119; 45ᵗʰ *ARSBPS* (1927), 40.

14. Ruth E. Bender, *The Conquest of Deafness,* 3d ed. (Danville, Ill.: Interstate Printers and Publishers, 1981), 98–103, 143, 147; Edward L. Scouten, *Turning Points in the Education of Deaf People* (Danville, Ill.: Interstate Printers and Publishers, 1984), 63–65. See also John Philbrick, 23ʳᵈ *Semi-Annual Report* (1871), in *ARSCB* (1871), 205–7, and *Report of Committee on School for Deaf-Mutes* (1873), 282–83.

15. *Report of the Committee on School for Deaf-Mutes* (1873), 283; *ARBS* (1891), appendix 272–73; quoted in *ARHMSD* (1890), appendix 293–94. See also Harry Best, *Deafness and the Deaf in the United States* (New York: Macmillan, 1943), 454. For more on Bell's views, see Van Cleve and Crouch, *A Place of Their Own,* 142–50. Douglas C. Baynton offers a more critical view of oralism in *Forbidden Signs: American Culture and the Campaign against Sign Language* (Chicago: University of Chicago Press, 1996).

16. Bender, *Conquest of Deafness,* 144–46; quoted by John Philbrick, in 23ʳᵈ *Semi-Annual Report* (1871), 206; "ARHMSD" (1881), in *ARSCB* (1881), appendix 316; *Report of Committee on School for Deaf-Mutes* (1873), 282–83; Philbrick, *23ʳᵈ Semi-Annual Report* (1871), 207.

17. *Report of the Committee on School for Deaf-Mutes* (1873), 287–90.

18. *Report of the Committee on School for Deaf-Mutes* (1873), 288–89; "Report of Ellis Peterson, Supervisor," supplement to *ARSCB* (1898), appendix 90; *ARHMSD* (1881), appendix 316–17.

19. *Proceedings* (1885), 185; 14ᵗʰ *ARBS* (1891), appendix 273.

20. 14ᵗʰ *ARBS* (1891), appendix 273–74; quoted in *ARHMSD* (1890), appendix 290; *ARSCB* (1874), 470–71.

21. Scouten, *Turning Points,* 222–23; 23ʳᵈ *ARSBPS* (1903), in *ARSCB* (1903), appendix 100; *ARSCB* (1874), 471; *ARHMSD* (1890), appendix 290, 294. Fuller's report on her work with Helen Keller can be found in *ARSCB* (1903), appendix 191–99. See also Helen Keller, *The Story of My Life* (Garden City, N.Y.: Doubleday, 1954), 60.

22. *ARSCB* (1905), 5; *Report of the Business Agent,* School Document no. 2 (1910), 35; *Annual Statistics of the Boston Public Schools* (hereafter referred to as *ASBPS*), School Document no. 12 (1915), 13 (the *ASBPS* also includes yearly enrollment statistics for the HMSD); *Rules of the School Committee and Regulations of the Public Schools of the City of Boston,* School Document no. 10 (1906), chapter 13, section 295; "RPHMSD" (1920), 119; 45ᵗʰ *ARSBPS* (1927), 40.

23. "RPHMSD" (1921), 99–100; "RPHMSD," in 42nd *ARSBPS,* School Document no. 17 (1924), 186.

24. "RPHMSD" (1921), 96; "RPHMSD" (1924), 187; 45th *ARSBPS* (1927), 41.

25. *ARSCB,* School Document no. 10 (1912), 30–31; 23rd *ARSBPS* (1903), appendix 100–2; *Proceedings* (1900), 221; *Rules of the School Committee and Regulations of the Public Schools of the City of Boston,* chapter 19, section 385.

26. 23rd *ARSBPS* (1903), appendix 99–100; *ARSCB* (1912), 30–31.

27. 45th *ARSBPS* (1927), 42; 23rd *ARSBPS* (1903), appendix 101–2; "RPHMSD" (1921), 100; *ARSCB* (1912), 31; "RPHMSD" (1921), 101.

28. "RPHMSD" (1924), 189; 45th *ARSBPS* (1927), 42. See also "RPHMSD" (1920), 123.

29. 23rd *ARSBPS* (1903), appendix 99–100; *ARSCB* (1912), 31–32; 32nd *ARSBPS* (1913), 50; *Proceedings* (1913), 69; 33rd *ARSBPS,* School Document no. 11 (1914), 31; quoted in "RPHMSD" (1920), 120; *Proceedings* (1912), 35, 87, 89, 100, 106, 221.

30. 23rd *ARSBPS* (1903), appendix 100; *Proceedings* (1912), 223; 33rd *ARSBPS* (1914), 31.

31. *ARSCB* (1912), 31; 45th *ARSBPS* (1927), 42; "RPHMSD" (1920), 122; "RPHMSD" (1921), 102–3; 45th *ARSBPS* (1927), 42.

32. "RPHMSD" (1924), 188–89; "RPHMSD" (1920), 121; 45th *ARSBPS* (1927), 42.

33. See for example *ARSBPS* (1927), 42–43; "RPHMSD" (1921), 99–101; *ARBS* (1891), appendix 273; "RPHMSD" (1920), 121–22; and 33rd *ARSBPS* (1914), 31.

34. "RPHMSD" (1920), 124; 45th *ARSBPS* (1927), 43.

35. "RPHMSD" (1924), 190; 45th *ARSBPS* (1927), 43.

36. "RPHMSD" (1921), 101–2; "RPHMSD" (1924), 190. A highly detailed account of the work in lipreading classes is provided in the "Report by Assistant Superintendent Augustine L. Rafter," in 45th *ARSBPS* (1927), appendix 193–95. See also "RPHMSD" (1920), 122.

37. "RPHMSD" (1924), 187–88; 45th *ARSBPS* (1927), 41. Adams had commented on low pay earlier: see "RPHMSD" (1920), 121. On pay scales see for example *Proceedings* (1910), 107–8, and (1915), 102.

38. *ARSCB* (1874), 469; "RPHMSD" (1921), 98–99; "RPHMSD" (1924), 187.

39. "RPHMSD" (1920), 120.

40. "RPHMSD" (1921), 97–98.

41. "RPHMSD" (1924), 186; 45<sup>th</sup> *ARSBPS* (1927), illustration between 40–41; 56<sup>th</sup> *ARSBPS* (1938), 158–59.

42. *Report of Committee on School for Deaf Mutes* (1873), 285; *ARSCB* (1871), 46–47; *Report of Committee on School for Deaf-Mutes* (1874), 472.

43. *ARSCB* (1884), 22; *ARSCB* (1888), 60; "ARHMSD" (1890), 294; 45<sup>th</sup> *ARSBPS* (1927), 41; "RPHMSD" (1920), 123; "RPHMD" (1921), 103.

44. *ARSCB* (1874), 468; Winzer, *History of Special Education,* 317–19; Winefield, *Never the Twain Shall Meet,* 20; "Report of Ellis Peterson, Supervisor," appendix 90.

## Chapter 7: Disciplinary Programs

1. Committee on Truant Officers for the Year 1883, in *Annual Report of the School Committee of Boston* (hereafter referred to as *ARSCB*), School Document no. 19 (1885), 24; *ARSCB* (1883), 36–37; *ARSCB* (1884), 26; 5<sup>th</sup> *Annual Report of the Superintendent of the Boston Public Schools* (hereafter referred to as *ARSBPS*), 1885, in *ARSCB* (1885), 24–25. On the delays in starting the Parental School, see *ARSCB* (1889), 45–47; *ARSCB* (1890), 39; *ARSCB* (1891), 31. See also 10<sup>th</sup> *ARSBPS* (1890), appendix 20. For information on the founding and original plans of the school see *ARSCB,* School Document no. 21 (1892), 21–23; 17<sup>th</sup> *ARSBPS* (1897), in *ARSCB* (1897), appendix 85–86.

2. 15<sup>th</sup> *ARSBPS* (1895), in *ARSCB* (1895), appendix 84–89.

3. *ARSCB* (1894), 37–38.

4. On the early release policy see 17<sup>th</sup> *ARSBPS* (1897), in *ARSCB* (1897), appendix 87–91. For school attendance data and information on student background see 23<sup>rd</sup> *ARSBPS,* (1903), in *ARSCB* (1903), appendix 116; *ARSCB,* School Document no. 17 (1906), 40; and the *Annual Report of the Children's Institutions Department for the City of Boston* (listed as City Documents and hereafter referred to as *ARCID*) for the various years. (Data for a given year are typically found in the report of the following year.) Information on the 1905 probation system is found in *ARCID,* City Document no. 9 (1905), 12–13.

5. Walter S. Parker, in 23<sup>rd</sup> *ARSBPS* (1903), in *ARSCB* (1903), appendix 117–18. Legislative action regarding the closure of parental schools can be traced through "Report of John D. Prince, Agent of the Board," appendix A to 70<sup>th</sup> *Annual Report of the State Board of Education* (hereafter referred to as *ARSBE*), Public Document no. 2 (1907), 186–87; "Report of John D.

Prince, Agent of the Board," in 72ⁿᵈ *ARSBE,* Public Document no. 2 (1909), 191–92; "Report of Commissioner David Snedden," in 74ᵗʰ *ARSBE,* Public Document no. 2 (1911), 83; Report of Commissioner," in 79ᵗʰ *ARSBE,* Public Document no. 2 (1916), 60–62.

6. The law cited was an Act of the General Court passed in 1889, as explained in 10ᵗʰ *ARSBPS* (1890), appendix 21. See also *ARSCB* (1890), 13; 16ᵗʰ *ARSBPS* (1890), in *ARSCB* (1890), appendix 15–16.

7. *Proceedings of the Boston School Committee* (hereafter referred to as *Proceedings*) (1906), 53, 74, 135, 143, 242; 26ᵗʰ *ARSBPS,* School Document no. 9 (1906), 36–37; *ARSCB* (1906), 38.

8. *ARSCB* (1906), 38–39; *Proceedings* (1906), 143; *Proceedings* (1908), 24; 1ˢᵗ *Annual Report of the Statistics of the Boston Public Schools* (hereafter referred to as *ASBPS*), School Document no. 9 (1910), 15; 28ᵗʰ *ARSBPS* (1908), 66–67.

9. *Proceedings* (1911), 86; for enrollment figures of 1907, 1908, and 1909 see *Semi-Annual Statistics of the Boston Public Schools,* School Document nos. 12, 6, and 11, 12, 12, and 12 respectively; for 1910, 1911, and 1912 see *ASBPS,* 1910–13, School Document nos. 9, 9, 6, and 9, 15, 14–15, 14, and 14 respectively; *Proceedings* (1912), 203; 32ⁿᵈ *ARSBPS* (1913), 49; 59ᵗʰ *ARSBPS,* School Document no. 11 (1941), 161.

10. 35ᵗʰ *ARSBPS,* School Document no. 19 (1916), 76; *Rules of the School Committee and Regulations of the Public Schools of the City of Boston,* Document no. 5 (1919), 69; 45ᵗʰ *ARSBPS,* School Document no. 12 (1927), 43.

11. "Report of Superintendent Augustine L. Rafter," Appendix B to 37ᵗʰ *ARSBPS,* School Document no. 17 (1919), 60; *Proceedings* (1915), 121; *ARSBPS,* School Document no. 17 (1919), 14; *ASBPS,* School Document nos. 12, 16, 10, and 10, 17, 18–19, 18–19, 18–19, respectively (1918–1921); "Report of Assistant Superintendent Augustine L. Rafter," appendix A to 38ᵗʰ *ARSBPS,* School Document no. 13 (1920), 28. See also "Report of the Chief Attendance Officer, Mr. Joseph W. Hobbs," in 42ⁿᵈ *ARSBPS,* School Document no. 17 (1924), 71; 45ᵗʰ *ARSBPS* (1927), 48; *Proceedings* (1914), 225; *Proceedings* (1916), 168.

12. "Report of Assistant Superintendent Augustine L. Rafter," appendix to 41ˢᵗ *ARSBPS,* School Document no. 20 (1923), 69–70.

13. "Report of the Chief Attendance Officer" (1924), 69–70; 45ᵗʰ *ARSBPS* (1927), 44–45, 47–48.

14. 45th *ARSBPS* (1927), 45; Report of Assistant Superintendent Augustine L. Rafter" (1923), 70.

15. 45th *ARSBPS* (1927), 43–45. See also "Report of the Chief Attendance Officer" (1924), 69–71; "Report of Assistant Superintendent Augustine L. Rafter" (1923), 69–70.

16. 45th *ARSBPS* (1927), 45–51.

17. 45th *ARSBPS* (1927), 46–47; "Report of the Chief Attendance Officer" (1924), 70.

18. "Report of the Chief Attendance Officer" (1924), 69–70; "Report of Assistant Superintendent Augustine L. Rafter" (1923), 69; 45th *ARSBPS* (1927), 47–48.

## Chapter 8: The Boston Special Classes

1. 20th *Annual Report of the Superintendent of the Boston Public Schools* (hereafter referred to as *ARSBPS*), 1900, in *Annual Report of the School Committee of Boston* (hereafter referred to as *ARSCB*) (1900), appendix 80–82; *Annual Statistics of the Boston Public Schools* (hereafter referred to as *ASBPS*), School Document no. 10 (1920), 6; *ASBPS,* School Document no. 11 (1930), 6.

2. R. C. Scheerenberger, *A History of Mental Retardation* (Baltimore: Paul H. Brookes, 1983), 83, 129–30; Seymour B. Sarason and John Doris, *Educational Handicap, Public Policy, and Social History: A Broadened Perspective on Mental Retardation* (New York: Free Press, 1979), 275–77, 296–309.

3. Daniel Calhoun, *The Intelligence of a People* (Princeton: Princeton University Press, 1973), 72–76.

4. *ARSCB* (1867), 15, 65–66; see also *ARSCB* (1866), 91.

5. "A Chronology of the Boston Public Schools," in 47th *ARSBPS, School* Document no. 7 (1929), 103; 20th *ARSBPS* (1900), appendix 79.

6. *Proceedings of the Boston School Committee* (hereafter referred to as *Proceedings*) (1898), 558, 568, 580.

7. Boston Finance Commission, *Report on the Boston School System* (Boston, 1911), 93–94; *ARSCB,* School Document no. 10 (1912), 28. For examples of similar arguments, see 20th *ARSBPS* (1900), appendix 79; Elizabeth Daniels, in 20th *ARSBPS* (1900), appendix 84; *ARSCB,* School Document no. 17 (1906), 37–38; "Report of Assistant Superintendent Walter S. Parker," appendix to 33rd *ARSBPS,* School Document no. 11 (1914), 105; *Report of the Special Commission on Education,* Massachusetts Senate Document no. 330 (January 29, 1919), 45–46.

8. 22nd *Annual Report of the Superintendent of the Boston Public Schools* (hereafter referred to as *ARSBPS*) (1902), appendix 54–55. On attempts to return special class children to the regular grades, see David F. Lincoln, "Special Classes for Feeble-Minded Children in the Boston Public Schools," *Journal of Psycho-Asthenics* 7 (1902/1903): 85; *ARSBPS*, School Document no. 10 (1912), 34; *Report of Certain Phases of the Boston School System by the Survey Committee of the Boston Public Schools*, School Document no. 12 (1929), 110.

9. 20th *ARSBPS*, in *Annual Report of the School Committee of Boston* (hereafter referred to as *ARSCB*) (1900), appendix 81–83; Lincoln, "Special Classes for Feeble-Minded Children," 84; Harriet Lyman, in 20th *ARSBPS* (1900), appendix 86. For information on the recruiting and hiring of Dr. Jelly see 22nd *ARSBPS* (1902), appendix 56; 23rd *ARSBPS* (1903), in *ARSCB* (1903), appendix 103; *Proceedings* (1903), 419; *Proceedings* (1906), 155; 26th *ARSBPS* (1906), 36; *ARSCB* (1906), 37.

10. Examples of such vague descriptions can be found in "Report of the Director of Special Classes," appendix L to 38th *ARSBPS*, School Document no. 13 (1920), 113; David F. Lincoln, "Special Classes for Mentally Defective Children in the Boston Public Schools," *Journal of Psycho-Asthenics* 14 (1909/1910): 90; *ARSCB*, School Document no. 10 (1912), 28; 33rd *ARSBPS*, School Document no. 11 (1914), 34; Ada M. Fitts, "How to Fill the Gap Between the Special Classes and Institutions," *Journal of Psycho-Asthenics* 20 (1915/1916): 78; Ada M. Fitts, "The Value of Special Classes for the Mentally Defective Pupils in the Public Schools," *Journal of Psycho-Asthenics* 25 (1920/1921): 120; 45th *ARSBPS*, School Document no. 12 (1927), 49; *Report of Certain Phases*, 110. On mental testing, see "Report of the Director of Special Classes," appendix to 42nd *ARSBPS*, School Document no. 17 (1924), 126; Boston Finance Commission, *A Study of Certain Phases of the Public School System of Boston, Massachusetts* (Boston: 1916), 58–59; *Educational Standards and Educational Measurement*, School Document no. 10 (1914), 6–7; "Report of the Department of Educational Investigation and Measurement," appendix A to 39th *ARSBPS*, School Document no. 11 (1921), 28–30. Arthur Jelly offers some general and very interesting observations on identifying feeble-minded children in Arthur C. Jelly, "Special Classes for Defectives in Reform Schools," *Journal of Psycho-Asthenics* 9 (1905): 158–64.

11. Elizabeth Daniels, in 20th *ARSBPS* (1900), appendix 82; 23rd *ARSBPS* (1903), appendix 102–3; 26th *ARSBPS* (1906), 36; Lincoln, "Special Classes for Mentally Defective Children," 91.

12. "Report of the Director of Special Classes" (1920), 113–14.

13. 22nd *ARSBPS* (1902), in *ARSCB* (1902), appendix 53–54; *ARSCB* (1904), appendix 298–99; data for 1907–1909 from *Semi-Annual Statistics of the Boston Public Schools,* 1907, 1908, 1909, School Document nos. 12, 6, and 11, 11–12, 12, and 12 respectively; *ASBPS,* School Document no. 9 (1910), 15; *ASBPS,* School Document no. 9 (1911), 14–15; *Proceedings* (1901), 380; *Proceedings* (1906), 254; 20th *ARSBPS* (1900), appendix 81.

14. Lincoln, "Special Classes for Feeble-Minded Children," 85; 23rd *ARSBPS* (1903), appendix 102.

15. *ARSCB,* School Document no. 15 (1911), 40–41; *Proceedings* (1911), 117, 124, 161; *Proceedings* (1912), 26. On the inadequate number of special classes see "Plan for Increased Efficiency and Greater Economy of School Time," in *Proceedings* (1913), 56; 32nd *ARSBPS,* School Document no. 19 (1916), 23, 26; "Report of the Director of Special Classes," appendix I to 39th *ARSBPS,* School Document no. 11 (1921), 85; 45th *ARSBPS,* School Document no. 12 (1927), 49.

16. All data compiled from page 6 of the *ASBPS* for the respective years, except for page 4 in 1916. See also 34th *ARSBPS,* School Document no. 17 (1915), 64.

17. *Proceedings* (1912), 44; 32nd *ARSBPS,* School Document no. 10 (1913), 60; 23rd *ARSBPS* (1903), appendix 102; *Proceedings* (1913), 118; "Report of Certain Phases," 110–11.

18. 33rd *ARSBPS* (1914), 34.

19. "Report of the Director of Special Classes," appendix L to 38th *ARSBPS,* School Document no. 13 (1920), 113; 34th *ARSBPS,* School Document no. 17 (1915), 11.

20. 32nd *ARSBPS* (1913), 60–61; 33rd *ARSBPS* (1914), 34–35; 34th *ARSBPS* (1915), 64–66.

21. Fitts, "How to Fill the Gap," 79; "Report of the Director of Special Classes" (1920), 115; 32nd *ARSBPS* (1913), 60–61; 45th *ARSBPS* (1927), 50; *Report of Certain Phases of the Boston School System by the Survey Committee of the Boston Public Schools,* School Document no. 12 (1929), 110.

22. 32nd *ARSBPS* (1913), 64–65; 34th *ARSBPS* (1915), 12, 68–69.

23. 36th *ARSBPS,* School Document no. 23 (1917), 37–38; "Report of the Director of Special Classes" (1920), 117–18. See also Fitts, "The Value of Special Classes," 121–22.

24. "Report of the Director of Special Classes" (1921), 88–90; 45th *ARSBPS* (1927), 50–51.

25. Elizabeth Daniels, in 20ᵗʰ *ARSBPS* (1900), appendix 83–85; Harriet Lyman, in 20ᵗʰ *ARSBPS* (1900), appendix 86.

26. Harriet Lyman, in 20ᵗʰ *ARSBPS* (1900), appendix 86.

27. Lincoln, "Special Classes for Feeble-Minded Children," 87.

28. *Rules of the School Committee and Regulations of the Public Schools of the City of Boston,* School Document no. 5 (1919), 111; *Proceedings* (1905), 405–6; *Annual Statistics of the Boston Public Schools* (hereafter referred to as *ASBPS*), School Document no. 13 (1927), 28; *Report of Certain Phases,* 111; Mary Burkhardt, "Special Classes in Boston," *The Training School Bulletin* 16 (1919/1920): 19.

29. Lincoln, "Special Classes for Feeble-Minded Children," 86–88; Lincoln, "Special Classes for Mentally Defective Children," 90–92.

30. 32ⁿᵈ *ARSBPS* (1913), 62–63; "Report of the Committee on Educational Objectives and Achievements in the Public Schools of Boston," June 1926, appendix to 44ᵗʰ *ARSBPS,* School Document no. 10 (1926), 128.

31. Fitts, "How to Fill the Gap," 79; 34ᵗʰ *ARSBPS* (1915), 65–66. "Report of Assistant Walter S. Parker," Appendix to 33ʳᵈ *ARSBPS* (1914), 106.

32. Accounts by Elizabeth Daniels and Harriet Lyman are found in 20ᵗʰ *ARSBPS* (1900), appendix 84–87; Lincoln, "Special Classes for Feeble-Minded Children," 85–90. On special class centers see Ada Fitts, in "Report of Assistant Superintendent Walter S. Parker" (1914), 106; "Report of the Director of Special Classes" (1920), 114–15; "Report of the Director of Special Classes" (1921), 87–88; "Report of the Director of Special Classes" (1924), 129–30; and "Report of the Director of Special Classes" (1920), 116. The quote is from Fitts, "The Value of Special Classes," 117.

33. *Syllabus for Special Classes,* School Document no. 4 (1914), *passim,* especially 3–5; Special Class Teachers of Boston, *The Boston Way: Plans for the Development of the Individual Child,* 4 ed. (Boston, 1928), *passim;* Katherine C. Covney, "The Growth of Special Classes in the City of Boston," *Training School Bulletin* 39 (1942–43): 57; Ada Fitts, quoted in "Report of Assistant Superintendent Walter S. Parker" (1914), 106. See also 36ᵗʰ *ARSBPS* (1917), 36.

34. Fitts, "How to Fill the Gap," 80; Fitts, "The Value of Special Classes," 117, 119; Lincoln, "Special Classes for Feeble-Minded Children," 84; "Report of the Director of Special Classes" (1920), 114; *The Boston Way,* 4. See also Lincoln, "Special Classes for Mentally Defective Children," 91.

35. Lincoln, "Special Classes for Feeble-Minded Children," 84; *Proceedings* (1902), 145–46, 227; Martin Barr, in Lincoln, "Special Classes for Feeble-

Minded Children," 90; Lincoln, "Special Classes for Mentally Defective Children," 89, 92; 22ⁿᵈ *ARSBPS* (1902), appendix 55–56.

36. *ARSCB* (1904), appendix 118; *Proceedings* (1913), 169; *Proceedings* (1915), 169, 178. For additional information on requirements for special class certification see *Proceedings* (1911), 131–32; 36ᵗʰ *ARSBPS* (1917), 74; and Burkhardt, "Special Classes in Boston," 22. On Boston certification examinations see for example Boston Public Schools, Board of Superintendents, *Examination Papers* (Boston, 1926), nos. 239–42; other years of this publication also list such exams. Information on the yearly number of qualifiers for special class certificates can be found in the annual school document entitled "Candidates Eligible for Appointment as Teachers."

37. On Gesell's talks see *Proceedings* (1912), 214, and 32ⁿᵈ *ARSBPS* (1913), 62. The Waverley program is detailed in *Proceedings* (1914), 166; 34ᵗʰ *ARSBPS* (1915), 66; and 33ʳᵈ *ARSBPS* (1914), 35. The short courses by Healy and Bronner are noted in *Proceedings* (1917), 161–62 and 36ᵗʰ *ARSBPS* (1917), 36. Information on the normal school is found in 49ᵗʰ *ARSBPS*, School Document no. 7, 1931, 25.

38. *Proceedings* (1911), 147; *ARSCB* (1911), 40; 34ᵗʰ *ARSBPS* (1915), 66–67; Burkhardt, "Special Classes in Boston," 23.

39. 43ʳᵈ *ARSBPS*, School Document no. 9 (1925), 70; *Proceedings* (1911), 73; *Proceedings* (1916), 4; *Annual Report of the Massachusetts State Board of Education*, 1928, Part 1, 54–55. Information on these conferences for succeeding years is available in Part 1 of the *ARSBE* for their respective years.

40. *ARSCB* (1906), 37; "Mrs. McNaught," quoted in "Report of the Director of Special Classes," in 42ⁿᵈ *ARSBPS*, School Document no. 17 (1924), 128.

## Chapter 9: Programs for Children with Other Disabilities

1. "Report of Robert C. Metcalf, Supervisor," in *Annual Report of the School Committee of Boston* (hereafter referred to as *ARSCB*), 1898, appendix 84–85; 17ᵗʰ *Annual Report of the Superintendent of the Boston Public Schools* (hereafter referred to as *ARSBPS)*, 1897, in *ARSCB* (1897), appendix 66–70; *Proceedings of the Boston School Committee* (hereafter referred to as *Proceedings*), 1912, 80, 115.

2. *Proceedings* (1913), 97, 150; 32ⁿᵈ *ARSBPS*, School Document no. 10 (1913), 65–67. Quote is from "Report of Assistant Superintendent Augustine L. Rafter," appendix to 33ʳᵈ *ARSBPS*, School Document no. 11 (1914), 130.

3. 32ⁿᵈ *ARSBPS* (1913), 65–66.

4. Taken from 32nd *ARSBPS* (1913), 66, 65; "Report of Assistant Superintendent Augustine L. Rafter" (1914), 130–31. See also 33rd *ARSBPS* (1914), 33–34, for more information on the classes.

5. 33rd *ARSBPS* (1914), 35; 32nd *ARSBPS* (1913), 65; *Annual Statistics of the Boston Public Schools* (hereafter referred to as *ASBPS*), School Document nos. 16 and 21 (1916 and 1917), 4 and 6 respectively; *Rules of the School Committee and Regulations of the Boston Public Schools,* School Document no. 5 (1919), 111 (Chapter 14, section 281, paragraph 5); *Organization and Administration of Intermediate Schools in Boston,* School Document no. 13 (1918), 62.

6. Frank W. Ballou, "Report of Assistant Superintendent," Appendix C to 37th *ARSBPS,* School Document no. 17 (1919), 64–65; *ASBPS,* School Document nos. 12, 16, 10, 10, 15, 23, and 18 (1918–1924 respectively), 6.

7. *Proceedings* (1928), 51–53; *ASBPS,* School Document no. 10 (1928), 6; *Report of Certain Phases of the Boston School System by the Survey Committee of the Boston Public Schools,* School Document no. 12 (1929), 48–51; *ASBPS,* School Document no. 11 (1930), 6.

8. 17th *ARSBPS* (1897), appendix 55.

9. Richard Harrison Shyrock, *National Tuberculosis Association 1904–1954: A Study of the Voluntary Health Movement in the United States* (New York: National Tuberculosis Association, 1957), 108, 117–20.

10. Printed in *ARSCB,* School Document no. 15 (1911), 14–20; 32nd *ARSBPS* (1913), 54–55; in "Report of Assistant Superintendent Walter S. Parker," appendix to 33rd *ARSBPS* (1914), 114.

11. *Proceedings* (1908), 160–61, 167.

12. *Tuberculosis Among School Children,* School Document no. 2 (1909), 9–11; *Proceedings* (1909), 5, 9, 176, 186.

13. *Tuberculosis Among School Children,* 11.

14. *Rules of the School Committee,* 68–69; *ARSCB,* School Document no. 15 (1909), 28; 32nd *ARSBPS* (1913), 55–56.

15. This information is drawn from 32nd *ARSBPS* (1913), 55–56, 59–60; 33rd *ARSBPS* (1914), 33; 34th *ARSBPS,* School Document no. 17 (1915), 69. The quote is from "Report of Assistant Superintendent Walter S. Parker," 114.

16. *Rules of the School Committee,* 111; 32nd *ARSBPS* (1913), 57–59; "Report of Director of Medical Inspection," Appendix E to 39th *ARSBPS,* School Document no. 11 (1921), 62.

17. 32$^{nd}$ *ARSBPS* (1913), 58–59; "Report of Director of Medical Inspection," 62, 49.

18. Data compiled from *ASBPS*, 6 of the respective years, except 1916, 4; 34$^{th}$ *ARSBPS* (1915), 69–70. Information on the national battle against TB is from Shyrock, *National Tuberculosis Association*, 193–97. See also 33$^{rd}$ *ARSBPS* (1914), 33.

19. This information is compiled from 32$^{nd}$ *ARSBPS* (1913), 60; 33$^{rd}$ *ARSBPS* (1914), 33; 34$^{th}$ *ARSBPS* (1915), 70. Dyer's quote is from the 1913 report. See also *Proceedings* (1914), 46–47; *Proceedings* (1913), 123, 150, 172.

20. Data compiled from *ASBPS*, 6 for the respective years; see also 45$^{th}$ *ARSBPS*, School Document no. 12 (1927), 55–56; "Report of Assistant Superintendent Augustine L. Rafter," appendix to 45$^{th}$ *ARSBPS* (1927), 196–97.

21. 70$^{th}$ *Annual Report of the Perkins Institution and Massachusetts School for the Blind* (hereafter referred to as *ARPIMSB*) (1900/1901), 15, 19; 45$^{th}$ *ARSBPS* (1927), 53; 85$^{th}$ *ARPIMSB*, Massachusetts Public Document no. 27 (1916), 20.

22. *Proceedings* (1913), 17, 37, 164; 82$^{nd}$ *ARPIMSB* (1913), 21; 32$^{nd}$ *ARSBPS* (1913), 54; "Report of Assistant Superintendent Augustine L. Rafter," in 36$^{th}$ *ARSBPS*, School Document no. 23 (1917), 90; *Proceedings* (1915), 27.

23. "Report of Assistant Superintendent Augustine L. Rafter" (1917), 90–91; "Report of Assistant Superintendent Augustine L. Rafter" (1927), 198; 32$^{nd}$ *ARSBPS* (1913), 54.

24. "Report of the Committee on Educational Objectives and Achievements in the Public Schools of Boston," appendix to 44$^{th}$ *ARSBPS*, School Document no. 10 (1926), 126–27; "Report of Assistant Superintendent Augustine L. Rafter," Appendix B to 37$^{th}$ *ARSBPS*, School Document no. 17 (1919), 58; *Rules of the School Committee*, 111; *ASBPS*, School Documents no. 9 and 6 (1913 and 1914), 4 and 5 respectively. On Sarah Lilley see 83$^{rd}$ *ARPIMSB* (1914), 26; *Proceedings* (1914), 109; and "Report of Assistant Superintendent Walter S. Parker," 107.

25. 34$^{th}$ *ARSBPS* (1915), 70; "Report of Assistant Superintendent Augustine L. Rafter" (1927), 197; "Report of Assistant Superintendent Augustine L. Rafter" (1917), 91; 45$^{th}$ *ARSBPS* (1927), 54.

26. 45$^{th}$ *ARSBPS* (1927), 53; "Report of Assistant Superintendent Augustine L. Rafter" (1927), 197–98; "Report of Assistant Superintendent Augustine L. Rafter" (1917), 93.

27. "Report of Assistant Superintendent Augustine L. Rafter" (1917), 92–93;

34th *ARSBPS* (1915), 70; "Report of Assistant Superintendent Augustine L. Rafter," Appendix A to 38th *ARSBPS,* School Document no. 13 (1920), 27.

28.   Data compiled from *ASBPS,* 6 for respective years; see also 45th *ARSBPS* (1927), 54.

29.   *ARSCB* (1896), appendix 189–90; *Annual Report of the Committee on the Horace Mann School for the Deaf,* School Document no. 10 (1904), 6–7; *Annual Report of the Committee on the Horace Mann School for the Deaf,* School Document no. 9 (1905), 7.

30.   32nd *ARSBPS* (1913), 50–51; *Proceedings* (1912), 35, 40, 43, 55, 83, 100, 106, 121, 194–95, 202–3, 231; *Proceedings* (1913), 164; 32nd *ARSBPS* (1913), 52–53; *ASBPS,* School Document no. 6 (1914), 5.

31.   33rd *ARSBPS* (1914), 32; "Report of Assistant Superintendent Walter S. Parker," 108; 34th *ARSBPS* (1915), 70–71. Enrollment data compiled from *ASBPS,* 6 for the respective years except for 1917, compiled from "Report of Assistant Superintendent Augustine L. Rafter" (1917), 95.

32.   All quotes from 32nd *ARSBPS* (1913), 51. On kinds of speech "defects," see also "Report of Assistant Superintendent Augustine L. Rafter" (1917), 95; 34th *ARSBPS* (1915), 71; 45th *ARSBPS* (1927), 52–53.

33.   36th *ARSBPS* (1917), 38; information on scheduling compiled from 45th *ARSBPS* (1927), 52; and 34th *ARSBPS* (1915), 71; Rafter's quotes are from "Report of Assistant Superintendent Augustine L. Rafter" (1920), 26.

34.   34th *ARSBPS* (1915), 71.

35.   "Report of Assistant Superintendent Augustine L. Rafter" (1917), 95; see also 36th *ARSBPS* (1917), 38; 45th *ARSBPS* (1927), 52. On success rates see for example 33rd *ARSBPS* (1914), 32–33; "Report of the Committee on Educational Objectives and Achievements in the Public Schools of Boston," 127; and 36th *ARSBPS* (1917), 39.

36.   "Report of Assistant Superintendent Augustine L. Rafter" (1917), 94; "Report of Assistant in Charge of Speech Improvement Classes, Miss Theresa A. Dacey," 42nd *ARSBPS,* School Document no. 17 (1924), 179–80; 45th *ARSBPS* (1927), 53.

37.   "Report of the Assistant in Charge of Speech Improvement Classes," 180–81, 184. Data on teachers and teacher-student ratios is from 45th *ARSBPS* (1927), 51–52 and "Report of Assistant Superintendent Walter S. Parker," 108, 110.

38.   Information and citation compiled from 36th *ARSBPS* (1917), 38; "Report of Assistant Superintendent Augustine L. Rafter" (1917), 96; 45th *ARSBPS* (1927), 52; *Proceedings* (1917), 48, 208; and 36th *ARSBPS* (1917), 39.

## Chapter 10: The Legacy of Special Education in Boston

1.  Marvin Lazerson, "The Origins of Special Education," in *Special Education Policies: Their History, Implementation, and Finance,* ed. Jay G. Chambers and William T. Hartman (Philadelphia: Temple University Press, 1983), 21.

2.  This summary draws on brief discussions found in Daniel P. Hallahan and James M. Kauffman, *Exceptional Children: Introduction to Special Education,* 4th ed. (Englewood Cliffs, N.J.: Prentice Hall, 1986), 468–71, and Susan McLean Benner, *Special Education Issues within the Context of American Society* (Belmont, Calif.: Wadsworth, 1998), 341–51.

# INDEX

Page numbers in italics indicate photographs.